The words of a living language are like creatures; they are alive. Each word has a physical character, a look and a personality, an ancestry, an expectation of life and death, a hope of posterity.

—Morris Bishop, Preface, *The American Heritage Dictionary*

Words give glass quality to glass, blood to blood, and life to life itself.

—Pablo Neruda, *The Word* (translated by Alistair Reid)

RANDOM HOUSE REFERENCE
New York   Toronto   London   Sydney   Auckland

the fascinating
ways words
are born,
live & die

the life of
language

SOL STEINMETZ AND
BARBARA ANN KIPFER

Please address inquiries about electronic licensing of any products for use on a network, in software, or on CD-ROM to the Subsidiary Rights Department, Random House Information Group, fax 212-572-6003.

This book is available at special discounts for bulk purchases for sales promotions or premiums. Special editions, including personalized covers, excerpts of existing books, and corporate imprints, can be created in large quantities for special needs. For more information, write to Random House, Inc., Special Markets/Premium Sales, 1745 Broadway, MD 6-2, New York, NY 10019 or e-mail specialmarkets@randomhouse.com.

Library of Congress Cataloging-in-Publication Data

Kipfer, Barbara Ann.
    The life of language : the fascinating ways words are born, live, and die / Barbara Ann Kipfer and Sol Steinmetz.
        p. cm.
    ISBN 0-375-72113-4 (pbk. : alk. paper)
    1. English language—Etymology. 2. English language—Terms and phrases. I. Steinmetz, Sol. II. Title.

PE1574.K46 2006
422—dc22
                                                    2006045131

Visit the Random House Reference Web site: www.randomwords.com

Design by Elina D. Nudelman

ISBN-13: 978-0-375-72113-7
ISBN-10: 0-375-72113-4

contents

PART 6

BORROWING:

ADOPTING WORDS FROM FOREIGN PLACES

PART 7

CONCLUSION

foreword

How words are formed and where they come from is a subject of universal interest. Yet, surprisingly, few books of a popular kind have dealt with this subject in an engaging or interesting way. Most popular books on language devote only a chapter or two to the formation and origination of words, while scholarly language books dealing with word origins remain inaccessible to the general public. Our goal, therefore, was twofold: to devote an entire book to describing the fascinating processes by which words come into being, and to discuss these processes in an interesting and entertaining way.

In pursuing this goal, we tried to be precise and accurate without encumbering the reader with the appurtenances of scholarly books, such as footnotes, appendices, and glossaries. We also attempted, perhaps not always successfully, to avoid using the terminology and especially the jargon of professional linguists, words like *morph, morpheme,* and *morphology.* Instead, we concentrated on imparting clear and simple information even if it meant having to use more words than strictly necessary to make a point.

Like people, new words are born every day. Dictionary editors make it their business to read regularly a variety of current periodicals and new books to underscore every new word or new meaning they come across. They collect the marked words on computers or in "citation files," and when any one of these words keeps reappearing in a number of sources, they slate it for inclusion in the dictionary's next printing.

To be sure, words also die regularly. Some, like many nonce words (words created for a particular occasion) die aborning. Others have their proverbial fifteen minutes of popularity in the media before vanishing. Still others fade away, first becoming old or archaic, then obsolete. This is not only natural but necessary, because the language always clamors for fresh modes of expression and for new names for all things new. As in life, there is a cycle of birth, growth, and death for words, which is one main reason for language change, and for Chaucer's and Shakespeare's English sounding so foreign to our ears.

Nevertheless, the growth of English over the past hundred years has been phenomenal. The 1909 edition of *Webster's New International Dictionary* boasted of some 400,000 entry words. But, as of November 30, 2005, the *Oxford English Dictionary* contains no less than 616,500 entries! Where do all these words come from and how are they produced? Though most people can tell a questioning child how babies are born, few can easily answer the question: how and why are words born?

The answer is that language changes as the world changes. New words and meanings are created by new technologies, new fashions, new problems, and new attitudes. English, in particular, is in the forefront of language change, it having become over the past half-century an international language, with almost a billion speakers worldwide. The term "World English" is now used by linguists for a language spoken in 104 countries, from Anguilla to Zimbabwe. Every day, year in and out, new words are invented or adopted from other languages. The formation and acquisition of new words does not happen at random. There are many distinct patterns and paths by which words come into the language, and in this book we show the ways English words are created, built, and shaped.

We wish to thank our editors at Random House, Jena Pincott, Rahel Lerner, and Julia Penelope, for helping us in every possible way to make this a readable, informative, and interesting book.

In closing, we each dedicate the book to our respective families, whose encouragement and support contributed greatly to its completion:

To wife Tzipora Steinmetz, and children Jacob and Debby, Abraham and Ettie, Steven and Liba

To husband Paul Magoulas, and children Kyle Kipfer and Keir Magoulas

THE AUTHORS

it's all about words
words

In a recent New Yorker cartoon, a lanky teenager asks his father: "How did you say 'Whatever' in the sixties?" The father looks puzzled, apparently no longer remembering how he, as a teenager, gave himself an air of aloof indifference, whether with a shrug or by rolling his eyes, or by saying, "Give me a break." The adolescent who responds to parental demands with a cool "Whatever," will in turn be asked someday by his own offspring, "Yo, Dad, how did you say [blank] when you were a kid?"

The way we use words marks our age as well as the age we live in. Our choice of words is a marker of our time. A time-traveler from the 19th century, dropping into our home, would not only be amazed at the sight of a television, radio, computer, microwave, cell phone, and other futuristic apparatus, but would shake his head in incomprehension at our strange vocabulary, filled with technical terms, words of foreign extraction, and slangy expressions. We enjoy Hollywood's versions of such 19th-century novels as *Great Expectations* and *Pride and Prejudice*, but would find reading the novels of Dickens and Jane Austen pretty hard going because of their highly formal and convoluted language.

"Vocabulary," wrote the American linguist Edward Sapir, "is a very sensitive index of the culture of a people, and changes of meaning, loss of old words, the creation and borrowing of new ones, are all dependent on the history of culture itself." As society changes, so does its word stock. The vocabulary of English has had an unprecedented expansion since World War II, owing in large part to the prestige English acquired during the postwar years as the favored language of communication, technology, scholarship, and international diplomacy.

Two hundred years ago, a British visitor to America haughtily declared to Noah Webster, "There are too many words already [in the language]." At that time, Webster's *Dictionary* included a mere 40,600 words, and even that was too many for this critic. But obviously there were never enough words for the needs of a growing population. The 1961 edition of *Webster's Third New International Dictionary* included 450,000 terms. And a contemporary standard college dictionary limits itself with great difficulty to about 160,000 entry words. But dictionaries hardly contain *all* the words of a language. Rough estimates place the size of the English vocabulary somewhere between half a million and one million words, but it is doubtful that any speaker of English knows or uses all of them. Estimates of average English speakers' active vocabularies range between 15,000 and 50,000 words, while their passive vocabularies (the words they understand but don't use) can be 100,000 words or more.

Where do all those words come from and how are they produced? It is the purpose of this book to touch upon every aspect of word formation and word creation, from baby talk to word roots, from acronyms to retronyms.

The study of words and the way they are formed began in ancient Greece and Rome. Philosophers like Aristotle and grammarians like Varro (Marcus Terentius Varro, 116–27 B.C.E., the author of *On the Latin Language*, in 25 books) studied the ways in which words were formed as a part of grammar, founding a long tradition that was inherited and extended over time.

We start by discussing the debate over "What is a word?" It sounds perhaps like a foolish question, since speakers recognize words by the way they are spaced in writing. But words are not so spaced in running speech, and in ancient texts there were no spaces or punctuation between words. We also discuss how etymologists reconstruct the history of a word and how readers can decipher the often cryptic etymologies in dictionaries to learn more about the origin and formation of words.

The existence of words is usually taken for granted by speakers of a language. They also tend to think that topics like word formation are beyond their grasp. Though new words enter our language and our minds on a daily basis, we accept and incorporate them without much analysis. We are, however, curious about how the language allows speakers and writers to create new words.

Our extraordinarily complex language is built on forty-four distinctive sounds that combine into hundreds and thousands of meaningful word elements. These, in turn, combine to form thousands and even millions of different words and phrases. There are patterns that explain the regularities in the new words we form and that also explain why certain formations would be unlikely or impossible. Most of us subconsciously recognize a certain number of these patterns. Knowing the pattern, we can guess a meaning—especially in the context of a sentence. Take, for example, the word *missing* in the following sentences: *I'm missing my pen. You're missing my point. Who is missing in the group? The child is missing.* All of these sentences share the core meaning of the word *missing*, which is "failing to find or to be found," and so we guess the meaning of each sentence effortlessly.

A final word: This book is for the layperson, not the linguist. It is for the multitudes of the word-curious, those who ask questions about where words come from, about word histories, how words get their meanings, and wonder about the cultural factors that influence the creation and acquisition of words. We conceive this work for all people interested in broadening their knowledge of the language they use in everyday life. We will avoid using the terminology, and especially the jargon, of professional linguists. When we feel an irresistible urge to use an arcane linguistic term, we will promptly translate the term into plain English. All we ask of our readers is to follow us as we embark on an exciting journey through the turbulent sea of words that make up the English language.

CHAPTER 1

what is a word?

"The difference between the *almost right* word and the *right word* is really a large matter," wrote Mark Twain in *The Art of Composition*, "—it's the difference between the lightning bug and the lightning." Few of us would confuse a lightning bug (a firefly) with lightning, yet many words, especially those that look or sound alike (*aboard/abroad, brake/break, corps/corpse*) are often and easily confused.

So are words with similar meanings. An old *New Yorker* cartoon shows a little girl on a high chair being urged by her mother to eat against her will. "But dear," the mother says, "it's broccoli." To which the little girl replies, "I say it's spinach and I say the hell with it!" Unlike this highly articulate child, most youngsters are slow to learn the differences between words. Those differences are due to some extent to the nature of words themselves.

To linguists, "What is a word?" is a loaded question. A "word" seems like such a fundamental term in language, but it's actually quite complex. In everyday talk, we speak about "words" without ever thinking that the notion is complicated or problematic. Statistics tell us that average speakers have around 50,000 words stored in their mind. But what is it that is stored? What do we mean when we speak of "words?"

Among dictionary definitions for *word*, you would likely single out the one saying a word is "an uninterrupted string of letters which is preceded by a blank space and followed by a blank space or punctuation mark." This is called an "orthographic word," and this definition is based on a word being a unit in a writing system. Intuitively, this is how many laypeople define *word*.

But if a word has an apostrophe or hyphen or other punctuation mark, you might believe it to be two words. This dependence on orthography—how a word is written—to determine what a "word" is becomes a problem because spelling is quite variable. The word *who's* is different from the word *whose*, though the two are pronounced the same way. So are *they're* and *their*. There are many words that can be written in two or three different ways: as a solid (without any spaces), or with a hyphen, or separated by a space (example: *girlfriend, girl-friend, girl friend*). So, it's a problem to define what a "word" is if its appearance in print depends on the fancies, education, region, and so forth of individual writers.

Another way to define a *word* could be by sound, but in listening to other people speak, you'll have a hard time figuring out what a "word" is by the pauses. Pauses are not just used between words but also between syllables. Any child who has recited in the classroom the Pledge of Allegiance might remember declaring "I pledge a legion to the flag (or sometimes, "I led the pigeons to the flag") of the United States of America and to the public for Richard Stans, one nation, under guard, invisible. . . ." So much for using sound to define a *word*.

Or, consider the *meaning* of a "word" as a possible guideline. Can we say that *word* can be defined as an utterance conveying a single meaning? Well, no—mainly because not every meaning corresponds to one particular "word." In fact, there are meanings that have no words to express them. That is where *Sniglets* (Rich Hall, 1989) and other such collections come from; these are books and lists of "words" that should be in English but are not. Two examples are *lapflap*, "a magazine subscription insert that falls into your lap while reading," and *pupkus*, "the moist residue left on a window after a dog presses its nose to it." These are concepts or meanings without words to express them, so one has to make up "words" for them. Besides, if you open a dictionary, you will find that some of the commonest words, words like *care, fill, new,* and *strike,* have a multitude of meanings; a typical dictionary lists over sixty meanings for *strike.* So to define a *word* as "a unit of meaning" doesn't really capture the essence of what a word is.

Yet another way to attempt to define a *word* is by its part of speech. Words are often considered to be the smallest elements in a sentence. They belong to certain categories—noun, verb, adjective, adverb, preposition, and so on. One might test whether something is a word by checking whether it belongs to a particular part of speech. This approach can *help* determine if something is a "word," but it is not definitive and it is a difficult concept for the layperson to use.

For linguists, the term *word* is often set aside and other terms are used such as *lexeme. Lexeme* is what one would also call a base, or root, word; in the series *shoot, shoots, shooting, shot,* for example, we would say instinctively that each of those is a "word," but the base word, or lexeme, is *shoot.* When we consult a dictionary, we know to look up *shoot* and not *shooting*. We are aware that *shoot* is the basic unit and ignore the inflected forms.

There is another sense of the term *word* that needs to be distinguished: the grammatical word. *Shot* is both the simple past tense and the past participle of *shoot*, thus representing two grammatical words. So, there you have it—one more distinction offered by linguists. But relax: the term *word*, from here on will be used in a deliberately vague way. In this book, *word* will be used to mean what a native English speaker would intuitively call a "word." In other words, if you think something is a word, we agree. We can be tolerant of the subtle ambiguities in the use of the term *word*.

What makes up a "word," then? The parts that make up words are called by linguists "morphemes," and they are the smallest units of meaning in a language. Morphemes include things like prefixes (*un-*, as in *unbelievable*) and suffixes (*-able*, as in *believable*). A word in English may be simple, composed of one morpheme only, like *bat* or *hammer*, or it may be complex, containing more than one morpheme, as in *blackboard* (*black* + *board*), *knowledgeable* (*knowledge* + *-able*), and *disestablishmentarianism*, a word meaning opposition to established order, made up of six morphemes: *dis-*, *establish*, *-ment*, *-ary*, *-an*, and *-ism*.

To the layperson, a dictionary definition of *word* describes the concept in a manner that is too technical to be wholly satisfactory. Here are the primary definitions from recent editions of two American and two British dictionaries:

Merriam-Webster's New Collegiate Dictionary, 11th edition (2003): a speech sound or series of speech sounds that symbolizes and communicates a meaning usually without being divisible into smaller units capable of independent use.

American Heritage Dictionary, 4th edition (2000): a sound or a combination of sounds, or its representation in writing or printing, that symbolizes and communicates a meaning and may consist of a single morpheme or of a combination of morphemes.

Collins English Dictionary, 6th edition (2003): one of the units of speech or writing that native speakers of a language usually regard as the smallest isolable meaningful element of the language, although linguists would analyse these further into morphemes.

Chambers Dictionary, 9th edition (2003): the smallest unit of language that can be used independently; such a unit represented in writing or printing, usu separated off by spaces.

While these attempts at defining a *word* are acceptable as far as they go, they are incomplete and rather bloodless. They fail to suggest the awesome beauty and power of words, their ability to bring language to life, the magical quality that turns them into poetry, history, and literature. No one definition has successfully answered the question, "What is a word?" and so it joins questions like "What is the meaning of life?" in a long list of philosophical conundrums. But this lack of consensus among linguists stands in sharp contrast to the general agreement of native speakers everywhere who seem to know intuitively what a word is when they see, hear, speak, or write one.

CHAPTER 2

building blocks:

how words are formed

There are a number of ways in which words are created or come into a language. This includes the formation of longer, more complex words from shorter, simpler words, as well as the formation of all words, simple or complex, from more basic elements of language.

Philosophers such as Aristotle and Plato and grammarians like Dionysius Thrax and Terentius Varro were among the first known to study the ways in which words were formed. Their studies were limited to Greek and Latin, but they influenced greatly the study of other languages, including English. At first, the study of word formation was part of grammar, but it later moved on to become part of morphology, or the study of the structure of words. By word formation, we mean the different devices used to build new words. Each type of word formation will result in the production of a specific type of word. So, an understanding of word formation is one way of learning about the different types of words that exist in English.

Terms used to describe the building blocks of words are important. A *root* or *base* word is the element left after all the prefixes, suffixes, and other parts have been removed from a complex word. Another way of describing a root word is that it is usually a monosyllabic word upon which another word or words are built. Others may use the terms *simple word, simplex,* or *base word* for this concept. For example, the word *heart* is the root or base word of *hearty, heartless, hearten, heartfelt, heartland, heartstrings, heartwarming, warmhearted,* and many more.

Stem is another term used to designate a part of a word that remains when inflections (i.e., grammatical parts of a word) are removed. For example, *sing* is the stem of *sings, singing, sang, sung,* and *be* is the stem of the regular and irregular forms *am, are, being, been, is, was, were.* English has relatively few inflections. In the word *unmentionables,* the stem is *unmentionable;* for *smallest,* the stem is *small.*

The creation of a new root, base, or simple word is rare compared with other types of word formation. If this does happen, the new root is usually improvised and either echoic or imitative. These are called "motivated" new roots. *Zap* and *vroom* represent real or imagined sounds. They are "echoic" or "onomatopoeic" and can either be imitative or symbolic. *Splish* and *sploosh* are variants or adaptations of *splash:* the consonants are retained but the vowels are changed. Other new roots are created by reversals, anagrams, or other adaptations of preexisting forms (e.g., *chaise lounge* from the French *chaise longue,* or the title of Samuel Butler's utopian novel *Erewhon*).

There are, however, other new roots for which there is no linguistic explanation and these are termed *ex nihilo* ("out of nothing"). Proper nouns, such as company and brand names (e.g., *Exxon, Nylon, Kodak, Kevlar*) may simply be invented. *Google*, the Internet search engine, is another such invented word, influenced, however, by *googol* (one followed by a hundred zeroes), which was an invented root word. Nonproper noun forms like *googol* are rare, found chiefly in fictional works, especially fantasy and science fiction. Some examples are *grok* ("to communicate meaningfully," coined by Robert Heinlein), *hobbit* ("a lovable elflike creature," coined by J. R. R. Tolkien), and *Grinch* ("a spoilsport or killjoy," coined by Theodor Seuss Geisel). These are purely arbitrary combinations of letters, not derived in whole or part from any existing word.

Then there are "complex" words and "compound" words, which are actually different things. Complex words are formed via derivation, the process by which a word like *unbelievable* is built up from the root or base *believe*, or by which *expedite* is built up from the base *-ped-* (Latin for "foot"). Other examples of derivatives are: *drinkable, gardener, gentlemanly,* and *unaware.* Compound words are formed by composition or compounding, the process by which *blackboard* is formed from the simple words *black* and *board,* and *geography* is formed from the combining forms *geo-* and *-graphy.* Words like *birthday, craftsman, download, freeze-dried, grandfather, highway, newborn, peach-flavored, red-hot,* and *safeguard* are compounds. However, as this book will show, derivation and compounding are just two of a large number of different word-formation processes.

New root formation is one of the five basic concepts and types of word formation. The others are: modification, semantic change, generation, and borrowing. The rest of this book is divided into parts covering these five types of word formation.

new root formation:

the birth of words

INTRODUCTION

Like a plant that grows in native soil, so a nation's language grows from its native elements, its stock of words. The terms *root* and *stem* are pretty metaphors, but they're not intended to be taken literally. Unfortunately, these terms have "taken root" in language studies and are hard to "uproot." Of course, if we continue to use them, it's with the understanding that these terms have technical meanings totally unrelated to farming and gardening.

When we speak of root formation, we simply mean the formation of new words or word elements. For example, in a recent science-fiction movie, someone created a robot in the shape of a woman and called it a *fembot*. Two word elements were combined in this word: *fem-* (from *female*) and *-bot* (from *robot*). The possibilities of word formation inherent in this coinage are many: *manbot* (man robot), *boybot* (boy robot), *hebot, shebot, catbot, dogbot,* and so forth. The form *-bot* is therefore a potential source of new words, as is, indeed, the form *fem-*. The fact that no one has used either of these forms in other words is not significant, since there are an infinite number of root forms available in English for the creation of new words.

In fact, no one knows all of the roots existing in English, or the age of those that have been identified. Hundreds of words listed in a dictionary as being "of unknown origin" have no identifiable roots and may be much older than we think. What we do know is that roots consist usually of one syllable, like *cat, dog, run,* and are the basis of other words. Roots may be freestanding forms with specific meanings like *black, blue, brown, green,* and *red.* Or they may be bound forms with vague meanings, like *-ceive* in the words *conceive* and *deceive,* or *-tain* in the words *contain* and *detain.* A new root, such as *-bot,* if used widely enough, might come to be used every day. The next chapter discusses the ways roots are formed and, in turn, form words in English.

CHAPTER 3

word roots:
from tiny shoots to a forest of words

How do words get to be words? Why is an aardvark called an aardvark and not something entirely different? Since this African anteater looks a bit like a pig and digs with its snout into soil, the Afrikaans people combined the word for "earth," *aard*, with their word for "pig," *vark*, to call the animal *aardvark*. Although in modern Afrikaans the word is spelled *erdvark*, it came into English in the 1830s in the earlier Afrikaans form *aardvark*. But this is not all you can say of this word. You can add the fact that Afrikaans got the two words from Dutch *aarde*, "earth" (related to English *earth*) and *varken* "pig" (related to English *farrow*). So in the 1830s, if someone had chosen to translate *aardvark* into English, we might have ended up calling this animal an earth-farrow instead of an aardvark.

Words don't just happen. Words, figuratively speaking, are born and they grow. Once you learn how they are born and grow—including which roots they come from—you will find it easier to learn and remember them. You will also get a deeper understanding of the words you look up in the dictionary rather than just memorizing their definitions. Weeks later, even though you may have forgotten the meaning of a word, your knowledge of its root will likely help you recall the meaning.

So what is this thing called a root?

THE ROOT OF THE MATTER

The easiest roots to identify are simple words like *he, she, boy, girl, hand,* and *foot.* Words like these are sometimes called bases, because they form the base on which other words are built. So, for instance, *hand* is the base of *handle, handy,* and *handsome* (yes, *handsome,* which originally meant "handy" or "convenient," then "of fair size or amount," and finally "of fine form or proportion"). But a root or base can also be a part of a word, the part left over after a prefix or suffix has been removed from it. For example, the root of *confer, refer,* and *prefer* is *-fer.* Such roots are usually of Latin or Greek origin and have no clear-cut meanings in English. It's only after you trace a root to its original form that its meaning or meanings are brought to light.

In the case of *-fer,* the original Latin form of the root is *ferre,* which means "to carry, bring, bear." This fact sheds light on the basic meanings of such words as *transfer* ("carry across"), *refer* ("carry back"), *prefer* ("carry forward"), *confer* ("bring together"), *infer* ("bring in"), and *offer* ("bring near"). A further look at the Latin word reveals that *ferre* is a close relative of the English verb *bear,* meaning "to carry, bring" (as in "Greeks bearing gifts").

Roots, then, carry the basic meaning from which the rest of the senses of a word can be derived. To take some words at random, *ballet, cardigan, chair, father, green, gun, ice, man,* and *powder* are roots, and these examples also happen to be independent words. Root words like these have basic meanings. For example: *arbor* means "tree," *vouch* means "give assurance," and *auspice* means "favor, support." Although these roots are words in and of themselves, you can also combine them with other word elements (like prefixes and suffixes) to make new words, as in *arboreous,* "treelike" (adding *-eous*), *voucher,* "one that vouches" (adding *-er*), and *auspicious,* "favorable" (adding *-ious*).

But more often, roots cannot stand alone as words. They are bound forms, like *card-* in *cardiac, gen-* in *genetics, micro-* and *-cosm* in *microcosm,* pter- in *pterodactyl,* and *seg-* in *segment.* Most roots of this kind are of classical origin: They were borrowed from Latin or Greek, or came into English through French. They were often borrowed "wholesale," meaning that they came into the language nested inside derived forms such as the root *-nom-* "law" (in *astronomy, autonomy, economy*). Other roots must be combined with other word elements to form words, as in the following examples: *capit-* + *-al* = *capital, carn-* + *-age* = *carnage, chrono-* + *-logy* = *chronology.*

A bound root is like a dollar bill torn in half. It's of no use unless it's glued onto the half that's missing. To become complete, the root requires a word, another root, or an affix (prefix or suffix) to be attached to it. It then comes to life, a newborn word. If another root is added, we get words like *biology* (*bio-* + *-logy*), *geography* (*geo-* + *-graphy*), *telephone* (*tele-* + *-phone*). If an affix is added, it only slightly modifies the meaning of the root, for example, *temporary, temporal,* and *contemporary*—all from the root *temp-* (from Latin *tempus, temporis,* "time") and all having to do with time.

Root words, which have clear-cut meanings, are modified chiefly by a change in their part of speech, as *child*, a noun, becomes an adjective in *childish*. Such words also commonly form compounds, for example, *bluebird*, *greenhouse*, and *wishbone*. (We will discuss them in detail in the chapter on **Compounding**.)

A root sometimes acquires importance as a combining form—a form frequently used in combination with other elements to form technical or scientific terms. For instance, the root *helio-*, "sun," appears in many scientific and technical coinages: *heliocentric*, *heliogram*, *helioscope*, and *heliotropic*. (For a discussion of these forms, see the chapter on **Combining Forms**.)

THE ELUSIVE ROOT

The idea that the root is a meaningful element should be refined a bit. Roots are seldom well-behaved and often can be complicated. An example is the root *-cur-*, "run," found in such words as *current*, *concur*, *incur*, *occur*, and *recur*. The fact that this root does not literally mean "run" in the word *concur* may not be too troublesome because it is easy enough to see the connection between the actual meaning of *concur*, "agree, go along with," and the image "run with." This example shows that recognizing literal meanings is only a first step in understanding roots. Instances of *-cur-* in words other than *concur* may present new images, related in other ways to the literal meaning of "run." In *recur*, whose prefix means "again," there is normally no running in the literal sense. But the running action denoted by the basic meaning of *-cur-* makes for a more picturesque image of the bland event "happen again."

Very often the use of roots relies on our ability to see ways in which one thing stands for another. The meaning of the root *-aster-*, "star," in the word *disaster* suggests an ill-starred accident.

The meaning "point," designated by the root *punct-* in *punctuation*, refers to a variety of small marks, including periods and commas. In *punctual*, the connection with "point" is figurative, as "a point in time." In *puncture*, we get the image of a hole caused by something pointed.

But there are also times when a root changes meaning. It may start out with a particular meaning, but once it is used in different words and those words come to be used in a variety of situations, the root may lose its original simple meaning. The root *ship* once meant "ocean-going vessel" but when it is part of *airship* it simply means "vessel." Thus, although roots remain meaningful elements from word to word, we cannot expect their meaning to stay constant from word to word. For example, *-pyr-* sometimes means "fire" (*pyrotechnics*) and sometimes "fever" (*antipyretic*). The meanings are not the same, but they are related.

DIVINING THE DICTIONARY

A good question is how to find roots in a dictionary. Dictionaries usually divide words into syllables. The division into syllables is done mainly to help the reader decide where to hyphenate at the end of a line. Dictionaries also indicate pronunciation, including marking where the accent falls in words with more than one syllable. But roots are not labeled as such. Rather, dictionaries give etymological ("word history") information from which the user is supposed to figure out what the root forms are. From this information, how do we find the roots?

Looking at a word's etymology, we can start to investigate the root. We must find the ultimate source of the word—the very last italicized word or words in the etymology. Let's look at an example:

MUNICIPAL *adjective* Latin *municipalis* of a municipality, from *municip-, municeps* inhabitant of a municipality, from *munus* duty, service + *capere* to take [*Merriam-Webster's Online Dictionary*]

Is the Latin word *capere* a root? No, because it is a verb, meaning "to take," indicated by the suffix *-ere*. Actually it doesn't matter what the suffix *-ere* is or what it signifies; it matters only that you can recognize that there is a suffix on *capere* and that it can be removed to find the root. In this case, the root is *cap-*, the same root that appears in words like *captive, captor, capture,* all having the basic meaning of "take, seize." The other root, *munus,* is a bit trickier. It has been traced back to an earlier root *mei-,* "duty, office," in Indo-European, the assumed prehistoric language that was the ancestor of many modern languages, including Latin and English. Some dictionaries, like the *American Heritage Dictionary* and the *Oxford English Dictionary* (*OED*), focus on the roots and have done extensive research to provide them. In the case of *municipal,* the *American Heritage* presents the roots as being *mei-* and *cap-,* but the *OED* makes the reader look at the entries for *capture* and *muneral* ("gladiator funeral service") to dig down to the roots.

The root is the form that cannot be broken down further, and that is fairly constant in form and meaning. The best first step in building one's vocabulary is to become familiar with word roots, because learning the root of one word often gives you a clue to dozens or even hundreds more. If you learn that *syn-* and *sym-* and *syl-* mean "together; with," you have a clue to at least five hundred more words, for example, *synonym, synthesis, symmetry, sympathy, syllable,* and *syllogism.* Having learned the roots, you will remember a word longer than if you had merely looked up the definition. Like Greek roots, Latin roots are often used as combining forms to devise new words needed in science and technology. The Latin root *ovi-*, "egg," for example, has been used in words like *oviduct, oviferous, oviform,* and *oviparous.*

A word can consist of more than one root. For example, *matriarch* contains the roots *matri-*, "mother," and *-arch*, "ruler." *Matriarch*, therefore, means "mother who is the ruler (of her family or tribe)."

The analysis of words to find the roots can provide reliable spelling clues for less familiar words. If we realize that *elevator* contains the root *-lev-*, "lift, rise" (also found in *elevate, lever, levy*), we will know that the second vowel is spelled with an "e" rather than an "a" or some other vowel. If we already know that *salient* means "sticking out" (as in "salient features"), we may not need to know that it is built on the root *sal-* "spring, jump." But knowing that this word is built upon an "image" of jumping may enhance its expressive power and help you recall words like *sally* ("spring forth") and *saltation* ("a jumping about") that are not yet familiar.

Aardvark, formed from two Dutch roots, is not a common word. Other English words formed from two roots are far better known. One such word is *astronaut*, formed from the Greek roots *astron-*, "star," and *nautēs*, "sailor" ("one who sails the stars"), used since 1961 to refer to U.S. travelers to outer space. The competing Soviet spacemen were given the more ambitious name of *cosmonaut*, formed from the Greek roots *kósmos*, "universe," and *nautēs*, "sailor." (So far neither spaceman has made it beyond the moon.)

root creation:

spam, anyone?

Every once in a while a word emerges that has no relationship whatsoever with any previously existing word. A famous one is *quiz*. It first appeared in the sense of "an informal exam" in the 1860s. An oft-repeated story has it that the word was made up by an Irish prankster who bet his friends that he could invent a meaningless word and have everybody in Dublin using it within a day. He wrote the word *quiz* all over the walls of the town, and soon everybody was asking what it meant. The prankster won the bet, while the word became synonymous with questioning. A more likely, but also discredited, theory is that *quiz* was an alteration of *quies*, meaning "to question," which may have come from the Latin *quīes?*, "Who are you?," supposedly the first question asked at Latin exams in grammar schools. Dictionaries long ago labeled the word "origin unknown."

Trade names are notable root creations. The name Spam for a popular canned meat made of pork and ham won the $100 prize in a naming contest at a New Year's Eve party sponsored by the food's manufacturer, Jay Hormel. It was supposedly formed from a contraction of *sp(iced h)am*. The name generated the compound *Spamburger* in 1991, and *Spammobile*, any of various vehicles shaped like a can of spam, in 2001. With the computer age, a generic form of the term, spelled *spam*, without the initial capital, became notorious as a disparaging word for any disruptive message or messages sent repeatedly over a computer network. Sending such messages is called *spamming*. The generic usage is attributed to a popular sketch in the British comedy series *Monty Python's Flying Circus*, in which a waitress, after reciting a long menu of dishes made with Spam, joins her customers in singing a song that repeats the word *spam* over and over ad nauseam, suggesting any endless and tiresome repetition, like that of unsolicited e-mail messages. The sketch inspired the title *Spamalot* for a Broadway musical satirizing King Arthur's Camelot, staged in 2005 by members of the original Monty Python group.

Root creation is a purely arbitrary combination of letters, not supposed to be derived in whole or part from any existing word. These creations are labeled *ex nihilo* ("out of nothing") and are the purest forms of word manufacture. A master of root creation was the British poet and author Alastair Reid (b. 1926), whose humorous coinages include *poose*, meaning "a glistening drop of water hanging from the nose of a person with a cold or after a swim," and *gnurr*, "the sticky matter that collects in pockets and trouser cuffs after a time." More usually, such forms are created in fictional works, especially fantasy and science fiction. Kurt Vonnegut's 1963 novel *Cat's Cradle*, a classic of the genre, contains a number of words created *ex nihilo* that have become familiar to many readers. These words are central to a fictional religion, Bokononism, and include a *karass*, "an identity or purpose shared by many otherwise unrelated people"; *wampeter*, "an object that is the focus of a karass"; *foma*, "the untruths that make people happy"; and *granfalloon*, "any group of people whose association is based on a shared but ultimately false premise." (See also the chapter on **Coinages**.)

HOW TO GROW A NEW ROOT

Compared with other types of word formation, the creation of a new root, base, or simple word is relatively rare. When this does happen, the new root is usually improvised and often imitative of a sound. These are called "motivated" new roots. *Arf* or *bow-wow* (a dog's bark), *baa* (of sheep), *buzz* (of bees), *meow* (of cats), *tweet* (of birds), and *vroom* (a motor's roar) represent real or imagined sounds. They are "echoic" or "onomatopoeic" and can either be imitative or symbolic. Symbolic words suggest or express a meaning more vividly than a description. *Zap* and *splash* are such words (*splish* and *sploosh* are variants or adaptations of *splash*, with the consonants retained but the vowels changed for effect). In his book *Language* (1933), Leonard Bloomfield includes the following words as examples of symbolic forms: *flip, flap, flop, flitter, flicker, flutter, flash, flare, glare, glitter, glimmer, bang, bump, thump, thwack, whack,* and *wheeze.* Among imitative sounds he includes the names of objects that produce such sounds, such as *cuckoo, bobwhite, whip-poor-will.* (See other examples in the chapter on **Onomatopoeia**.)

More marginal are words, particularly scientific words, that are abstracted from long technical phrases in a manner reminiscent of blending and acronym creation, but where the motivation is far less clear. An example is *pemoline*, a central nervous system stimulant, which was apparently derived from *phenylimoxazolidinone*, its chemical components. Other examples are *Kepone*, a pesticide, *Keflex*, an antibiotic, *Kenalog*, a steroid, and *Kevlar*, a synthetic fiber, whose origins are uncertain (though words beginning with the syllable *Ke* are much favored in product names). Such formations, while possibly derived from the names of chemical ingredients, are far less obviously motivated than other categories. The process of forming them is best described as "word manufacture."

There are a number of trade names and scientific names, however, that may look like root creations, but are really formed from or suggested by already-existing words. Examples of trade names are *Vaseline*, created from German *Wasser*, "water," and Greek *élaion*, "oil," and *Windex*, derived from *window* and the brand-name suffix *-ex* (as in *Kleenex*). Examples of scientific names are the two natural pain suppressants *endorphin* (formed by contraction of *endo*genous mo*rphine*) and *enkephalin*, coined from Greek *enképhalos*, "brain," and the chemical suffix *-in*.

The bottom line is that, while comparatively few words have had their origin in root creation, this remains an original and intriguing type of word formation in English.

CHAPTER 5

inheritance or pattern formation:

dial-a-word, prosewise

In his book on Americanisms, *Never Enough Words* (1999), the language columnist Jeffrey McQuain lists a series of "Web words," words about the World Wide Web formed on the model or analogy of older words. The list includes *Webaholic*, "one addicted to the Web" (after *workaholic, golfaholic*, etc.), *Webcast* (after *broadcast, newscast*), *Webhead*, "a devotee or fan of the Web" (after *hophead, filmhead*, etc.), *Webmercial* (after *commercial, infomercial*), and *Webzine*, "a magazine on the Web" (after *fanzine, newszine*, etc.). These compounds of *Web* could not have been formed without the earlier words serving as models or pattern-setters. Words formed by analogy with other words are said to be inherited, and inheritance is the process by which word parts and their meanings are transferred to a new whole.

Inheritance of word parts is pretty common and much simpler than it sounds. If you read an article about *bigorexia*, describing a condition in which a person is obsessed with developing a big, muscular body, such a person being called *bigorexic*, it takes only a moment to realize that these words were formed on the model of *anorexia*, the well-known eating disorder, and *anorexic*, one who has anorexia. Similarly, a *New York Times* article described an addiction to suntans as *tanorexia*. "Some tanorexics," it went, "appear orange or leathery, but more often they're just unseasonably or consistently overbronzed. Tanorexics are in constant fear that their color is fading." Clearly the word parts *-orexia* and *-orexic* were each transferred to new wholes, *bigorexia* and *bigorexic*, *tanorexia* and *tanorexic*.

Or take another new word, *Wi-Fi*, referring to high-speed wireless transmission. The word was clearly patterned on *hi-fi*, or high-fidelity sound transmission. Here again the word part *-fi* (for *fidelity*) was transferred to a new whole. The transferred parts are sometimes called analogical forms or patterned forms. Words with *Franken-* and *Mc-* are prime examples of such forms.

FRANKENWORDS

The combining form *Franken-* was first used about 1992 in *Frankenfood*, referring to genetically modified food. *Franken-* was derived from *Frankenstein*, the creator of a monster in Mary Shelley's 1818 novel of the same name, and popularly used as a synonym for any monstrous creature that inflicts ruin upon its creator. The coiner of *Frankenfood* clearly intended the word to be disparaging of the production of genetically modified food by comparing it to the creation of a monster. But once the name was launched, *Franken-* became neutral shorthand for any genetically modified food, including vegetables like *Frankenbeans, Franken-*

corn, *Frankenrice*, and *Frankentomatoes*, various kinds of *Frankenfruit*, *Frankenplants*, and *Frankentrees*, and even *Frankenfish* such as *Franken-salmon*. Not only was the word part *Franken-*, but its meaning, "genetically modified," transferred to new whole words. One such word is *Frankenword* (also spelled *frankenword*), a disparaging term coined in the 1990s to denote words formed by blending two or more words. From the University of Tennessee student newspaper *The Daily Beacon* (Aug. 30, 1996): "Words I particularly detest are those *Frankenwords* . . . that combine two others to make one horrific abomination . . . like *edutainment*, my 'favorite' *frankenword*, a cross-breeding of education and entertainment." According to the writer Kerry Maxwell, "The fun thing about the term *frankenword* . . . is that it is self-referring, i.e., the term *frankenword* is itself a *frankenword* . . . , coined by analogy with terms such as *Frankenfood* and *Frankenfruit*."

The combining form *Mc-* has had even wider application. *Mc-* came into being when the American writer Paul Dickson, in a 1982 book titled *Words*, coined the word *McWord* for the Scots-Irish-surnamed foodstuff (*Egg McMuffin*, *Chicken McNuggets*, etc.) produced by the entrepreneur Ray Kroc's fast-food giant McDonald's. The use of *Mc-* expanded vastly after the word *McJob* was popularized in Douglas Coupland's 1991 novel *Generation X*, which defines the word as "a low-pay, low-prestige, low-dignity, low-benefit, no-future job in the service sector." Dictionaries soon added *McJob* to their latest editions. As McWords multiplied, Tom McArthur, the editor of *The Oxford Companion to the English Language* (1992), perhaps influenced by his own Mc-Name, thought the usage worthy enough to receive full entry in the book (p. 636, entry **McWord**).

By analogy, Kroc's business has been referred to facetiously as a *McEmpire*, and related coinages suggest the quick, cheap, and superficial, as with *McFashion*, 'pre-packaged clothing', *McPaper* (a dismissive name for) the newspaper *USA Today*, *News McNuggets* its news reports, *McLatin* classical studies made easy. . . .

He might have added *McMansion*, referring mockingly to any of the pretentiously large but superficially built suburban houses that spread like McDonald's franchises across the United States since the 1980s; *McTheater*, any of the numerous cheaply produced theatrical productions staged by college students everywhere; *McNews*, the superficial snippets or sound bites of information claiming to be news that is broadcast over the networks; and *McWorld*, coined by Benjamin Barber, a Rutgers University political science professor, as a cover term for the commercially homogenous world created by corporate globalization.

The success of *Mc-* illustrates the power of inheritance, how a small but meaningful word part is inherited by countless new words. These words owe their existence as much to the original McWord as to the words it spawned.

PATTERNS

Lots of coined words are patterned on others, as seen in the following examples:

AQUANAUT, "underwater navigator," and *astronaut*, "outer space navigator," patterned on *aeronaut*, "airship navigator"

BLOODMOBILE, *bookmobile*, patterned on *snowmobile*

CHILDPROOF, *foolproof*, *leakproof*, patterned on *waterproof*

DIGERATI, "people skilled in using digital computers," and *glitterati,* "wealthy fashionable people," patterned on *literati,* "scholarly or literary people"

GRAPHICACY, "skill in graphic arts," *oracy,* "skill in oral expression," and *numeracy,* "skill with numbers," patterned on *literacy,* "skill in reading and writing"

HESIFLATION, "hesitant inflation pattern," *slumpflation,* "business slump combined with inflation," and *stagflation,* "stagnant inflation," patterned on *inflation* and *deflation*

PINK-COLLAR, "involving mainly women employees," *blue-collar,* "involving factory workers," *gray-collar,* "involving service workers," and *steel-collar,* "involving robots," all patterned on *white-collar,* "involving professional or clerical workers"

Societal and political changes have led to other pattern formations: *black power* became the pattern for *gray power,* "political power of the elderly"; *man-year* and *man-hour* set the pattern for *woman-year* and *woman-hour,* and eventually for the gender-neutral *person-year* and *person-hour,* all measures of work performed by a single individual. And *women's lib* inspired the coinage of *gay lib, animal lib,* and *kids' lib.*

Often, in dictionaries, you will find in the etymology an indication that a word was formed on the pattern of another or others. Such forms are shown in the etymology by the phrase "patterned on," "based on the pattern of," or "after." The *OED* uses the indication "after."

When a new word or expression becomes established or popular, it will become the model for words or expressions of a similar character. Thus, *sexism* and *sexist*, which in the 1960s became a byword of those fighting discrimination against women, was modeled on the older, 19th-century words *racism* and *racist*. Once the new words gained a foothold, they became the models for words like *ageism* ("discrimination against older people") and *ageist*, *heightism* ("discrimination based on one's height") and *heightist*, *speciesism* ("discrimination against various animal species") and *speciesist*, and other words in *-ism* and *-ist* in which these suffixes denote discriminatory practices. Through this process, *-ism* acquired the new meaning of "prejudice or discrimination against," used for instance in *ableism*, "prejudice or discrimination against the disabled." In turn, *-ist* acquired the meaning of "one who practices (a form of) discrimination," as in *ableist* "one who practices ableism."

A FIX OF AFFIXES

Prefixes and suffixes often acquire new meanings. The prefix *pre-* acquired the meaning "previously, before the usual time" from its use in words like *preboard* (a plane, etc.), a *preowned* car, *prepay*, *prequalify*, *prerecord* (a message), *presort* (letters, etc.), and *prewashed* jeans. The suffix *-net*, "network," first appeared in *Arpanet* (acronym for "Advanced Research Project Agency Network"), and was then used to form terms like *Internet*, "the global computer network," *Ethernet* "a local-area computer network," *intranet*, "a corporate or other restricted computer network," and *Usenet*, "a worldwide network of newsgroups."

Some affixes burst into fashion at a particular time, infecting the language with much repetitive jargon. An example of this is the suffix *-wise*, whose proliferation in the sense of "with regard to" in words like *costwise*, *marketwise*, *percentagewise*, *profitwise*, *securitywise*, *saleswise*, *qualitywise*, and *timewise* has been much criticized since the 1950s. In *The Elements of Style*, E. B. White makes fun of the usage by rewording Thomas Paine's famous sentence, "These are the times that try men's souls," as "Soulwise, these are trying times." And in a letter he wrote in 1959, he complains, "This has been the summer of the great discontent and widespread confusion, weatherwise, healthwise, and otherwisewise." Wilson Follett, in his *Modern American Usage* (1966), writes about the overuse of the suffix:

> What was handy as a device has thus been made hideous as a mannerism, and it deserves to be outlawed from decent use. Until the rage abates, a sensible writer will resort to such coinage in *-wise* only to make fun of them, as S. J. Perelman does when he speaks of *what was going on, prosewise, from 1930 to 1958.*

Not just single words, but compounds and phrases are often patterned formations. For example, the *credit card* set the pattern for *bank card, charge card, debit card,* and *smart card*; and *baby-sitter* became the pattern for *house-sitter, pet-sitter,* and *car-sitter.* The adjective *run-of-the-mill*, meaning "average" or "commonplace," was the template for such varied formations as *run-of-the-alley hoodlums, run-of-the-house animals, run-of-the-scale musical performers,* and *run-of-the-universe galaxies.* A more familiar formation is one based apparently on the trademark *Dial-A-Phone* for an automatic phone-dialing system introduced in Great Britain in the 1950s. Many other *dial-a-* forms have appeared since then for any service or information obtained by dialing a telephone number, among them *Dial-A-Flight, Dial-A-Joke, Dial-A-Law, Dial-A-Meal, dial-a-park, dial-a-program, dial-a-ride, Dial-A-Shrink, Dial-A-Song, Dial-A-Teacher,* and so on.

modification:

how words grow and thrive

INTRODUCTION

The great word-makers of English literature—
poets like Chaucer, Spenser, Shakespeare, and Milton, and Bible
translators like Tyndale and Coverdale—owed much of their
greatness to a bold and imaginative use of language. With a limited stock of words, they molded and shaped old, familiar English into new forms that yielded novel expressions and images.
Chaucer called a pie *bake-mete*, "bake-food," and described a constable as having *a fyr-reed cherubynnes face*, "a fire-red cherubim's
face." Where Chaucer used the phrase *derring doe* to mean "dar-
ing to do," Spenser used it as a noun meaning "valor," which
gave us *derring-do*. Shakespeare's many coinages include *never-ending*,
which Milton used in *Paradise Lost* ("the never-ending flight of
future days"), *cold-blooded*, *heaven-kissing* ("a heaven-kissing hill"),
world-without-end, and *breathing one's last*. And to Tyndale and

Coverdale we owe many of the words that made the language of the King James Bible a model of simplicity and sublime beauty, words like *beautiful, long-suffering, lovingkindness,* and phrases like *the burning bush, the golden calf,* and *Is there no balm in Gilead?*

The common characteristic of these writers was that they made up new words by modifying existing ones. To be sure, they also borrowed extensively from other languages; but before reaching out for a foreign word to express an idea, they explored their native English to, in Shakespeare's words, "suit the action to the word, the word to the action." Robert Clairborne, in *Our Marvelous Native Tongue* (1983), gives this example of the versatile use of the native tongue in Old English:

> The single word hēah, high, was incorporated into more than a dozen expressions, including hēah-borg, 'high-hill'—mountain; hēah-bliss, 'high-bliss'—exultation; hēah-burg, 'principal town'; hēah sæ, 'the high seas'—deep sea; hēah-heort, 'high-hearted'—proud;... and hēah-strēt, highway (from the Roman strata via).

The process of changing an existing word or word sequence to form a new word is called *modification.* The formation of abbreviations and acronyms, back-formations, clipped forms, and so on, are common modifications. All words, whether they are nouns, verbs, adjectives, or other parts of speech, seem to be able to undergo modification. Certain modifications, such as doublets (*guarantee/warranty*), are historical oddities due to different routes of transmission of a word from a single source. Others, as those modified by folk etymology (for example *muskrat,* from an Algonquian word unrelated to either *musk* or *rat*) are the product of simple misunderstanding. Rather than English having specific rules for these modifications, there are a number of totally free processes and any word can undergo one or more of these as the need arises.

CHAPTER 6

abbreviations and acronyms:

bcnu l8r in no-ho, ok?

Words are abbreviated to save space and time. It is far easier to write and pronounce *DNA* (dee'-en'-a') than to write or pronounce *deoxyribonucleic acid*. The oldest English abbreviations, which were borrowed from Latin, were created for the same reason, to spare writers and readers the trouble of having to spell out long words or phrases repeatedly. These included common abbreviations like *etc.* (for Latin *et cetera*, "and the rest"), *e.g.* (for Latin *exemplī grātiā*, "for the sake of example"), *i.e.* (for Latin *id est*, "that is"), and *q.v.* (for Latin *quod vidē*, "which see"). Among English abbreviations, certain ones, like *Dr., Prof., Rev.,* have always been acceptable, since they stand for pronounceable words. But as a general and fashionable practice, abbreviating and clipping English words has been criticized since the 1700s by writers like Jonathan Swift and critics like George Campbell. It was not until the mid-19th century that abbreviation became acceptable.

OK AND A-OK

A vogue to create abbreviations broke out in the United States in the late 1830s. How this became fashionable, somewhat like slang, was studied and described in 1963–64 by the scholar Allen Walker Read in a series of articles in the journal *American Speech*. His greatest discovery was the origin of *O.K.*, which started out as a jocular abbreviation, but became over time a nearly universal affirmative, used in many languages throughout the world. Professor Read traced the usage to the city of Boston, where in the late 1830s it became faddish to abbreviate certain common phrases, such as *no go* or *no good*, which were rendered *N.G.*, and *Our First Men* (meaning "original settlers"), which was abbreviated *O.F.M.* The fad took a humorous turn when jocular misspellings of common phrases began to be abbreviated, leading to such forms as *O.W.* for *oll wright* ("all right"), *K.Y.* for *know yuse* ("no use"), and *O.K.* for *oll korrect* ("all correct"). While the other abbreviations vanished, *O.K.* achieved national currency in the name of the Democratic Party's "O.K. Club." This club was formed in New York City in 1840 to promote the reelection of President Martin Van Buren, and although the "O.K." in the club's name was actually an abbreviation of *Old Kinderhook*, a nickname of Van Buren, whose birthplace was the village of Kinderhook, near Albany, N.Y., the abbreviation became firmly established in the sense of "all right" that is used today.

Postscript: 120 years later, in 1961, a group of astronauts on the Mercury Project popularized a fresh and more intensive variant of *O.K.* It was *A-OK*, meaning "excellent, perfect," and it was coined by blending a century-old adjective, *A-one* or *A1,* meaning "first-class" with the equally old *O.K.* In effect, two old abbreviations were combined to create a new one.

THE ALPHABET AGENCIES

The biggest boost to the use of abbreviations was the creation of the so-called "alphabet agencies" during the early years of President Franklin D. Roosevelt's administration. Beginning in 1933, the New Deal launched over 20 agencies that got to be known primarily by their abbreviations. Some of the most important ones were the *AAA* (for Agricultural Adjustment Administration), *CCC* (Civilian Conservation Corps), *FCC* (Federal Communications Commission), *FDIC* (Federal Deposit Insurance Corporation), *FHA* (Federal Housing Administration), *NLRB* (National Labor Relations Board), *NRA* (National Recovery Administration), *PWA* (Public Works Administration), *SEC* (Securities and Exchange Commission), *TVA* (Tennessee Valley Authority), and *WPA* (Works Progress Administration). The mix of letters was also somewhat facetiously referred to as an "alphabet soup." Nevertheless, abbreviations continued to proliferate not only in government but in business and technology, with no end in sight.

The information explosion that began in the 20th century made abbreviation a common practice in communication because a major factor in their use is that of economy. They contribute to conciseness, precision, and succinctness. The downside of abbreviating, if it's excessive, is a loss of literateness and good prose.

TXT MSGS

Text messaging, instant messaging, e-mail—these are big areas for abbreviations. Text messaging (also called "texting") is transmitting very short messages (hovering about 160 characters) from one cell phone to another or others, a limitation on space that calls for frequent abbreviations, such as BCNU ("be seeing you"), NE1 ("anyone"), RUOK ("are you OK"), OIC ("Oh, I see"), MS U ("miss you"), and CU L8R ("see you later"). Such abbreviated forms are also used routinely in instant messaging (abbreviated "IM," and referred to as "IM-ing"), in e-mails, and who knows? maybe in letters sent by snail mail, if people are still old-fashioned enough to write letters to one another.

Here, for the record, are some popular e-mail abbreviations:

BFN—Bye for now
BTW—By the way
HSIK—How should I know
IMO—In my opinion
IOW—In other words
LOL—Laughing out loud
NBD—No big deal
ROTFL—Rolling on the floor laughing
TIC—Tongue in cheek

On the upside, abbreviations have the advantage of conveying a sense of social identity and being "in the know," as would be the case with computer and Internet buffs. In telegraphy, for example, as well as in computerized communications, the extra time, space, and materials required for rendering long words and phrases is an important concern. It is well-known that most speech is filled with redundancies, unnecessary repetitions and circumlocutions, and the redundancy increases considerably in long messages. The fact that much information in long communications is redundant makes abbreviation convenient, even necessary. Long descriptive terms can be shortened into easily remembered units. The need for speed in shorthand and the desire to avoid redundancy in codes makes abbreviation an important element in stenography and cryptography as well.

Another factor in the growing use of abbreviations is the proliferation of new companies and organizations that need to be named. Long names like Archer Daniels Midlands Company are easier remembered as *ADM* by consumers of its agricultural products, not to mention its shareholders. In recent years many corporations, aware of the value of abbreviated names as mnemonics or easily remembered units, have named themselves simply *CIB, SBC, BMW, ING*, without ever explaining what the letters stand for, if indeed they stand for anything. Many organizations and government agencies are best remembered by their abbreviated names as well. Some well-known ones beginning with the letter *A* are

AAA *(American Automobile Association)*

AARP *(American Association of Retired Persons)*

ABA *(American Basketball Association)*

ACLU *(American Civil Liberties Union)*

AFDC *(Aid to Families with Dependent Children)*

AFL-CIO *(American Federation of Labor-Congress of Industrial Organizations)*

The examples so far illustrate the kind of abbreviations known as *initialisms* (and sometimes as *alphabetisms*) because they are formed from the initial letters of a string of words and are pronounced as a sequence of letters. For example, the slang abbreviation *BYOB* (for "bring your own booze/bottle") is pronounced /bee'wy'o'bee'/, and popular communication and entertainment staples like *CD, DVD, VCR,* and of course *TV,* are pronounced respectively as /see′dee′/, /dee′vee′dee′/, /vee′see′ar′/, and / tee′ vee′/. And we are indebted to the automobile industry for popularizing the abbreviations *APR* and *SUV,* which, for the noncognoscenti, stand for "annual percentage rate" and "sports utility vehicle," respectively. A glance at the daily paper will easily turn up numerous initialisms, such as *DWI* ("driving while intoxicated"), *PG-rating* ("Parental Guidance" movie rating), *CIA* ("Central Intelligence Agency"), *GOP* ("Grand Old Party," nickname of the Republican Party), *UN* ("United Nations"), *EU* ("European Union"). The names of medical conditions are usually long and are therefore commonly abbreviated, for example, *ADD* ("attention deficit disorder"), *ADHD* ("attention deficit hyperactivity disorder"), *CFS* ("chronic fatigue syndrome"), *OCS* ("obsessive-compulsive disorder"), *STD* ("sexually transmitted disease"), *MSBP* ("Munchausen syndrome by proxy"), and *PTSD* ("post-traumatic stress disorder").

Abbreviations can be used as verbs, nouns, adjectives, or other parts of speech. The initialism *ID* for *identification* is also used as a noun (*Show him your ID*), as a verb meaning "to identify" (*The police ID'd the suspect*), and as an adjective (*I lost my ID card*). The word *overdose*'s medical abbreviation, *OD,* has become a verb (*He OD'd on heroin*) and a noun (*died of a fatal OD*). Abbreviations are also used to form compounds like *A-bomb, H-bomb, B-movies,* and *an R-rating.* Or they can be used to form derivatives such as *UFOlogy* and *UFOlogical* (*UFO* standing for "unidentified flying object").

ACRONYMANIA

The term **acronym** was coined about 1943 to denote a wordlike type of abbreviation that became widespread during World War

II, like *radar* (from *radio detection and ranging*), *sonar* (from *sound navigation ranging*), *loran* (from *long range navigation*), *jato* (from *jet-assisted takeoff*), *WAVES* (for *Women Accepted for Volunteer Emergency Service*), and *UNRRA* (from *United Nations Relief and Rehabilitation Administration*). The term *acronym* was formed from the combining forms *acro-*, "tip, end" and *-onym*, "name," on the analogy of words like *synonym, homonym,* and so on. Unlike initialisms, which consist of the initial letters of a string of words and are pronounced letter by letter, acronyms are formed from the first letters or syllables of a string of words and p*ronounced as a word.* Some famous acronyms include:

NASA /nas'a/ *(for National Aeronautics and Space Administration)*

NASCAR /nas'kär/ *(for National Association for Stock Car Racing)*

NASDAQ /nas'dak/ *(for National Association of Securities Dealers Automated Quotations)*

NATO /nay'tow/ *(for North Atlantic Treaty Organization)*

Because they are pronounced, acronyms often share the grammar of standard words, taking on plural endings and shifting to new parts of speech. Hence, they are a productive source of new vocabulary, as seen almost daily in the media by the appearance of novel coinages, for example, *dink* ("double income/no kids"), *POTUS* ("President of the United States"), and *NIMBY* ("Not in my back yard"). Some acronyms are themselves based in part on already-existing acronyms, for example, *guppie* for "gay urban professional," based on the earlier *yuppie*, "young urban professional." The acronym *WASP* ("White Anglo-Saxon Protestant") yielded the derivatives *WASPy* and *WASPish*, meaning "like a White Anglo-Saxon Protestant." And because acronyms are so much like words, they can produce variant forms with their own meanings. For example, the acronym *WYSIWIG*, pronounced *wizzywig*, used in computer technology for "What you see is what you get," was the basis for the acronym *WYSIWYP*, pronounced *wizzywip*, which stands for "What you see is what you print."

Most acronyms are spelled at first with capital letters but rarely appear with periods. When they become very common, they are frequently spelled in lower case: *quasar* (from *quasistellar*), *laser* (from *lightwave amplification by stimulated emission of radiation*), *sitcom* (from *situation comedy*), *biopic* (from *biographical motion picture*). But when they have an ambiguous appearance, and especially when they resemble common words, they retain the capitalized form: *AIDS* (from *acquired immune deficiency syndrome*) and *SARS* (from *severe acute respiratory syndrome*). If they are proper names, they usually retain the initial capital: *Anzam* (from *Australia, New Zealand, and Malaysia*), *Soweto* (from *South West Townships*). Acronyms are sometimes deliberately modeled on older acronyms: the acronym *maser* (from *microwave amplification by stimulated emission of radiation*) was followed by the coinage of *laser*, which in turn led to the coinage of *graser* (from *gamma-ray amplification by stimulated emission of radiation*). Though the acronym *taser*, a gunlike device that fires electrified darts, derives its name from *Tele-Active Shock Electronic Repulsion*, its form was influenced by *laser*.

Acronyms are coined in English in many fields of activity: science, technology, sports, politics, military, and the media. Examples from electronics and computer technology include *GIGO* (from *garbage in garbage out*), *MIPS* (from *million instructions per second*), *RAM* (from *random-access memory*). Other fields have given us *SWAT* (from *Special Weapons and Tactics*), *ESOL* (from *English for Speakers of Other Languages*), *TESOL* (from *Teachers of English to Speakers of Other Languages*), *REM* (from *Rapid Eye Movement*). Politics and wars have generated many acronyms including *WAC*,

GI, MP, SALT, some intended as slogans, *WIN* (from *Whip Inflation Now*), and others unintentionally funny or intentionally derisive, like *CREEP* (from *Committee to Reelect the President*) and
MEOW (from *moral equivalent of war*).

DISASTROUS ACRONYMS

*Here are two examples of nearly disastrous acronyms de-
scribed in a 1982 article in the language quarterly* Verba-
tim:

During the Nixon administration, the White House staff
invented the acronym NISSIM for certain memorandums
titled National Security Study Memorandum. When the
Carter Administration took over, the title of these memos
was changed to Presidential Security Study Memorandum. Not a moment too soon, it was wisely decided to
scuttle the corresponding acronym.

During the 1982 Memorial Day weekend, the Massachusetts authorities, trying to maintain highway safety for visiting motorists, deployed on the roads helpful teams
bearing the title of Fatal Accident Re-education Teams.
Rather than use the obvious acronym, they prudently
chose the not-exactly-acronymic FARE.

New groups or organizations looking for a memorable name
often choose a catchy acronym such as *MADD* (*Mothers Against
Drunk Driving*) and *NOW* (*National Organization of Women*). This
phenomenon is called a "reverse acronym." The creators start
with a word they want as their name and then they work from
its letters to find the words that represent something like the

idea they want to be associated with. Another widespread recent phenomenon is acronyms based on some popular phrase. One can make an acronym or initialism from any common phrase and just about any string of words. The restaurant chain TGI Friday's is one; starting a memo with FYI is another.

Acronyms are especially popular in naming geographical areas and locations. *SoHo*, an avant-garde section in lower Manhattan, was so named from its being *South of Houston Street*, but the name was clearly influenced by the Soho district in London. Soon after, the section situated *North of Houston Street* was christened *No-Ho*. This inspired local wits to rename Houston Street *Ho-Ho*. The acronym by which the populous Boston–New York–Washington axis or corridor has come to be known is the whimsical-sounding *Bosnywash*. Other large urban corridors have since considered similar acronyms for themselves: *Chipitts* for the Chicago–Pittsburgh axis, *Sansan* for the San Francisco–San Diego axis.

Humorous acronyms are in a class of their own. *BOMFOG* or *bomfog*, meaning pompous, bombastic rhetoric, was coined by Nelson Rockefeller from the initials of "brotherhood of man and fatherhood of God," a high-sounding expression used in speeches by members of his own family. Another acronym critical of excessive rhetoric is *MEGO*, which stands for "My Eyes Glaze Over." Political decisions are sometimes sarcastically said to be made by *BOGSAT*, meaning a "Bunch of Guys Sitting Around a Table." In hospital parlance, a *GOMER*, or *gomer*, is a whining or obnoxious patient, a name thought to be an acronym for "Get Out of My Emergency Room!" And let's not forget the famous acronyms *FUBAR* for (polite form) "Fouled Up Beyond All Repair" and *SNAFU* for (polite form) "Situation Normal All Fouled Up."

back-
formation:
finding short roots
in long words

If you were asked which word came first into English, *gloom* or *gloomy, reminisce* or *reminiscence, resurrect* or *resurrection,* you would probably say the shorter word came first. You would respond that way because in English it is common to form a new word by adding an ending to an older and shorter word. But sometimes, as in the examples just mentioned, it works the other way around and a shorter word is derived from a longer one by removing a part of it, such as a suffix or prefix. Thus, *gloom* came from *gloomy, reminisce* from *reminiscence,* and *resurrect* from *resurrection.* Another such word is *editor.* It looks like it came from *edit,* the verb, but actually the noun *editor* is the older word. Similarly, *television* gave rise to *televise,* and *babysitter* preceded *babysit.* The verb *sculpt* came from *sculptor* by analogy with an established pattern, for example, *act/actor, direct/director.* This process is considered abnormal, since it reverses the way people usually make up new words. The usual rule of word formation is expressed in the formula X + A → Y *(agitate + -ion → agitation)*. The reverse, however, is expressed as Y - A → X *(intuition – -ion → intuit)*. The noun *couth* and the verb *intuit* were formed from the words *uncouth* and *intuition*.

The editor of the *Oxford English Dictionary* (*OED*), Sir James Murray, coined the term back-formation for words like these since they reverse the usual way words are formed. Some have called them back-derivations or inverse-derivations. But most dictionaries prefer the term *back-formation* to describe both the process by which such words come about and the words themselves. Linguists have defined *back-formation* as "the formation of new words by the deletion of actual or supposed affixes in longer words," which can be termed a special case of clipping or shortening (see the next chapter).

ENTHUSED ABOUT BACK-FORMATIONS?

Often, back-formations are criticized when they first arrive on the scene. Some offend the aesthetic sense ("such an ugly-looking word") or the desire to conserve the "purity" of the language. Examples of those denounced include *enthuse* from *enthusiasm*, *intuit* from *intuition*, and *liaise* from *liaison*. To *back-form* is itself a back-formation. Back-formations of all kinds, unless very well-established, are more frequently found in informal rather than formal language. The main reason for the initial dislike of a new back-formation is its unusual formation, regarded as aberrant jargon or slang. This is exemplified by the controversial reception of the verb *enthuse*, "to show enthusiasm," in various usage books. Robert C. Pooley, in *The Teaching of English Usage* (1974), quotes the following passage from a 1902 usage manual: "*Enthused* is not only a monster, but a useless creature in company with such well-bred words as *stirred, aroused, inspired, excited, transported, ravished, intoxicated.*" Pooley points out that, despite such early condemnation, *enthuse* has been growing more frequent in popular speech and is occasionally found in writing. Yet he admits that its status remained uncertain in the 1970s, as seen in the comments of several usage writers of that period:

as a back-formation from *enthusiasm,* it is one that has not won full acceptance. (Theodore M. Bernstein, *The Careful Writer*)

The formation of this word is unsystematic . . . . Lopping off 60 percent of a word without analogical precedent has undoubtedly stood in the way of ultimate acceptance of *enthuse* . . . (J. J. Lamberts, *A Short Introduction to English Usage*)

Enthuse is not well established in writing on a serious level. (*American Heritage Dictionary*)

Enthuse, enthused . . . . Many readers find these words annoying. Avoid. (Hans P. Guth and Edgar H. Schuster, *American English Today*)

This attitude had softened considerably by the 1980s, and the article on *enthuse* in the 1989 *Webster's Dictionary of English Usage,* after pointing out signs that the stigma on this word had begun to disappear, ends on this positive note: "In another hundred years or so, who knows?—maybe everyone will have forgotten why there was ever any fuss over *enthuse.*"

The same *Webster's* reports that *donate,* an American English back-formation from *donation,* was roundly condemned throughout most of the 19th century (the verb had been around since 1785). But by 1917, the scholar J. Lesslie Hall, in his book, *En-*

glish Usage, after citing the critic T. L. K. Oliphant's condemnation of *donate* as "a new-fangled word," gave this ringing defense to the maligned verb:

> The form *donate* appeals to the American *sprachgefühl*; it fills the mouth better than *give*; sounds "bigger" in the papers and on the street, and also comes, by a familiar process, from the noun *donation*. . . . Some good scholars forget that most of our words were once new-fangled, or rather, neologisms. Others think that no good thing can come out of America. If the millionaire-philanthropists and their clients need a new word, why not let them have it? Words, like politicians, may have a constituency.

Webster's last word on the word: "It is no longer controversial."

OTHER FORMS OF BACK-FORMATIONS

Not all back-formations fit the pattern by which *couth* and *intuit* were formed—by dropping a prefix or suffix. Sometimes a new word is formed by a grammatical back-formation, as when a singular word ending in *-s* is mistaken for a plural, so that when the *-s* is dropped, a new singular is formed. This is how *pea* was formed from *pease* (pronounced *peez*), even though historically *pease* was a singular. Similarly, *riddle* was formed from Middle English *redels*, and *skate* from an earlier *skeates*, a singular word borrowed from Dutch *schaats* and mistaken for a plural.

A notable example of this process is *sherry*, the wine. The word first appeared as *sherris* in Shakespeare's *Henry IV, Part II* (1597), where Falstaff gives a long speech in praise of "your excellent sherris." The spelling *sherris* was borrowed from Spanish (*vino de*) *Xeres*, "wine from Xeres," Xeres being the town in Spain where the wine was made. But shortly after its appearance in English, *sherris* was taken to be a plural, and the new singular *sherry* was formed, appearing in 1608 in a play by Thomas Middleton, *A Mad World, My Masters*.

The great majority of English back-formations are verbs, such as *surveille* from *surveillance, diagnose* from *diagnosis, swindle* from *swindler, peddle* from *peddler,* and *beg* from *beggar*. The most successful of the back-formed verbs are those coined by analogy with standard verbs. For example, *escalate* was a back-formation from *escalator,* on the analogy of such pairs as *elevate/elevator* and *decorate/decorator*. Nouns ending in *-ion* frequently give rise to corresponding verbs. The verbs *abduct, appreciate, electrocute, investigate,* and *negate* all appeared later than the corresponding nouns *abduction, appreciation, electrocution, investigation,* and *negation,* suggesting that back-formation played a part in their coinage.

Each year sees a new crop of back-formations: *carjack,* verb, from *carjacking, Iraqify* from *Iraqification, weaponize* from *weaponization, call-forward* from *call forwarding*. Also, unusually, nouns were back-formed from adjectives: *sleaze* from *sleazy, raunch* from *raunchy, grunge* from *grungy*. In 2003, the term *embedded reporter* or *embedded journalist* suddenly filled the media as a large number of Western war correspondents became "embedded" with military units, living and marching with them into Iraq. Within months, such journalists came to be called *embeds,* by back-formation from *embedded*: "[Chris] Ayres managed just nine days as an embed in Iraq . . . in the back of a Humvee" (*New Yorker,* Sept. 12, 2005).

Some back-formations are coined because they meet a real need, as the verbs *jell* from *jelly, grovel* from *groveling, automate* from *automation, jubilate* from *jubilation*. Others are playful formations, such as a whole group of words created by the whimsical dropping of what looks like a negative prefix. Examples of these are *ertia* (from *inertia*), *sipid* (from *insipid*), *armingly* (from *disarmingly*), *scrutable* (from *inscrutable*). Such words are coined either for effect or because people think they exist or ought to exist. Some, like *ept* and *eptitude* (from *inept* and *ineptitude*), have actually gained some currency, perhaps by influence of the pair *apt/aptitude*. Yet serious back-formations far outweigh the playful ones, with fully established new verbs like *emote* (from *emotion*) and *laze*, derived from *lazy*, possibly by analogy with such pairs as *craze/crazy*. *Lech* was formed from *lecher* as a parallel to *love/lover*. Similarly, *lase* comes from *laser* and *surreal* from *surrealism*.

THE FUTURE OF THE FORM

Interestingly, fifty or sixty years ago back-formations were dismissed by usage writers as rarities, few of which were destined to survive. This is what Porter G. Perrin's widely used *Writer's Guide and Index to English* (1950, revised edition 1959) thought about back-formations:

> A number of back formations have made their way, like *diagnose* from *diagnosis*, *edit* from *editor*; some, like *enthuse*, are slowly making their way; but most are formed in fun, like *burgle*, and are used either in humor or in a derogatory sense, like *orate*. *Donate* seems unnecessary, since we have *give*, but *enthuse* is more justifiable, since it takes the place of the clumsy *be enthusiastic over*.

By now we know that most back-formations are not formed in fun, but rather to fill some needy niche in the vocabulary. *Burgle*, derived from *burglar*, has been used in British English since it was coined in the 1870s (American English prefers *burglarize*, coined about the same time). *Orate*, derived from *oration*, has been indeed used in American English since the 1860s mainly as a humorous word meaning to engage in excessive oratory. But these are exceptions. A more recent work, *The World*

Almanac Guide to Good Word Usage (1959, edited by Martin H. Manser with Jeffrey McQuain), presents the current view:

> Back-formations often arise as a result of false assumptions about the composition of a word. People hearing the word *scavenger* might assume incorrectly that the noun comes from a verb *scavenge* and so come to use this verb . . . . New verbs are regularly being formed in this way: *televise, automate.* Many, such as *liaise* (from *liaison*) are disliked when newly coined, but when such verbs are created from a genuine need for them in the language, they tend to be retained.

FUNNY FORMATIONS

The process of back-formation, because it reverses the norm, has been used sometimes to create comic effects. The British lexicographer Diane Nicholls gives several examples of the humor elicited from back-formation. When a friend of hers complained that he had been asked to be an usher at three weddings in one year, he exclaimed indignantly: "Do I look like a man who likes to ush? Do they think I enjoy ushing?!" Another example is the old joke, which starts "Do you enjoy Kipling?" and the answer comes "I can't rightly say. I've never kipled." Since a word like *intrepid* might be construed as a negative (on the analogy of negative words like *indecent* and *incredible*), it would take little effort for someone to create the facetious back-formation *trepid* ("I consider myself a trepid explorer"). Similarly, *delible* ("a delible pen") is a possible back-formation from *indelible*. While there is no evidence of a positive adjective *gruntled* being derived from *disgruntled*, the back-formation *disgrunt*, verb, did show up in a piece in *The New York Times Book Review* of April 30, 1972: "The other two jurors went on to give the prize to . . . the collator, leading one critic to disgrunt that next year they'll give it to a Xerox machine." This is apparently a nonce word, coined for the occasion, suggesting other possible nonce coinages, such as *pensable* from *indispensable* and *gainly* from *ungainly.*

BACK-FORMATIONS IN ACTION

Verb compounds are among those that are frequently formed by back-formation. Such verbs usually have noun or adjective compounds as their sources. To *globetrot*, for example, is probably derived from the noun *globetrotter* or *globetrotting*. To *free-associate* appears to be from the noun *free association,* and to *henpeck* and *spoonfeed* were derived from the adjectives *henpecked* and *spoon-fed.* Other examples of compound verbs formed by dropping a noun ending include:

> air-condition (from *air conditioner*)
> babysit (from *babysitter*)
> gift wrap (from *gift wrapping*)
> housekeep (from *housekeeper*)
> house-sit (from *house sitter*)
> mass-produce (from *mass production*)
> proofread (from *proofreading*)
> safekeep (from *safekeeping*)
> sightsee (from *sightseeing*)
> spring-clean (from *spring-cleaning*)
> stage-manage (from *stage manager*)
> tape-record (from *tape recorder*)
> typewrite (from *typewriter*)
> window-shop (from *window-shopping*)

FILLING A VOID

As one might expect, back-formations play an important role in scientific and technological word-making. Space scientists originally used the verb *self-destruct* (back-formed from *self-destruction*) when a rocket or other device was designed to destroy itself under certain conditions. The term was adopted by the military and, as every TV-watcher knows, *self-destruct* was popularized by the series *Mission Impossible*. Some less well-known examples of scientific back-formation include verbs like *back-mutate*, "to revert to the original genetic form" (from *back mutation*), *mitose*, "to undergo mitosis" (from *mitosis*), *immunosuppress*, "suppress (someone's) immune system" (from *immunosuppression*), *thermoregulate*, "to regulate one's body temperature" (from *thermoregulation*), and *vasoligate*, "to tie off (someone's) sperm-bearing tubes" (from *vasoligation*).

Back-formation has by now achieved standing as a traditional source of new words. When coined naturally and out of genuine need, it contributes substantially to the vocabulary of the English language. In a *New York Times Magazine* column titled "Back-Formation" (Oct. 12, 2005) the language writer William Safire goes even further:

> *Back-form* is a verb formed from the noun *back-formation*, just as *edit* is a verb created by editing the end of the noun *editor*. Try it yourself, become a neologist. You can even front-form: computerese has brought us *unsubscribe* (cancel my subscription!) and *uninstall* (rip it out of the wall!). By paring down words and shuffling the parts of speech you may coin a word that fills a void and catches on.

CHAPTER 8

clipping or shortening:

back, fore, and fore-and-aft

Etymologists, who study the origin of words (not to be confused with entomologists, who study insects), have traced the practice of clipping or shortening words to the early 1700s, when the fashion arose in England to truncate long words when talking informally—*phiz* for *physiognomy, poz* for *positive, hip* for *hypochondriac, rep* for *reputation,* and *mob* for *mobile,* meaning "the fickle throng, rabble" (from Latin *mobile vulgus,* "common people").

The practice was sharply criticized by Jonathan Swift, who thought that "we are already overloaded with monosyllables, which are the disgrace of our language." Though he was backed in this by other famous writers, such as Joseph Addison, the practice of clipping words became more popular, and while most of the voguish clippings of his day fell out of use (*mob* was the exception), the floodgates had been opened for clipped words to inundate the mother tongue.

In truth, however, cutting words short was not invented in the 18th century. We find earlier instances of words that had been lopped off longer ones and actually replaced the original. *Wig*, for example, was clipped (no pun intended) in the 1600s from *periwig*, a word borrowed from Middle French, and the shorter word soon eclipsed the long one. Also in the 1600s, the word *pun* appeared in John Dryden's comedy, *The Wild Gallant*, very likely as a clipped form of *pundigrion*, meaning an ambiguity, a play on words, which was borrowed from Italian *puntiglio*, the source of English *punctilio*. In the same period, *brandy* was shortened from the earlier *brandy-wine*, which came into English from Dutch *brandewijn*, "burnt wine," and *withdrawing room* became *drawing room*. Even earlier, in the 1500s, *gent* was shortened from *gentleman*, *lunch* from *luncheon*, and *coz* was a popular shortening of *cousin*. Perhaps the oldest example of clipping was the word *patter*, "to talk rapidly, chatter" (originally, "recite a prayer rapidly"), which appeared in the 1300s and was derived from *pater*, a clipped form of *paternoster*, "the Lord's prayer" (literally, "Our Father"), a prayer usually recited at a good clip.

CUTS THAT CHANGE MEANING

There is a basic difference between clipping and back-formation. The process of back-formation consists of both a change in form and a change in the part of speech: The noun *intuition* begets the verb *intuit*; the adjective *sleazy* engenders the noun *sleaze*. In clipping, the part of speech of the clipped word does not change: Whether you hail a *cab*, a *taxi*, or a *taxicab*, all three remain nouns. The only change that occurs is that the original form is clipped: *mayonnaise* becomes *mayo*, *delicatessen* becomes *deli*, *rehabilitation* becomes *rehab*.

There are, however, exceptions.

One exception is that some clipped words get meanings that differ from the words they derive from. For example, *narc* or *narco* (clipped from *narcotic*) doesn't mean a narcotic but a government narcotics agent, and *mod* (from *modern*) denotes a style of dress of the 1960s featuring minidresses, boots, and other fashions of the time. An early example is *extra*, "additional," which in the late 1700s was shortened from *extraordinary*. A recent example is *hype*, "excessive publicity," which is ultimately a clipped form of the combining form *hyper-*, "over, excessive." This form of shortening should not be confused with those that often occurred in early English by aphesis, which is the loss of an unstressed vowel or syllable at the beginning of a word. Examples of such words are *mend* (from *amend*), *tend* (from *attend*), *lone* (from *alone*), and *squire* (from *esquire*). The shortened words usually had meanings that differed markedly from the longer ones, which is why both forms are retained in the language.

Another exception is that clipped forms sometimes undergo a change in spelling. Some spelling changes are based on pronunciation: *nuke*, "nuclear weapon," was shortened and altered from *nuclear*, *fax* from *facsimile*, *trank*, "tranquilizing drug," from *tranquilizer*, *perk* from both *perquisite* and *percolator*. Such forms also occur in slang (*natch* from *naturally*, *Jeez* from *Jesus*, *pard* for *partner*). Other clipped forms are altered by the addition of a diminutive or other ending: *weenie* or *wienie* from *wiener* (an early synonym of *frankfurter*, now often clipped to *frank*), *veggie* from *vegetable*, *cabbie* from *cabdriver*. Other examples of "irregular" clippings in which the spellings have changed are: *bike* from *bicycle*, *mike* from *microphone*, *pram* from *perambulator*. Clipped forms that have a *-y* or *-ie* suffix are *Aussie* from *Australian*, *bookie* from *bookmaker*, *commie* from *communist*, *hanky* from *handkerchief*, and *movie* from *moving picture*.

Clipping in scientific and technical terminology is often much more complex. Some examples are: *phorate* (an insecticide) from *phosphorodithioate*; *hycanthone* (an antibacterial drug) from *hy*droxymethyl thio*xanthenone*; and *phencyclidine* (an immobilizing drug) from *phenylcyclohexyl piperidine*. There seem to be no limitations on this type of clipping other than the clipped form should resemble a word.

VULGAR AND IMPERTINENT?

The practice of clipping syllables from longer words continued well into the 19th and 20th centuries to the present. Among such "stump words," as the Danish linguist Otto Jespersen called them, were *vet*, clipped from *veterinarian* and also from *veteran*; *van*, clipped from *caravan*, *cab* from *cabriolet*, *exam* from *examination*, *fan* from *fanatic*, *pants* from *pantaloons*, *brig* from *brigantine*, *canter* from *Canterbury gallop*. The now standard word *bus* was shortened in the 1830s from *omnibus*, a word borrowed from French, which took it from Latin *omnibus*, "for all." And *zoo* appeared about 1840 as a shortening of *zoological garden*. Clipped words multiplied especially in the United States. Writing in the 1920s, H. L. Mencken reported in *The American Language*:

> We have thus witnessed, within the past few years, the genesis of scores [of clipped words] now in wide use and fast taking on respectability: *phone* for *telephone*, *gas* for *gasoline*, *co-ed* for *co-educational*, *pop* for *populist*, *frat* for *fraternity*, *gym* for *gymnasium*, *movie* for *moving picture*, *plane* for *air-plane*, *prep-school* for *preparatory-school*, *auto* for *automobile*. . . .

Yet critics on both sides of the Atlantic continued to look askance on clippings. To most of us, the word *bike* is a common and acceptable short form for *bicycle* and, by extension, *motorcycle*. But in 1906, H. W. and F. G. Fowler's *The King's English*, frowning on "shortenings by the lower classes," reluctantly predicted that "*bike* will very likely be good English also in time. But though its brevity is a strong recommendation, and its uncouthness probably no more than subjective and transitory, it is as yet slang. Such words should not be used in print . . . ." Mencken himself expressed reservation about some shortenings that "linger on the edge of vulgarity," such as *flu* for *influenza, pen* for *penitentiary, con* for *convict* and for *confidence* (as in *con-man, con-game, to con*), *beaut* for *beauty, champ* for *champion, coke* for *cocaine, wiz* for *wizard, hon* for *honey,* and *barkeep* for *barkeeper.*

In 1966, Follett's *Modern American Usage* commented:

> Shortenings . . . always carry a tone of vulgarity or impertinence, and if they are applied to persons they are resented by those whom they mean to designate. Among the vulgar ones are *glads* for *gladioli, mums* for *chrysanthemums, nympho* for *nymphomaniac, psycho* for *psychological* (or more exactly, *psychiatric) case* or *patient,* and so forth. The curtailed titles *Doc* and *Prof* can only be uttered as a sort of joke between intimate friends; and the supposedly collegiate words *grad, undergrad,* and *frat*(ernity) are chiefly in favor with makers of movies and other strangers to campus life.

And as recently as 1985, Hans P. Guth, in his *New English Handbook,* writes: "Avoid clipped forms like *bike, prof, doc, fan, mag, exec, econ.*" Yet he admits that "other shortened forms, like *phone, ad,* and *exam* are now commonly used in serious writing."

Times have changed. Standard English has become less formal than in the past, and though dictionaries often label clipped words as "Informal" or "Colloquial," implying a conversational level a notch or two below formal, current usage tends to overlook such niceties. *Bus, cab, chimp, bra, exam, gym, lab, phone,* and *plane* have become Standard English. Words like *ad* and *adman* and *want ad, memo, info, combo, limo,* and *celeb* (from *celebrity*) no longer raise eyebrows, and clippings that originated in college slang have become standard as well: *dorm, lab, math, poly-sci, grad, prof, prom, pre-med,* and so on. Most people are not even aware that *burger* was clipped from *hamburger* or that *polio* is a shortened form of *poliomyelitis,* nor do they give any thought to *taxi* being clipped from *taxicab* or *piano* being a shortening of *pianoforte.* How many know that *cute* is a clipped form of *acute,* or that *squash,* the vegetable, was mercifully shortened from *isquoutersquash,* a word borrowed from Algonquian meaning "green things that can be eaten raw?"

CUTS OF THE TIMES

Starting in the 1960s, clipped forms began burgeoning in English: *deli, disco, lib* (*women's lib, gay lib, kids' lib*), *mayo, mod, fab* (for *fabulous*), *narc, perp* (for *perpetrator*), *hood* (for *neighborhood*), *op-ed* (for *opposite-editorial page*), and *photo-op* (for *photo opportunity*). Examples run the gamut of uses, depending on the social, economic, and political activities and happenings of the time. The rise in alcoholic and narcotic addiction standardized clippings like *detox* (from *detoxify* and *detoxification*), *rehab* (from *rehabilitation*), *meth* (from *methadone*), *dex* (from *dexedrine*). In intellectual circles, a *pseud* and sometimes *pseudo* (from *pseudointellectual*) denoted someone with intellectual or artistic pretensions. In popular culture, *zines* (from *fanzines*) were magazines devoted to science fiction, popular music, or other interests. In art and literature, *pomo* came to stand for both postmodern and postmodernism. Businesspeople invested millions in *munis* (from *municipal bonds*) and cancer patients underwent *chemo* (from *chemotherapy*). Computer use reduced the *Internet* to the *Net,* and the *World Wide Web* to the *Web.* A recent example is *bot,* a clipping of *robot,* used in computer technology, especially in compounds like *mailbot* and *searchbot,* for time-saving programs performed with robotlike precision.

THE THREE CUTS OF CUTS

Analysis of clippings shows that they tend to fall into three categories, which have been called "back-clippings," "fore-clippings," and "fore-and-aft clippings." Back-clippings are those in which the end of the word is clipped off and they are the most common type. Examples of back-clippings include:

ad(vertisement) and (in British English) advert(isement)
bi(sexual)
bra(ssiere)
champ(ion)
chimp(anzee)
condo(minium)
coop(erative)
decal(comania)
demo(nstration)
disco(theque)
exam(ination)
frank(furter)
gym(nasium)
hippo(potamus)
lab(oratory)
lunch(eon)
math(ematics)
max(imum)
mayo(nnaise)
memo(randum)
piano(forte)
porn(ography) or porno(graphy)
pro(fessional)
prof(essor)

pub(lic house)
reg(ulation)
rep(utation)
tech(nical), tech(nician), tech(nology)

Note that *pub* is an example of a clipped phrase. Other examples of this are: *perm* from *permanent wave, op art* from *optical art, pop* from *popular music, prefab* from *prefabricated building,* con from *confidence trick,* and zoo from *zoological garden.* From *perm* and *con,* verbs (*to perm, to con*) have been formed.

"Fore-clippings" are those in which the front of the word is clipped off, as in the following:

(a)*cute*
(air)*plane*
(alli)*gator*
(earth)*quake*
(ham)*burger*
(heli)*copter*
(motor) *car*
(oleo)*margarine*
(omni)*bus*
(o)*possum*
(rac)*coon*
(tele)*phone*
(tele)*scope*
(turn)*pike*
(violon)*cello*

The third type is *"fore-and-aft clipping,"* in which parts are clipped from the front and end (and sometimes from the middle) of a word:

Amer(ican) Ind(ian) = Amerind
binoc(ular)s
bio(graphical) pic(ture) = biopic
(French) frie(d) (potatoe)s = fries
(in)flu(enza)
op(tical) art
(re)frig(erator) = fridge
sci(ence) fi(ction)
sit(uation) com(edy)

Earlier in this chapter, we pointed out that some clipped forms have origins which have been forgotten, like *mob.* This is an example of semantic "dissociation" from the full form. A word like *mob* (from Latin *mobile vulgus)* and *pants* (from *pantaloons)* are no longer felt to be clippings since the longer forms are not used. *Curio* (from *curiosity)* and *fan* (from *fanatic)* have acquired meanings that are quite different from their earlier full forms and are also not regarded as shortenings.

The bottom line is that most of the time the result of clipping will be a synonym which is often more convenient to use than the longer word and that the longer word will fall into less frequent use. In modern English, we tend to clip words which we use a lot, as in the area of education (*gym, math, trig)* and eating (*burger, Coke, lunch, shake)*. Clipped words are often used casually and informally, but they obviously serve a useful purpose in communication, else they would not endure for as long as they do.

CHAPTER 9

contractions:

its do's and don'ts

George Bernard Shaw, an ardent promoter of spelling reform (he financed a public competition in the 1950s for the creation of a new alphabet that came to be known as the "Shavian Alfabet"), famously published the texts of his plays with spellings like *dont, shouldnt,* and *hadnt,* in which he omitted the apostrophes in words that were clearly contractions of phrases (*do not, should not, had not*). Others have followed Shaw's example without success. Porter Perrin gave Shaw this ambiguous defense: "The apostrophe is one of the most useless anachronisms in our traditional system of spelling, as Bernard Shaw demonstrated in his printed works; but you must know how to use it."

Perrin was right. English has long shown a fondness for marking contractions with apostrophes. Shakespeare is chock-full of contractions like *'tis, 'twas, 'twere,* and *'twill,* only two of which have been replaced by modern equivalents: *'tis* by *it's* and *'twill* by *it'll,* the other two having fallen out of use, along with others, like *if't* ("if it"), *in't* ("in it"), *'tween* ("between"), *e'en* ("even"), *o'er* ("over"), and many others. Poets still use contractions like *o'er* and *e'er* ("ever"), and we find a word like *and* reduced to *'n'* in certain phrases ("coffee 'n' cake," "rock 'n' roll"), and *of* becoming *'o'* in words like *o'clock* and *will-o'-the-wisp,* and in Irish family names like *O'Brien* (where it means "descendant of").

Mark Twain reportedly had a habit of omitting punctuation marks and apostrophes in his manuscripts. He just didn't think they were all that important. His frustrated editor finally wrote him a note insisting that he insert the proper marks in their proper places. To which the author responded by sending him a page filled with punctuation marks, apostrophes, and diacritics, and the attached note, "Put them in wherever they seem to fit." The editor never complained again.

Contractions are words formed by compressing two (or more) words. The word *contraction* comes from Latin *contraction-, contractio* "a coming or drawing together," and, as applied to words, it involves the dropping of a sound in speech, or of a letter or syllable in writing. When you write *don't* instead of *do not,* or *she's* instead of *she is* or *she has,* you're doing two things: (1) imitating speech, which drops unstressed syllables, and (2) forming in writing one word in place of two. This is a kind of shortening, but entirely different from the kind of shortening represented by abbreviations (*AAAA, ABA, TNT,* etc.) and by clippings (*ad, auto, cab, zoo,* etc.).

Other languages also have contractions. Spanish, for example, contracts *de el,* "of the" to *del.* But English contractions are remarkable for their use of the apostrophe (') to show the omission of a vowel or syllable: *didn't, don't, he's, they're.* While contractions like *doesn't, they'll, haven't, didn't, won't,* and *would've* are acceptable in most writing, some writers suffer twinges of discomfort in using them. In *Garner's Modern American Usage* (2003), Bryan Garner explains: "The common fear is that using contractions can make the writing seem breezy. For most of us, though, that fear is nil. What you gain is a relaxed sincerity—not breeziness." And to bolster this point, Garner cites, among others, John R. Trimble, in *Writing with Style:* "Use occasional contractions. They'll keep you from taking yourself too seriously, tell your reader that you're not a prude, and help you achieve a more natural, conversational rhythm in your style."

Any survey of the use of contracted forms would show that they are widely accepted in informal speech and writing, but are generally unacceptable in formal writing. The acceptability depends on the context in which they are used. There is no reason, really, not to use them, but they do have to be used with care. It often depends on whether you would use the contraction in speaking that particular sentence. It also depends on whether the contraction would help or hinder the rhythm and emphasis in the sentence. Contractions have to be used by "feel," not by "rule."

COMMON CONTRACTIONS

There are various types of contractions, the most common involving the verbs *be (am, is, are), have, has, had; will, shall, would,* and *should.* They include such contractions as *I've* for *I have, he'll* for *he will, there'll* for *there will,* and *who'd* for *who would* or *who had.* There are many "had" contractions, *he'd, I'd, it'd, she'd, they'd, we'd,* and *you'd,* as well as *am/are/is* forms, *I'm, he's, she's, it's, they're, we're,* and *you're. Has* and *have* create contractions like *he's, I've, it's, she's, they've, we've,* and *you've.*

A number of contractions contain the word *not*, such as *don't* (*do not*), *haven't* (*have not*), *isn't* (*is not*), and *won't* (*will not*). A list of the most common negative contractions includes:

aren't (are not)

can't (cannot)

couldn't (could not)

doesn't (does not)

don't (do not)

hadn't (had not)

hasn't (has not)

haven't (have not)

isn't (is not)

shouldn't (should not)

wasn't (was not)

weren't (were not)

won't (will not)

wouldn't (would not)

Other, less frequent, contractions are: *ain't* (*am not*), *let's* (*let us*), *c'mon* (*come on*), *bo'sun* for *boatswain*, *fo'c'sle* for *forecastle*, and *nor'easter* for *northeaster*.

Shorthand or stenography often involves contractions and abbreviations, though they tend to be personal and inconsistent. Examples are *dept* (*department*), *quotns* (*quotations*), *sthg* (*something*), and *wout* (*without*).

Another type is called *wanna*-contraction, after its most prominent example: *wanna* from *want to*. Examples are *gonna* (*going to*), *oughta* (*ought to*), *shoulda* (*should have*), and *woulda* (*would have*). These spelling contractions are used mainly in representing informal or slang speech or dialogue. Here are a few examples of *wanna*-contractions:

"What's gonna happen next, Em?" said Lou hollowly. "What's he gonna do?" (Kurt Vonnegut, Jr., *Tomorrow and Tomorrow and Tomorrow*).

"Take the money an' get outa here." "Lemme go!" he cried, struggling to his feet. (Liam O'Flaherty, *The Informer*).

Contractions can have different meanings depending on their "context," the words around them. *What's* can mean "what is" or "what has":

What's (What is) the origin of black holes in the universe?
What's (What has) that child done now?

There are some contractions that should be avoided, mainly because they are not instantly "readable." These include wild ones like *I'd've* (*I would have*), *she'd've* (*she would have*), and *there're* (*there are, there were*). Others, like *should've, might've, may've, must've,* and *would've,* in which the *'ve* is easily mistaken for *of,* will often be erroneously changed to *should of, might of, may of, must of,* and *would of,* a common error in the writings of children. In literature, though, they are often used intentionally to transcribe the language of illiterate speakers or writers, as in the following:

If Milt hadn't of been so hoggish, he'd of ordered a half a cantaloupe instead of a whole one and it might not of stuck in his throat. (Ring Lardner, *Haircut*).

The contraction *I'd* and *I've* are used differently in American and British English. In British usage, sentences like *I'd run out of ideas* or *I've to write home* are normal, whereas in American English the same sentences would require *I had* and *I have*. Likewise, the contraction *I'll* is used differently by Americans and Britons. In American English, *I'll* can stand for either *I shall* or *I will*; in British usage, *I'll* can stand only for *I shall*. Such differences are based mainly on tradition.

One contraction that has been the object of much heated controversy is *ain't*. To begin with, the word has a strange appearance; while the apostrophe indicates that it is a contraction, it is unclear which words were contracted: *am not? are not?* If either one, why is it spelled the way it is? Then, the many uses to which it is put are baffling. How can it mean *am not, is not, are not, have not,* or *has not* at the same time?

AIN'T A STIGMA? SAY IT AIN'T SO.

The facts, as far as they're known, are these: *Ain't* developed in the 1700s as a variant form of *amn't*, which was a contraction of *am not*, and of *an't*, which was a contraction of *are not*. This explains such usages as *I ain't ready* and *They ain't here*. To complicate things, *ain't* may have also evolved from the contraction *i'n't* for *isn't* or *is not*, which would explain the usage *he (she, it) ain't here*. Finally, *ain't* could have also been a variant of the dialectal form *hain't* (for *have not* and *has not*), yielding such usages as *You ain't heard nothing yet*.

While many writers used *ain't* in its various meanings through the 1800s and 1900s, language critics steadily objected to its use on various grounds: that it was vulgar, inelegant, uneducated, illiterate, and so on. The stigma attached to its use was nevertheless generally ignored by writers until 1961, when treatment of the word (along with some others, like *irregardless* and *finalize*) in the newly published *Webster's Third New International Dictionary* erupted in a public—and much publicized—controversy. The dictionary divides the entry for *ain't* into two definitions. The first, covering the senses "are not," "is not," and "am not," is followed by the note "though disapproved by many and more common in less educated speech, used orally in most parts of the U.S. by many cultivated speakers esp. in the phrase *ain't I*." The second definition carries the label *substandard* for the senses "have not" and "has not."

Despite these caveats, newspaper and magazine writers pounced on this entry (as well as others) to condemn or ridicule *Webster's Third*. For example, *Life* magazine wrote: "Webster's, joining the say-as-you-go school of permissive English, has now all but abandoned any effort to distinguish between good and bad usage." Yet many scholars came to the dictionary's defense, both in the United States and abroad. In the long run, despite the immediate negative reactions it received, *Webster's Third*'s entry for *ain't* has withstood the test of time, as has the dictionary itself.

---

CHAPTER 10

diminutives:

smallness is (sometimes) cute and endearing

In the 1960s, various grocery stores began to call themselves *superettes* to distinguish themselves from the large *supermarkets* that were threatening to engulf them. No one seemed to realize the contradiction inherent in the name *superette*, which literally meant "large-small," the prefix *super-* meaning "large" and the suffix *-ette* meaning "small." The coiners simply wanted a word that suggested a smaller version of the supermarket, and so they looked for an appropriate diminutive, which they found in *-ette*.

Most usage books omit discussion of diminutives because they are not considered very productive in English. Only dictionaries, which deal with the history of words, call attention to diminutives. When looking up a word in a dictionary, it is not unusual to come across the abbreviations *dim.* or *dimin.* or the written-out *diminutive*. These words denote "something little" (from Latin *diminutivus* "making less") and are applied to words expressing something small. This information is often contained in etymologies and is not evident to those using the words.

Many languages have diminutives, some to a greater degree than others. Italian, for example, has *momentino* (diminutive of *momento*), Spanish has *momentito*, German has *momentchen*, Dutch has *momentje*, and so on. Notice that the diminutive is always formed by adding a suffix: *-ino, -ito, -chen, -je*. In all these cases, the diminutive means "little moment," and is used literally to mean that something will take a very short time. But the same diminutive ending can indicate affection or familiarity, as in Italian *ragazzino*, "little boy" (*ragazzo*, "boy"), Spanish *hijito*, "little son" (*hijo*, "son"), and German *Kindchen*, "little child" (*Kind*, "child").

Australian English is noted for its affinity to diminutives, which occur in greater number than in any other dialect of English. The suffixes *-ie* or *-y*, *-o*, and *-s* are frequently attached to words to form diminutives. For example: *tinnie* ("a tin of beer"), *barbie* ("a barbecue"), *cuey* ("a cucumber"), *Aussie* ("an Australian"), *ambo* ("an ambulance"), *reffo* ("a refugee"), and *turps* ("turpentine"). These Australianisms are colloquial expressions of familiarity and good-fellowship.

Diminutives formed with other suffixes include words ending in *-let*, as in *booklet* (*book*), *piglet* (*pig*), *rivulet* (*river*), and *starlet* (*star*); *-et(te)*, as in *kitchenette* (*kitchen*), and *cigarette* (*cigar*); and *-ie* or *-y*, as in *doggie, doggy* (*dog*), *kitty* (*cat*), *laddie* (*lad*), and *lassie* (*lass*). But prefixes can also indicate a diminutive, as *mini-* in *minivan*, and *micro-* in *microeconomics*. Diminutive words can be literal or metaphorical, are often terms of endearment or affection, familiarity or intimacy, but sometimes also suggest condescension or dismissal. The diminutive suffix *-ling* is "neutral" in *duckling* (*duck*) but affectionate in *darling* (*little dear*) and dismissive in *princeling* (*prince*).

The contrasting word form is "augmentative," whose general meaning is "large," often implying awkwardness or ugliness. Augmentatives are common in Latinate languages, such as Italian and Spanish; for example, Italian *nasone*, "big nose" (*naso*, "nose") and Spanish *perrazo*, "large dog" (*perro*, "dog"). English has no augmentatives.

A number of English words have suffixes such as -*elle*, -*ette*, and -*let*, denoting smallness or inferiority. Diminutives are said to be "denotative"—indicative or designating—if the basic meaning is smallness. They are called "connotative" —implying or adding significance—if the basic meaning is endearment or dismissal. Most diminutive formations apply to nouns. The addition of the diminutive suffix does not change the part of speech of the base word, which is why this topic falls under Modification.

FOREIGN AND HOME-GROWN DIMINUTIVES

When you browse a dictionary, you will be surprised to find many etymologies indicating diminutive forms, but these may occur in other languages leading up to the English word. Here are some examples:

The word *glossary* comes from the Latin *glossarium*, which comes from Greek *glossarion*, "difficult word," which is a diminutive of *glossa*, "tongue, language."

The word *seamróg*, which gave us *shamrock*, is a diminutive of Irish *seamar*, "clover."

The word *aileron,* one of the hinged flaps on the trailing edge of an airplane wing, comes from French *aileron,* a diminutive of *aile,* "wing."

Animalcule, a small or tiny animal, is a diminutive of *animal* and ultimately derives from Latin *animalculum.*

Bagel, the familiar roll with a hole, came to us from Yiddish *beygl,* from dialectal German *beugel,* which is a diminutive form of *boug-/bouc-* "ring, bracelet."

The word *globule* comes from Latin *globulus,* the diminutive form of *globus,* "ball, pill, round lump."

There are about a dozen diminutive endings found in English words, but most of them are not productive of new words. Let's take a look at each. The ending *-aster* expresses "resemblance" and is often used to indicate that something is inferior or petty, as in the following examples: *astrologaster, criticaster, grammaticaster, philosophaster, poetaster, politicaster.* (The suffix is unrelated to the *-caster* in *broadcaster.*) This suffix first appeared in the 1500s, but it is little used today. The best known word in *-aster* is *poetaster,* meaning an inferior poet. A satirical comedy by Ben Jonson, titled *The Poetaster,* produced in 1601, deals with the rivalries of minor poets of Jonson's time, and its notoriety has helped perpetuate the word, which is still used occasionally to put down a second-rate poet.

The endings *-cule, -culus, -ule,* indicating something small, originated in Latin and first appeared in English in the late 1500s. Words like *animalcule, calculus, capsule, corpuscule, floccule, flocculus* ("small tuft of wool"), *globule, granule, homunculus* ("small human body"), *module, molecule,* and *nodule* are typical examples. Many scientific and medical terms have these endings.

The ending *-el* is from French and first appeared in English in the 1200s. The words *bowel, chapel, colonel, crenel, fennel, fontanel, grapnel, hovel, kernel, pimpernel, roundel, spinel,* and *tunnel* have this diminutive suffix.

The ending *-elle* came into English via French in the 1400s, while *-ella* is Italian and appeared in English in the 1700s. Both indicate something short, small, or insignificant, such as: *bagatelle* ("a trifle"), *chanterelle* (a kind of mushroom), *fustanella* ("short skirt"), *membranelle* ("small membrane"), *novella* ("short novel"), and *umbrella* (ultimately from Latin *umbra*, "shadow").

The ending *-en* was Saxon and became part of English before the Norman Conquest (1066). It creates nouns that mean something is "made of" or is an early version of the original. Examples are: *chicken, kitten,* and *maiden.*

The diminutive endings *-et* and *-ette* derive from French and were masculine and feminine, respectively, but do not necessarily carry a gender implication in English. After the 1600s, *-ette* became the dominant form. Words with these endings are: *baronet, barrette, bimbette, chaplet, cigarette, diskette, flannelette, fleurette, kitchenette, (drum) majorette, novelette, nymphet, palette, pipette, statuette,* and *towelette.* In this group, only *bimbette* (a synonym of *bimbo*) is a derogatory slang word, offensive to women.

The endings *-ie* and *-y* are from Scottish. They have been used in English since the 1500s to form diminutives of common nouns and proper names: *birdie, daddy, doggie, doggy, kitty, mousie, mousy, pussy, sonny,* and many others, as well as such nicknames or pet names as *Charlie, Charley, Debbie, Debby, Sallie, Sally, Willie, Willy,* and so forth. The endings *-ie* and *-y* are productive suffixes, especially common in Australian English.

Because the *-ing* ending has many other uses, its use as a diminutive suffix is harder to spot. It comes from Old English and indicates something that is fractional or a part of a larger thing. Instances of this are *farthing* and *tithing.*

The ending *-kin,* which first appeared in Middle English, was attached to nouns to form diminutives, but is rarely used to create new words. The ending was derived chiefly from Dutch and German. Words using it include: *bodkin* ("small dagger"), *bumpkin, cannikin, catkin, firkin* ("small tub"), *gherkin, lambkin, manikin,* and *napkin.* The pet name *babykins* is modern, formed with the endings *-kin* and *-s* (used in pet names like *Babs* and *Sweetums*). The word *munchkin,* meaning "a small person, dwarf, or elf," derives from the *Munchkins,* a dwarfish people in L. Frank Baum's 1900 book, *The Wonderful Wizard of Oz,* and was popularized by the book's 1939 film version, *The Wizard of Oz..*

The ending *-let* was borrowed from French and indicates a diminutive when attached to a common noun, but when appended to the name of a body part (as the ankle, arm, or wrist), it usually means "ornament." This suffix was not used for diminutive forms until the 1700s and now is mainly used to form occasional diminutives, like *bomblet* and *caplet.* Common examples are: *anklet, armlet, booklet, bracelet, coverlet, cutlet, droplet, leaflet, moonlet, piglet, ringlet, rivulet, starlet, streamlet,* and *wristlet.*

The ending *-ling* is found in Old English and Middle English but is rare in modern English. It can mean affiliation with someone or something superior, as in *atheling* ("a man of royal blood"), *fosterling* ("a foster child"), *hireling,* and *underling.* It can indicate youth, as in *birdling, codling, duckling, foundling, gosling,* and *sapling.* It can also connote contempt, as in *godling* ("a minor god"), *lordling* ("a petty lord"), and *princeling* ("a young or minor prince").

The least common diminutive ending is *-ock,* which comes from Old English, but not every *-ock* noun is a diminutive. Examples of diminutives with this ending are: *bullock, hillock, paddock,* and *tussock.*

Not every word that ends with a so-called diminutive suffix

is, in fact, a diminutive; several such suffixes have other uses. For example, *-ette* may denote a feminine form, as in *bachelorette*, or show that something is an imitation, as in *leatherette*. Also, a diminutive suffix may appear on a word that is not a diminutive of anything (*jerkin*—the garment is not a small *jerk*).

The prefixes *micro-* and *mini-* are very happy to serve modern English in the creation of diminutives. These are now common: *minibike, minibus, minicam, minicar, minidisc, minigolf, minipark, mini-recovery, miniskirt,* and *minivan.* This prefix combines with even more words involving appliances, electronics, and other objects. *Micro-* goes with not just nouns but also verbs and adjectives to make such word forms as: (nouns) *microanalysis, microbrew, microchip, microdot, microeconomics, microfiber, microhabitat, microinstruction, micromanage, micronutrient, microprocessor,* and *micro-recession;* (adjectives) *microanatomic, microcosmic, microcrystalline, microenvironmental,* and *micrometric;* (verbs) *microfilm, micromanage, microminiaturize, microprogram, micropublish,* and *microwave.*

Names, usually nicknames or pet names also suggesting smallness, affection, dismissal, and so on, often have diminutive forms: *Amanda* turns into *Mandy, Andrew* is shortened to *Andy, Charles* becomes *Charlie, Patricia* becomes *Patty,* and *William* may be called *Bill, Billy, Will, Willie, Willikins, Wills, Willy.* Mainly, though, diminutive names are used to express familiarity and affection—a positive attitude toward the person or thing referred to. Another word for "pet name" or a diminutive endearment, as in baby talk, is *hypocorism* (from a Greek word for "pet name").

A parting thought: It does remain somewhat of a mystery why the English language has such a liking for diminutives, and, unlike other languages, shows little or no interest in things large and ugly that would produce augmentative endings.

CHAPTER 11

doublets:

why is a muscle like a mouse?

Before we answer the question why a muscle is like a mouse, we should explain what a doublet is. A doublet is one of a pair of distinct words having a common origin. In other words, doublets derive from the same single source, but somewhere along their line of development they diverge and take different paths, somewhat the way two species of plants or animals evolve from a single source.

Generally, doublets resemble each other in form, and even in meaning, but they are unquestionably different words, and unless we know their histories, we wouldn't necessarily think that they are related. Which brings us to the words *muscle* and *mouse.*

Both words go back to a common ancestral source, the Indo-European word *mūs,* meaning "mouse." Indo-European is the name of the reconstructed prehistoric language from which many of the great language families of the world, including Germanic (the ancestor of English) and Italic (the ancestor of Latin) developed. Old English *mūs* and Latin *mūs* are thus cognates, or first cousins, and both words mean "mouse." Now a diminutive form of Latin *mūs* was *mūsculus*, meaning "little mouse." This word was applied by speakers of Latin to a muscle, partly because of the resemblance of some muscles, such as the biceps, to the shape of a mouse, and partly from the resemblance of a muscle's rippling motion to the scurrying movements of a mouse. English speakers agreed that a muscle is similar to a mouse, and so, in the 1300s, they borrowed Latin *mūsculus*, spelling it *muscle*. And that is how the words *mouse* and *muscle* became a doublet.

CONQUESTS OF LANGUAGE

If English had remained a static language, resistant to foreign words, it might have very few doublets. During the Old English period (c. 450–1100 C.E.) the language was relatively static, adopting only a handful of Latin words spread by merchants and Christian missionaries, words like *cuppe*, "cup" (from Latin *cuppa*), *munuc*, "monk" (from Latin *monachus*), *weall*, "wall" (from Latin *vallum*), *biscop*, "bishop" (from Latin *episcopus*), and *scōl*, "school" (from Latin *schola*). The Danish conquest of Britain in the late 700s introduced a number of Scandinavian words into English, among them the word *skirt*, a doublet of *shirt* (Old English *scyrte*). Both words meant originally "a shirt," but eventually the Scandinavian word *skirt* developed its present English meaning. This early example shows why many doublets remain in the language instead of one of them disappearing: Each of the pair serves as a new word with a meaning of its own.

The year 1066 marked the beginning of the most important

change in the English language. That was the start of the Norman Conquest, when England was invaded by William I of Normandy (later known as William the Conqueror), and the beginning of the influx of Norman-French and Latin words into English. Over the next two hundred years, English borrowed from Norman French and Latin an enormous stock of words, including household terms like *chair, furniture, table*; food terms like *beef, fruit, roast, veal*; architectural terms like *arch, castle, column*; gaming terms like *ace, cards, dice*; hunting terms like *leash, falcon, quarry, sport*; religious terms like *angel, religion, saint, virgin*; ethical and moral terms like *blame, grace, mercy, pity, virtue*; cultural terms like *art, beauty, color, paint*; military terms like *arms, battle, enemy, force, officer*; judicial and legal terms like *accuse, crime, judge, jury, justice, plea*; and governmental terms like *court, crown, prince, state*, and many more.

The wealth of words that entered English from Norman-French and Latin resulted in the introduction of many doublets such as *abbreviate* and *abridge, aptitude* and *attitude, fragile* and *frail, castle* and *chateau, cloak* and *clock, cohort* and *court, coy* and *quiet, faction* and *fashion, guardian* and *warden, inch* and *ounce, legal* and *loyal, poison* and *potion, regal* and *royal, tradition* and *treason,* and *vine* and *wine.* Three such words are called triplets, for example, *capital, cattle, chattel,* all ultimately from Medieval Latin *capitale,* "property," or *salary, sauce, sausage,* all ultimately from Latin *sāl,* "salt."

What has happened in most cases is that the root word was acquired by two different languages (or two varieties of the same language) and then, when these words were borrowed by English, duplicates started popping up. In some cases, one of the words supplanted the other; in others both were retained but developed slightly different meanings or connotations, as *shirt* and *skirt* did. French doublets often came into English in two forms, one a learned or scholarly borrowing from Latin, with slight alterations in the form, the other an older form inherited from Latin and greatly altered in the process. Typical examples of such doublets are *legal/loyal, regal/royal,* and *tradition/treason.* Hundreds of English words were gained and lost in this way. This is partly why English is the only language that has books of synonyms like *Roget's Thesaurus.* In short, a doublet is one of two (or more) words in a language that are derived from the same ultimate source, but usually by different routes.

An example of closely related doublets are *gubernatorial* and *governor*; the first was borrowed from Latin *gubernātor* into English, while the second went from Latin to Old French and then to English, and the form *governor* results from changes the word underwent in French. *Gubernatorial* and *governor* are close in meaning and somewhat close in form. However, doublets can vary widely in both form and meaning. Some doublets show only a vague resemblance in form, as for example *thesaurus* and *treasure,* both ultimately from Greek *thesaurós,* "a store," with the first going through Latin to English and the second coming from Latin through French to English. Other doublets may vary in closeness of meaning as well as form: *guarantee* and *warranty* are fairly close in form and have almost the same meaning; *abbreviate* and *abridge* are quite different in form and have almost the same meaning; *costume* and *custom* and *cloak* and *clock* are fairly close in form but quite distinct in meaning. An extreme pair, *inch* and *ounce,* have different meanings and very different forms.

The word *doublet* itself is from the early 1300s, borrowed from Old French and meaning "a man's close-fitting garment" (literally, something doubled or folded). It was formed in Old French from *double* and the diminutive suffix *-et.* In the linguistic sense of a pair of words deriving from the same ultimate source, the word was reborrowed from modern French in the 1860s.

DIGGING FOR DOUBLETS

How does one find out about these incongruous pairs of words that derive from a single source? Where does one find out that *galaxy* and *lettuce* both come from words meaning "milk"? What connects *canary* with *cynic*? (answer: both come from words meaning "dog"). What links *bugle* to *cow*? (answer: both come from words meaning "ox" or "cow"). There are 112 incongruous pairs in the book *Dubious Doublets* (Stewart Edelstein, ed., 2003). The book covers doublets from *aardvark* (matched with *porcelain*) to *zodiac* (which shares an origin with *whiskey*). Some pieces are brief; others lead into longer discussions about words, such as acronyms, eponyms, portmanteau words, and toponyms. Many doublets have no "obvious" common root, and a number of them (such as a link between *bully* and *friar*, between *pregnant* and *king*, and between *vegetable* and *witch*) are dubious, which is why the author named his book *Dubious Doublets* and focused on unlikely word pairs.

The rest of one's investigations into doublets would have to be done in dictionaries, but no dictionaries explicitly indicate (even in the etymologies) which words are doublets. Don't think it will be easy. In the *Oxford English Dictionary*, only 69 entries contain the words "a doublet of" in the etymology. Very useful are such books as *The Barnhart Dictionary of Etymology* (H. W. Wilson, 1988), *The Roots of English* (Robert Claiborne, 1989), *The American Heritage Dictionary of the English Language* (4th edition, 2000) and its index of Indo-European roots, and *The American Heritage Dictionary of Indo-European Roots* (by Calvert Watkins, 2000). The 1984 edition of *The World Book Dictionary* also marks many doublets with "see etymology (etymol.) of doublet ~."

Etymologists study words from different languages having a common meaning, called cognates, and work backward by deduction to discover the root. By comparing such cognates, etymologists search for the *etymon* ("true source of a word"), a word or word-part from which compounds or derivatives are formed. However, since Indo-European is a reconstructed language based on the family of languages derived from it (most of the languages spoken in Europe, India, and western Asia), etymologists do not always agree on the roots of words. We also have no written records of Old English earlier than the 7th century. About 80 percent of our English lexicon comes down from Indo-European word roots. The rest are derived from foreign languages unrelated to Indo-European.

DOUBLING BACK

Let's look at the stories of the previously mentioned doublets in this section.

ABBREVIATE, ABRIDGE: Both words come from Latin *brevis*, "short," with *abridge* taking a trip through Old French.

APTITUDE, ATTITUDE: Both derive from Latin *aptitūdō*, "fitness," the first through French, the second through a French borrowing of Italian *attitudine*.

CASTLE, CHATEAU: These derive from Latin *castellum*, a diminutive form of *castrum*, "fort"; *chateau* is the modern French version that has been borrowed into English as is.

CLOAK, CLOCK: Both originate in Medieval Latin *clocca*, "bell," by way of Old French *cloque*. A cloak was so called because its shape resembled that of a bell. *Clock* meant originally a timepiece in which each hour is marked by the sound of a bell.

COHORT, COURT: These derive from Latin *cohortem* (later, *cortem*) "court, enclosure," with *cohort* entering French first (*cohorte*). *Court* is the living descendant of Latin *cortem* in French.

COSTUME, CUSTOM: These words come from Latin *cōnsuētūdinem,* "habit, custom," with *costume* making its way through Italian and French before entering English, and *custom* moving from Latin to Old French before reaching English.

COY, QUIET: Both derive from Latin *quiētus,* "at rest, in repose," with *coy* coming from the Old French form *coi* (earlier *quei*), and *quiet* coming straight from Latin.

FACTION, FASHION: These come from Latin *factiōn-, factiō,* "a doing or making" (from *facere,* "to do, make"). French *faction* was a learned borrowing from Latin before coming into English with the meaning "a class or party of people," while *fashion* took the longer route through Old French *façon,* in the sense of "form, shape, appearance, fashion."

GUARANTEE, WARRANTY: *Guarantee* is from Old French *garant,* "a warrant," while *warranty* is from Old North French *warantie,* derived from *warrant,* "a warrant." Both *garant* and *warant* came from Frankish (the West Germanic language spoken in the 400s and 500s in the region of ancient Gaul that became France), represented by Old High German *weren,* "to confirm, warrant."

GUARDIAN, WARDEN: *Guardian* is from Old French *gardein,* "protector, custodian," while *warden* is from Old North French *wardein,* "guardian, custodian." Both words came from Frankish, represented by Old High German *warten,* "to watch, guard."

INCH, OUNCE: *Inch,* the unit of length, was adopted in Old English from Latin *uncia,* "twelfth part (of a foot, pound, etc.)", while *ounce* came into Middle English through

Old French from the same Latin *uncia*, meaning, in Troy weight, "a twelfth of a pound." In avoirdupois or ordinary measure, it is a sixteenth of a pound.

LEGAL, LOYAL: Both come from Latin *lēgālis*, "legal" (from *lēg-, lēx*, "law"), *legal* through a French learned borrowing of the Latin word, and *loyal* by way of Old French *loial, leial*, meaning "faithful, loyal," derived from the same Latin word. The meaning "faithful" referred originally to allegiance to a country's law.

POISON, POTION: These words derive from Latin *pōtiōn-, pōtiō*, "a drink, potion, poisonous drink," both coming into English through the Old French variant forms *poison*, "poisonous drink," and *pocion*, "drink, potion."

REGAL, ROYAL: Both come from Latin *rēgālis*, "of or fit for a king, kingly" (from *rēg-, rēx*, "king"), *regal* through a French learned borrowing of the Latin word, and *royal* through Old French *roial*, derived from the same Latin word.

TRADITION, TREASON: These derive from Latin *trāditiōn-, trāditiō*, "delivery, handing over, surrender" (from Latin *trādere*, "to deliver, hand over, betray"), *tradition* through a French learned borrowing of the Latin word, and *treason* through Old French *treson, traïson*, derived from the same Latin word.

VINE, WINE: *Vine* came through Old French from Latin *vīnea*, "vine, vineyard" (from *vīnum*, "wine"); *wine* was an early Old English borrowing from Latin *vīnum*, "wine."

There is more to doublets than these concise histories tell us. For example, if we looked a little deeper into the histories of *gubernatorial* and *governor*, we would find that the Latin verb from which they derive, *gubernāre*, "to direct, manage, govern," came from Greek *kybernân*, "to steer, direct," which was the source of English *cybernetics*, the term that gave us the combining form *cyber-* (*cyberspace, cybersex, cybersquatter*, etc.). Then there are some pairs that seem to be doublets but turn out on investigation to be variant forms. One such pair is *fancy* and *fantasy*. *Fancy* did not come from another language but was formed by contraction of *fantasy*, which came into English through Old French *fantasie* from Latin *phantasia*. Originally both *fancy* and *fantasy* meant "imagination, image, appearance," but gradually *fancy* came to mean "liking, inclination," as in "to take a fancy to (something)" while *fantasy* retained the original meaning.

Doublets came into English as a result of the historical process of borrowing. This process involved acquiring sometimes the same vocabulary from two different sources, usually Latin and French. These recycled words could be introduced into English and retained because they were different in form and meaning from each other. Doublets resulted from the early history of English; it is unlikely that these days we should be acquiring more than an occasional doublet. Yet doublets will continue to be a fascination and major topic of investigation to those interested in the growth and development of English words.

CHAPTER 12

folk etymology:
word history misunderstood
or mistaken

In *The Origin and Development of the English Language*, Thomas Pyles and John Algeo illustrate the nature of folk etymology with an amusing story. While visiting an American ballet school to observe its teaching techniques, a German ballet teacher heard a student describe a particular ballet jump as a "soda box." After some inquiries, the mystified visitor found out that what the student and her class had misheard from their instructor as "soda box" was the standard ballet term *saut de basque* or "Basque leap." While the authors wonder how widespread the misunderstood term might be in American ballet schools, they are certain that a common term like *chest of drawers* is often misheard as Chester drawers. They even quote a classified ad in an Athens, Georgia, newspaper to prove the point.

Examples of such misunderstandings are fairly common, and

they really have little to do with etymology, the term used in linguistics for the history and development of a word. But because the new words formed this way create in a sense a new history, linguists decided to call it *folk etymology* (since the coiners of such words are plain folks) or, less frequently, *popular etymology*. In his book *On Language*, William Safire gives a number of examples of current folk etymologies. "In today's language," he writes, 'harebrained' is often giddily and irresponsibly misspelled 'hairbrained,' *perhaps* on the notion that the hair is near the brain."

Other examples are phrases produced by the slurred "and," as when "hard 'n' fast rules" gets transformed to "harden-fast rules," or when "the whole kit 'n' caboodle" is occasionally written as "the whole kitten caboodle," which may be a good name for a satchel in which to carry a cat.

That misunderstandings of this sort can become implanted in the language is illustrated by the phrase *spitting image*, "exact likeness." This phrase, which is first attested in 1901, was an alteration of the earlier phrase *spit 'n' image*, in which *spit* meant "exact likeness." How *spit* came to mean "exact likeness," is a matter of conjecture. Some have suggested that *spit* in this context derived from a mispronunciation of *spirit* as *spi't*. The lexicographer Eric Partridge believed that the phrase *spit 'n' image* came from the idea of a "speaking likeness," the reference being, for example, to a son's speech being an exact replica of the father's, down to the spit they eject when they speak.

Folk etymology is, thus, the result of changes based on a naïve misunderstanding of a word or phrase and changing it to a familiar-sounding one with a similar meaning. Some examples are *sparrow-grass* replacing *asparagus, plantar wart* (from Latin *planta*) reinterpreted as *planter's wart*, and *Jerusalem artichoke*, altered from the Italian *girasole*, "sunflower."

BEST GUESSES

Folk etymologies exist because, when people hear an unfamiliar word, they try to understand it by relating the word to others they know well. They often guess at the meaning and, if enough people make the same wrong guess, the erroneous meaning can become part of the language. If the word really confuses them, they may change the form so that it resembles, at least partially, a more familiar word (or words). In most cases, though, the product of folk etymology is objectively not much help toward understanding what the word means and may be downright misleading. But one of the most basic of human traits is to find reasons for why things are as they are. That is the fascination with etymologies in general, "Where did the word *sandwich* come from?" People cannot resist making up explanations for the origins of words and phrases, especially if they cannot find an etymology or it does not "make sense" to them.

People are prone to draw false conclusions on the basis of superficial resemblances and this is the most common form of folk etymology. This is especially true for foreign words, which are changed to make them sound more like English words. *Belfry*, "bell tower" has nothing to do with bells, for example. The early spelling was *berfrey*, from Old French *berefrei, berfrei*, a word of Germanic origin, meaning a "movable tower used when attempting a siege." The sense shifted to "tower for protecting watchmen," then to "watchtower, beacon tower, bell tower," and eventually to "place where a bell is hung!"

The conversion of words from foreign languages into English and from older forms of English into modern English frequently results in redundancies. *Foremost*, which looks like a combination of *fore* and *most*, actually comes from Old English *fyrmest*, meaning "earliest, first," and the superlative of *forma*, related to *fruma*, "beginning." The cliché *first and foremost* is actually redundant. The same is true for *salt cellar*, as *cellar* derives from Latin *salaria*, "salt," and has no relation to the *cellar* in root or wine cellar.

UNCERTAIN ORIGINS

One of the difficulties faced by etymologists is that some words are not related to ancient forms and it is therefore difficult to establish their origins. Consequently, the forms from which such words are said to derive can only be produced by analogy. Similarly, the fallacy in folk etymologies is that the earliest or an earlier meaning of a word is the "correct" one, as when it is argued that the "true" meaning of *history* is "inquiry, investigation" since that was the classical Greek meaning. This view is false because in many or most cases there is no record of the earliest senses of a word.

False conclusions about the origins arise—affecting the meanings—as a result of the conversion of Old English and Middle English terms into modern English. A *crayfish* is not a fish but a crustacean (from Middle English *crevis*, "crab"). A *helpmate* may be a help and a mate, but the word is actually an alteration of *help meet*, "suitable helper." Another example is *bridegroom*. In Middle English, the original spelling was *bridegome*, a combination of *bride* and *gome*, "man." But the second element ceased to be understood and was changed to *groom* to make *bridegroom*.

FAVORITE FOLK ETYMOLOGIES

There are about 300 folk etymologies recorded in a typical unabridged dictionary. Among them are *buckaroo*, cockroach, depart, female, frontispiece, gridiron, hangnail, humble pie, Lemon sole, penthouse, shamefaced, and sovereign. Let's look briefly at their stories.

Buckaroo, "cowboy," is an alteration (influenced by buck, "male deer, goat, etc.") of Spanish vaquero, from vaca, "cow."

The Spanish word cucaracha entered English as cockroach because of the influence of the familiar words cock and roach. The insect resembled neither, the latter being a type of fish up to that point. Roach, in the sense "cockroach," is actually a later shortening of the word.

The etymology of depart starts with its initial use being restricted to wedding ceremonies to mean "separate" in the expression, "'till death us depart." Later, the verb became obsolete and was analyzed as do and part, hence the changed expression, "'till death do us part."

Female came from Old French femelle, which derived from Latin fēmella, "young woman," a diminutive of fēmina, "woman." The spelling female was formed by folk etymology on the analogy of male.

Frontispiece meant originally the front of a building, and was borrowed as frontispice from Old French, but the last syllable was assimilated by folk etymology to piece.

Gridiron was an alteration (influenced by iron) of the earlier spelling gridire, "griddle," which was a variant of gridil, a variant of Old French greil, gril, "grill."

Hangnail was an alteration (influenced by hang) of Middle English angenayle, "corn on the foot," derived from Old English angnægl, a compound of ang, "corn," and nægl, "nail."

People who eat humble pie are humbled only figuratively. The name of the dish comes from numbles or umbles, meaning the "liver, heart, and other edible (but inferior) animal innards." The original phrase, *a numble pie* became *an umble pie* when the article and the noun redivided at some point (the same way that *a nadder, a napron, a noumpere* became *an adder, an apron, an umpire*). *Umble pie* became *humble pie* when someone changed it on the basis of its having been served to *umbles* (figuratively and transferred to mean those of lower rank, women and children) while men were served the "best" meat.

Lemon sole is not a sole but a flatfish or flounder, assimilating its English name from the etymology of *limande* in French.

Penthouse was borrowed from Middle French *pentis*, from Old French *apentis*, "attached building," from Latin *appendicium*, "appendage." The alteration to *penthouse* was formed by folk etymology, which associated the first syllable, *pent*, with being confined, and the second syllable with *house*.

Shamefaced was an alteration by folk etymology of the earlier *shamefast*, from Old English *scamfæst*, "bound by shame," a compound of *scamu*, "shame," and *fæst*, "fastened, bound."

Sovereign came from Old French *soverain*, derived from Vulgar Latin *superanus*, from Latin *super*, "over." The English word acquired the *g* by association with the etymologically unrelated *reign*.

FALSE ETYMOLOGY

There is another sense in which the term "folk etymology" has been used, though not by language scholars to be sure. This other sense might better be called "false etymology," since it refers to any popular but mistaken idea of the origin of a word. Many slang words are explained by contriving etymologies for them that sound reasonable but are entirely baseless. For example, the verb *snooze* is falsely etymologized as a blend of *sneeze* and *doze*. A famous example of a false etymology is the widespread belief that the word *posh*, "stylish, elegant," is an acronym of "port outward—starboard homeward," presumably referring to the more desirable and expensive section of a ship traveling between England and India. This etymology, though widely discredited, is still occasionally found in some reference books. The actual origin of *posh* is unknown; some have connected it with a British slang noun meaning "a dandy," which is of unknown origin.

Other categories of false etymologies have been pointed out by Hugh Rawson, the author of *Devious Derivations: Popular Misconceptions and More than 1,000 True Origins of Common Words and Phrases* (1994, reprinted 2002). He describes "imaginary eponyms" as those that come about because someone wants to place blame or credit for something on a famous person. This type of hypothesis has led to questionable etymologies for *bogus, condom, Nosey Parker,* and *shyster.* The popular notions that *condom* was named for a Dr. Condom who invented the contraceptive device, or that *shyster* was named after an unscrupulous lawyer called *Scheister,* have no basis in fact. The word *condom* first appeared in 1706, and many attempts have been made to trace it to a source, all without success. On the other hand, *shyster,* first recorded in 1843, turned out to be an alteration (influenced by the suffix *-ster*) of German *Scheisser* "incompetent person," derived from the vulgar word *Scheisse* "excrement." Sometimes the popularity of a word may have been helped by identification with a real person, for example, *crapper* and *hooker.* Words that truly derive from names of real people are *bloomer, bowdlerize, boy-cott, chauvinist,* and *diesel.* For examples, see the chapter on **Eponyms.**

Another of Rawson's categories is "spurious acronyms." *Cabal* has been interpreted as an acronym from the first letters of the last names of five of Charles II's ministers: Clifford, Arlington, Buckingham, Ashley, and Lauderdale. *News* has been said to derive from North, East, West, and South. You've probably heard the story for *tip* being said to stand for, "To Insure Promptness," but it is much more likely that its origin is the notion of touching lightly as it is the offering of a small gratuity. *SOS (S.O.S.)* has been explained as meaning "Stop Other Signals," "Save Our Ship," and "Save Our Souls." The true story is that the letters were chosen because they were easily transmitted in Morse code.

Then there are "geographic ghosts," words associated falsely with place names. Though there are many terms that are derived legitimately from the names of places—*denim, jeans*—there are just as many whose etymology is assigned incorrectly to a place name. Examples of this are *guinea pig, turkey, sedan,* and *tobacco.* The *guinea pig* has been mistakenly associated with Guinea in West Africa, the *turkey* with an unrelated Old World bird, *sedan* with a French city instead of an Italian word *sede,* "chair," and *tobacco* does not come from the island of Tobago.

JOHNSON'S AND WEBSTER'S ETYMOLOGIES

Both Samuel Johnson and Noah Webster made some egregious errors in writing etymologies. To prepare for etymological research for his big dictionary, Noah Webster studied Greek, Latin, Hebrew, French, German, Dutch, Anglo-Saxon, Welsh, Old Irish, Persian, and seven Asiatic and Assyrian-based languages, for a total of 20 different alphabets and languages. He maintained that all modern languages could be traced to a single tongue he called Chaldee and he accepted as historic truths the biblical accounts of the Tower of Babel. But Webster's etymological techniques were misguided and he developed some strange theories as the basis of tracing etymologies. It took him about ten years to develop his theory of etymology but he went very far astray. Though Webster set new, high standards with the scholarship of his etymologies, they are not viewed as entirely accurate by modern standards. Webster was contemptuous of the principle of regularity of sound change and ignorant of the discoveries based upon it. Much criticism has also been leveled at Samuel Johnson for the supposed inferiority of his etymologies. The discovery that sound change was regular has guided philological study since around 1932. Modern etymologists must explain how every sound in the current form of each word developed from older forms. If they cannot explain certain changes on the basis of systematic sound change according to established principles, then they must have some other plausible explanation to offer.

Sometimes folk etymologies are formulated on superficial resemblances between words and complicated explanations are given where simpler ones will do. Then there are times when words have "boring" or low origins and amateurs and professionals go out of their way to refine the explanations. And no one likes to see "origin unknown," so stories are sought out to fill those gaps. Those stories are often created or embellished to give them the air of authenticity. Some stories even start as jokes and end up being recorded!

One common etymology claims that *marmalade* is derived from "Marie malade." The story is that when Mary, Queen of Scots, was ill, this orange preserve—once a rare delicacy—was one of the few things she could eat. The truth is that *marmalade* came into English from French around the time of the Norman Conquest and is traceable to Greek *melimelon*, "honey apple." The preserve was originally made of quinces, which resemble large yellow apples, but is now made with oranges.

It is worth studying folk etymology, though, not just for entertainment but also because many common words and phrases have been shaped in form and meaning by mistaken notions about their origins. These etymologies tell us much about the way people think.

semantic change:

the split personalities of words

INTRODUCTION

A famous passage in Lewis Carroll's *Through the Looking Glass* contains this exchange between Humpty Dumpty and Alice:

> *"When I use a word," Humpty Dumpty said in rather a scornful tone, "it means just what I choose it to mean—neither more nor less."*
>
> *"The question is," said Alice, "whether you can make words mean so many different things."*
>
> *"The question is," said Humpty Dumpty, "which is to be master—that's all."*

This bit of dialogue illustrates the problem of finding out the exact meaning of words. If every word had just one meaning, people would need a huge vocabulary to understand each other, and dictionaries would be twice or triple their present size. Fortunately, most words do not have a single meaning, and this fact enables us to communicate with a fairly limited stock of words. But first we have to learn those meanings.

How do words acquire so many different meanings?

The answer lies in *semantic change*, which is the gradual change that words undergo over time. (*Semantic* comes from Greek *sēmantikos*, "having meaning, signifying" from *sēma* "sign.") For example, we use the word *luggage* to mean the suitcases and trunks we take along on a trip. But in Shakespeare's play *Henry IV*, the word is used in its basic sense of "something that is lugged." When Prince Hal tells Falstaff, "Come, bring your luggage nobly on your back," he is referring to the body of Hotspur, whom the prince had killed in battle. Similarly, our use of the word *addiction* is negative, meaning an unhealthy dependence on drugs or other bad habits. In Shakespeare, however, the word is neutral and means simply "a strong tendency or inclination," as in *Othello*, where the king's herald encourages "each man to what sport and revels his addiction leads him."

The meaning of an existing word can change in many ways, and one meaning can give rise to another or others. One way of changing the meaning or use of a word is by changing its part of speech, as when a verb is turned into a noun, or a noun is turned into a verb. This process is known as functional shift or conversion. Common subdivisions of semantic change include: generalization (or extension or radiation); specialization (or narrowing); and metaphor. We also discuss elevation (or amelioration) of meaning and degradation (or pejoration) of meaning, as well as euphemism, or the use of a mild or pleasant word in place of one that is harsh and offensive.

CHAPTER 13

transformations:

how changes in meaning alter words

Everyone knows that words can change their meaning. It is a fact of life, not only in English but in all languages. Most of the time we fail to see the changes, since they are often as gradual and imperceptible as those in a growing plant. But with the number of words and infinite variation in everyday language, there is the potential for constant change. Our language varies constantly in response to complex interactions of different factors in different situations. At any one time, words can convey a multitude of different meanings along with a whole lot of associated baggage that arises from our experiences and personalities. The meanings of words are linked to the life and culture of speakers.

Some words go through a long history with very little change; they mean approximately what they did originally or have gained only a few additional senses over the years. Words like *amethyst* (the gem), *cruse* (of oil), and *fawn* ("young deer") have not changed their meanings since the Middle Ages. Other words progress through a remarkable series of transformations, alternately broadening and narrowing in meaning, sometimes ending up with a sense that seems to have no relation to the original. The word *nice* meant originally "stupid, ignorant," and went on to mean "fussy, extravagant," then "precise, punctilious," and finally "good, agreeable." Still other words retain their core meaning but add many new senses, all clearly relating to the original.

A source of new vocabulary, then, is the development of new meanings in existing words, usually either through figurative uses, such as "a *hailstorm* of criticism," or in technical coinages such as the specialized meanings of *charm* in particle physics ("one of the quantum properties or flavors that distinguish different quarks") and *word* in computers ("consecutive string of bits that can be transferred and stored as a unit").

New technology changes the way we conduct our daily life and the words that refer to it change, also. As computers became common, many words changed their meanings because they could conveniently be used to refer to aspects of computing: *clipboard, command, memory, customize, icon, mouse, paste,* and *surf* are just a few.

A typical word does not have just one meaning; it has a cluster of meanings that have been acquired during its lifetime. There is at least one core meaning to which the others are related. Check in a dictionary to see how many meanings are listed for common everyday words like *about, beak, chair, devil, eat, fine, get, go, happy,* and *set.* The decisions of lexicographers to give separate entries for senses (or meanings) is based on usage in context. Each of the senses of a word is appropriately used in certain contexts. *Context* is the environment in which a word appears in a sentence and this is how a word acquires its meaning.

As a word interacts with other words, it acquires meaning from them. Since most words have more than one sense, one cannot discuss meanings without paying attention to the words' usage in sentences. But it is also not true to say that context always gives an indication of a word's meaning.

PATTERNS OF CHANGE

No one has been able to systematize the ways by which changes in meaning take place, but a few major types of change are well known. Generalization (or extension) occurs when a word widens its meaning. Specialization (or narrowing) happens when a word becomes more specialized in meaning. Amelioration occurs when a word develops a positive sense. Pejoration (or deterioration) is when a word develops a negative sense. Metaphor is a method by which a word's meaning is extended to other things to which it is comparable.

An example of generalization or extension is a figurative sense, which can provide a vivid comparison. *Adrenalin,* which refers to a hormone used to stimulate the heart when used literally, can be extended to mean "something that stirs to action; a stimulant or stimulus" when used figuratively, as in *A plentiful supply of money is adrenalin for the stock market.* The figurative use of *launder* extends its meaning to the "cleansing" of money from illegal or disreputable sources. *Clone* used to be confined to the scientific meaning of two or more individuals duplicated or propagated asexually from a single ancestor, but now it has figurative senses such as "a replica" and "an automaton or robot." Generalization can also come about by transference. Transferred senses involve changes in the area or scope of a word's use, as when *altruism* describes "self-sacrificing behavior among animals."

Fabulous is a word that once meant "based on or pertaining to a fable." It came to mean "incredible" or "marvelous" since those adjectives could describe fables. Another example is *awful*, which specifically meant "inspiring awe" but now has been generalized to mean "disagreeable, objectionable." If you look up the etymologies of words, you will find many that have broadened their meanings considerably: *assassin* (originally, "hashish-eater"), *companion* (originally, "bread-sharing person"), *construe* ("pile up"), *depend* ("hang down"), *educate* ("lead up"), *paper* ("papyrus"), *thing* ("meeting, assembly"), and *understand* ("stand between").

A restricted meaning can be broadened, as the noun *executive*, meaning an administrative officer in a corporation, has been extended to describe anything sophisticated and expensive, as in *executive suite, executive jet*, and *executive housing*. Even the word *metaphor* has been broadened to apply to anything that represents or symbolizes something else, as in *For them, football is a metaphor for understanding the world.*

Conversely, the scope of a word's reference may be narrowed by specialization. Narrowing takes place quite frequently when common words with nonspecialized meanings are borrowed into some scientific field or area of technology in which they are given a highly specialized meaning. In the field of nuclear or particle physics we find common words like *beauty, flavor*, and *truth* that have acquired highly specialized transferred senses. In molecular biology, the concept of a genetic alphabet has stimulated the transfer of the meanings of *palindrome, sentence, synonym,* and *word* to specific applications associated with the genetic code. Slang and argot also put common words to specialized uses: CB (Citizens Band) radio has attached new meanings to *apple, break, ears*, and *hammer*. Computers have given specialized meanings to many common words (*bootstrap, desktop, software, toggle, virus, window*), as have business and economics.

When a word becomes specialized in meaning, its scope narrows to become more specific. Examples of this process are: *corn, deer,* and *flesh.* Each meant something quite general (*corn,* "any grain or seed," *deer,* "any animal," *flesh,* "any meat") and have since come to mean something more specific. Other examples are *corpse* ("a body"), *doctor* ("teacher"), *garage* ("shelter"), *ghost* ("spirit, soul"), *lumber* ("disused articles"), and *science* ("knowledge").

Other changes in meaning come about because of social factors. Certain words develop derogatory meanings as a result of changes in customs, values, and specific events. The word *warehouse* has come to have a derogatory meaning when applied to a large, impersonal institution, especially as a verb meaning "to institutionalize (people) in usually deficient housing and in conditions in which medical, educational, psychiatric, and social services are below par or absent," as in *warehousing the mentally ill.*

FINDING MEANING IN CONTEXT

Reading experts tell us that we should look for definite contextual patterns in sentences. These are the most important suggestions:

1. Look for the restatement of an unknown word in the context that follows it. The restatement may be made by a known word or by an accompanying phrase, clause, or sentence, for example, "While some *abolitionists* concede that the prison system is a necessary evil for now, their immediate goal is to *do away with* as many prisons as possible."

2. Look for contrasting words or statements that may help explain the unknown word, for example, "If the very idea seems hopelessly *utopian,* consider a *real-world* case."

3. Look for key words that may limit the possible meanings of an unknown word. If sentence context does not tell anything about a word's meaning, take a close look at the word itself, for example, "Advocates of *mainstreaming* do recognize the need of having some special facilities and programs in schools."

4. Memorize the most common prefixes, suffixes, and roots used to form English words. Analyze the component parts of words you read, for example, *automobile, chronology, microscope, multivolume, psychopath,* and *telephone.*

5. Look for a shorter word that you "know" inside a long, unfamiliar word, for example, "Most people are the same except for a few *happenstantial* differences."

It is fairly common for meanings to change from neutral to derogatory. Degradation or pejoration can be seen clearly when looking at names for common people in the Middle Ages, like *boor* (originally, "countryman"), *homely* ("of the home, domestic"), *knave* ("boy, male servant"), *villain* ("of a villa or country house"), and *vulgar* ("of the common people"). All of these words have derogatory meanings.

Adjectives seem particularly susceptible to degradation. *Egregious* and *notorious* are words that have gone from meaning "well-known or outstanding in a good way" to "well-known or outstanding in a bad way." Others that have acquired new derogatory meanings are: *artificial* (originally, "man-made"), *indifferent* ("impartial, neutral"), *officious* ("eager to please, obliging"), *silly* ("soulful, blessed"), and *smug* ("trim, neat"). Pejoration or degradation is a change in social scope and status. An earlier, higher-class or neutral meaning came first and then the word acquired a lower-scale meaning.

Then again, words formerly considered derogatory or negative are sometimes "rehabilitated" and given positive meanings, and the new meanings completely reverse the established ones. *Fulsome*, used previously to mean "grossly excessive, offensive to good taste," is now commonly used to mean "very flattering or complimentary," probably due to misinterpretation of the syllable *ful-* to mean "full" or "abundant." Changes in meaning stimulated by social factors also include euphemism, the use of mild or indirect expressions to avoid harsh or offensive ones, but this is actually a meaning acquiring a different word rather than a word acquiring a different meaning.

Contrary to common belief, words can improve in reputation. Some words signify something quite humble or low early on, but as time goes by they change to designate something elevated. *Angel* first meant "messenger," *constable* meant "keeper of horses," and *governor* meant "pilot, steersman." *Halo* once described "a threshing floor where oxen tread in a circle." From the idea of a circle came the word's use describing the ring of light seeming to encircle the moon or sun, then later the ring of light around a saint's head. Words with improved reputations include: *meticulous* (originally, "fearful, timid"), *minister* ("servant, attendant"), *mischief* ("injury, harm, misfortune"), *naughty* ("having nothing, needy"), *sensitive* ("having or feeling sensation"), *shrewd* ("wicked, evil"), and *smart* ("painfully sharp, stinging"). These "social climbers" have attained an improved status. There are not, however, as many instances of this type as pejoration.

The word *face* has taken on the metaphorical meaning of "reputation" and "the surface of anything." When a metaphor is so common that people usually take it for granted, it is called a "dead metaphor." *Understanding*, for example, is a dead metaphor, having its origins in the idea that "standing between" something was akin to having a good *grasp* of it (another, slightly less dead metaphor) or knowing it thoroughly. Etymologically, *consider* is a metaphor meaning "take the stars into account" (from Latin *sīder-, sīdus,* "constellation"), *manure* means "to work with the hands" (related to *maneuver*), and *gorge* means "throat, gullet," and there are thousands more whose history reveals a transition from the concrete and literal to the figurative and metaphorical. Originally, *metaphor* was a Greek word meaning "transfer" and its etymology is *meta,* "change" and *phérein,* "to bear, or carry." Thus, the word *metaphor* itself has a metaphorical meaning in English, "a transfer of meaning from one thing to another."

Another mechanism for change of meaning is accidental association. *Scripture* meant "writing" originally but by association with religious writing, in particular the Bible (which itself just meant "book"), it came to mean "religious writing." Analogy is another such mechanism, involving the perception of similarity between some concrete object or process and some abstract concept or process. Common examples are "the *head* of the Republican Party," "the *flight* of the population from the war-torn area," "the east *wing* of the house," "the *foot* of the stairs."

Semantic change is in many ways unpredictable. It is unlikely that scholars will ever be able to foresee the direction in which particular words will change their meanings. But by looking at a wide range of examples of changes in meaning, one can begin to develop a certain sense of what kinds of change are likely.

CHAPTER 14

euphemism:
careful language in the age of political correctness

A best-selling college dictionary published in the late 1990s, bowing to the spirit of political correctness, found it necessary to include an appendix titled "Avoiding Insensitive and Offensive Language." The appendix includes, among other suggestions, tips on how to avoid sexism ("replace *mankind* with *humankind* or *homo sapiens*"); tips on the use of "gender-neutral" terms (*anchor* instead of *anchorman*, *housecleaner* instead of *cleaning lady*, *ancestor* instead of *forefather*); on avoiding racial or ethnic names like *Oriental* and *Eskimo* (replace with *Asian* and *Inuit*); on describing "sexual orientation" (*life partner*, *same-sex*, to avoid reference to a *gay* or *lesbian* relationship).

The use of indirect, tactful, and sometimes purposely deceptive language to make an idea or concept more acceptable is, of course, not new. For example, the porcelain plumbing fixture used for defecation and urination in a bathroom was originally called a "water closet" or "W.C.," then delicately renamed a "toilet" (which originally referred to a dressing room), which in turn was considered too indelicate and had to be renamed in a variety of ways: *bathroom, washroom, powder room, restroom, lavatory, latrine, commode, privy, ladies room, Gents,* and (in slang) *heads, jakes, john,* and so on.

While changes in usage like these evolved over centuries, the advent of political correctness over the past several decades accelerated such changes to an extent never seen before, affecting every area of language. Some examples are: the use of *gender* instead of *sex, neutralize* instead of *kill, pro-choice* instead of *pro-abortion, pro-life* instead of *anti-abortion, erectile dysfunction* instead of *impotence, domestic violence* instead of *wife-beating, physically challenged* or *differently abled* instead of *handicapped, Third World* instead of *underdeveloped nations, person with AIDS* or *P.W.A.* instead of *AIDS victim.*

All of these are what linguists call euphemisms. Linguistically, a euphemism (from Greek, "speaking good") is a mild or acceptable word or phrase used to replace a harsh or inappropriate one. Socially, the motives for using euphemisms are complex: they may be used to avoid offending the feelings or sensibilities of one's listeners (e.g., *underachiever* instead of *poor student, seniors* instead of *old people, attendance teacher* instead of *truant officer*), but they may be used also to upgrade a job or position, as for example, the use of *correction officer* instead of "prison guard."

The word *dysphemism* (from *dys-* "not" + *(eu)phemism*) is used to describe a negative or derogatory expression that is used to replace a neutral one. Dysphemisms are the opposite of euphemisms. For example, derogatory names for homosexuals, such as *"homo," "fairy,"* and *"pansy"* are outdated dysphemisms, whereas *"gay," "lesbian,"* and *same-sex (same-sex marriage)* are euphemisms that have become acceptable in the standard language. Ethnic names are especially prone to change through euphemism: *Native American* and *African American* have largely replaced names now considered disparaging, such as, respectively, *American Indian* or *Redskin*, *Negro* or *Colored* or *Black*. And old ethnic slurs like *Mick*, *Wop*, *Dago*, *Yid*, and *Hebe* are no longer tolerated in print and are only used jocularly, and then often only by the people the names were used to disparage.

LANGUAGE OF DECEIT

Euphemism, however well-intentioned, is often the language of deceit, evasion, hypocrisy, and prudery. It conveniently allows us to use mild, roundabout, or vague expressions in place of those that are uncomfortably accurate, blunt, or precise. Euphemistic language can be found in all aspects of life: age, alcohol, death, drug-taking, marriage, money, politics, race, sexuality, work, and much more. Often slang words are used to mask sensitive or taboo subjects.

POPULAR EUPHEMISMS AND DYSPHEMISMS

Here are some examples of euphemisms and dysphemisms in a walk through the alphabet:

adult bookstore for a store selling pornographic books

athletic supporter for a jockstrap (pouch supporting male genitalia)

break wind for "expel intestinal gas"

collateral damage for the death or injury of civilians by mistake in wartime

do away with for kill

drag queen, a dysphemism for a male transvestite

evasion for a lie

full-figured (or *plus-sized*) for fat or heavyset

four-letter word for an obscenity

grass (or *pot, reefer, weed,* etc.) for marijuana

hit the bottle for "get drunk"

infidelity for adultery

john for a lavatory and also for a potential customer
    for a prostitute

knockers (or *boobs, jugs,* etc.), dysphemisms for
    women's breasts

lived-in for untidy

massage parlor for a brothel

non-white for a person of African or Asian ancestry

organ for the penis

pickled for drunk (there are hundreds of euphemisms
    for *drunk*)

queen, a dysphemism for a male homosexual, especially
    an effeminate one

road apples for horse manure in the street

skinny-dip for "bathe in the nude"

technicolor yawn for vomiting due to drunkenness

unhinged for insane or psychotic

wet dream for nocturnal seminal emission

X-rated movies for pornographic films

yellow for cowardly

zoo for a crowded and confused place

New words and expressions are often coined to replace ones that are felt to be too direct, harsh, unpleasant, or offensive. In an effort to avoid giving offense, various circumlocutions are formed, for example, the use of "colored," "nonwhite," "African American," "Afro-American," "Negro," or "member of a minority group." Similarly, Spanish-speaking Americans are variously described as "Hispanic," "Latinos," or "Hispanic-Latinos," instead of specific names like "Mexicans," "Puerto Ricans," or "Dominicans." Many speakers avoid the word *Jew*, choosing to speak instead of "Hebrews" or "Jewish people." However, one should not generalize about ethnic names, as members of a specific group may disagree on the terms they find offensive.

Euphemisms are also created for superstitious reasons, as by using the coinage *moonchild* to describe a person born under the sign of Cancer, in order to avoid mentioning the name of the dreaded disease. The word *cancer* is often replaced by some euphemism, such as "the C-word" or "the big C." Another example is *hospice*, originally meaning a guest house for the poor or sick, now used as the name of an institution for the care of the dying, "the terminally ill." The fear of death is one of the great reasons for indulging in euphemisms. Most of us will say almost anything to avoid saying that someone has died: "passed away," "passed on," "left us, "is gone," "gone to heaven," "gave up the ghost," "gone to his eternal reward," and so on. A metaphoric phrase like "buy the farm" is sometimes used to mean "to die," and even Catholic churches have replaced the sacramental term "extreme unction," with the more acceptable "anointing of the sick." The sacrament of penance was also renamed "rite of reconciliation," and the confessional is euphemistically called a "room of reconciliation."

EUPHEMISMS AND DYSPHEMISMS

Prudery, or an excessive desire to appear proper or respectable, has always been a prime motive for employing euphemisms. Direct reference to sexual activities and functions is still frowned upon by many. Thus, pornographic stores, theaters, and so forth are often referred to as "adult," a sexual affair is a "relationship" or "tryst," and unmarried lovers living together are "cohabiters," "cohabitees," "partners," "domestic partners," "live-in friends," "roommates," "significant others" (SOs), and so on.

The names of bodily parts associated with sex are particularly avoided, despite the liberal trends that permit the use of the words *breast* and *legs*, which were scrupulously avoided in the 19th century even when referring to parts of a chicken. The word *buttocks* is replaced by "butts," "buns," or "backside"; women's breasts are referred to dysphemistically as "boobs," "jugs," "knockers"; and to have sexual intercourse is described as "going to bed with," "making out," "making love," "sleeping with," not to mention a host of slang dysphemisms.

Another motive for euphemisms is the wish to make a position, occupation, or institution look or sound better by changing its common name to one thought to confer greater dignity or importance upon it. A prison guard is thus renamed a "correction officer" and solitary confinement in a prison is made to seem less dehumanizing by calling it an "adjustment center." Garbage collectors are renamed "sanitation engineers" or "sanitation workers." The personnel department of a business is now "human resources." Barbers and haircutters became "hair stylists." Airline stewards and stewardesses became "flight attendants." The low esteem attached to old age brought on the coinage of "senior citizen" and other terms like "third age" and "middlescence."

Euphemisms have also become important manipulatory devices in political and military discourse. The Nazis employed the euphemism *Endlösung* ("Final Solution") for their program of mass extermination of Jews throughout Europe. The Vietnam War produced euphemisms like "body count" for the number killed in combat and "pacification" for the destruction of an area to eliminate guerrilla activity. *Apartheid,* which originated in the Republic of South Africa as a euphemism for a policy of separation between the black population and the white, came to mean racial segregation of the worst sort. Governments and agencies that are supposed to be protecting us from terrorists are now referred to as "homeland security." The underhanded activities that led to the Watergate scandal were euphemistically termed, "dirty tricks." A foreign government trying to overthrow another is in the process of "destabilizing" its target. The physical destruction of an unwanted ethnic group in a country has been called "ethnic cleansing." Some of these euphemisms were originally "code words," used to convey meaning only to insiders.

Often euphemisms are created not so much to hide an unpleasant fact of life, but to provide a more accurate or refined description, as when "disadvantaged" is used for poor people, "underachievers" for poor students, and "learning-disabled" for the mentally slow or backward. Such a motivation is evident in new definitions in psychiatry that attempt to replace "blanket" categories with more specific terms, for example, "bipolar disorder" replacing "manic depression." This was also the motivation in world politics that replaced words like *rich* and *poor* as applied to countries with specific descriptive words like "developed countries," "underdeveloped countries," "developing countries," and "emerging countries."

It is not always clear when a word is a euphemism and when it is not. Vulgarisms, slang, acronyms, jargon, and technical terminology may be euphemistic, but this depends on the speakers or writers and their audience. For example, a vulgarism may become a euphemism when it is less distressing to the speaker and the listener than the more orthodox term it disguises. Thus, the words *hooker* and *call girl* are felt to be less disturbing than the standard term *prostitute*. Slang is often euphemistic when it is sufficiently arcane and the property of an insider group. In the underworld, the word *kill* is usually replaced by such slang synonyms as *waste, hit, whack, ice, pop off, rub out,* and *dump*. In the narcotics world, one who sells drugs is called a *dealer, pusher, connection, peddler, source, bagman, broker,* and *fixer*. In these cases, the substitution of a slang term for a more widely known one that is unacceptable allows slang to function as euphemism.

The same is true of jargon, which, because of its limited accessibility, is particularly effective as concealing language. Acronyms and abbreviations are euphemistic when they cover obscenities, like "snafu" (abbreviation of *situation normal: all fucked up*), when they cover up something unpleasant, like *DOA* (*Dead on Arrival*), or when they neutralize something frightening, like *WMDs* (*Weapons of Mass Destruction*). Usually the speaker or writer, the conditions surrounding the speech or writing, and the person or group to whom it is addressed will determine whether a word or phrase is a euphemism.

The earliest euphemisms were probably religious. Since the names of the gods were considered identical to them, to speak a name of a god was the equivalent of evoking the deity. This was considered a dangerous practice, even for priests, so they came up with indirect forms of reference to avoid the wrath of the deity: *the Almighty, the Creator, the Deity, the Eternal, the Lord*. The instinct here extends into many other domains of taboo that are dominated by a strong conviction about the magical power of words such as *death* and *birth*. Which subjects and what parts of them were acceptable or forbidden vary both from culture to culture and from one historical period to another within a culture. There have been many linguistic revolutions tied to cultural, social, economic, and political change.

HOW EUPHEMISMS ARE MADE

The formation of euphemisms is based on linguistic and psychological patterns that have fundamentally remained the same. Meaning can be defined as the sum of the responses to a word or phrase; words and phrases may be regarded as responses to stimuli. After a word has been associated for a long time with the stimulus that provokes it, the word itself picks up aspects of the response elicited by the stimulus. When unpleasant elements of response attach themselves strongly to the word or phrase used to describe them, then we tend to substitute another word or phrase that is free of these negative associations.

Some ways in which euphemisms are formed include borrowing words from other languages that have less negative associations, like *halitosis* (formed in the 1800s from Latin *halitus* "breath" + *-osis* "abnormal") for "bad breath." Euphemisms may also be made by a semantic process called widening or generalization, when a specific term is too vivid or painful. For example, instead of referring explicitly to a disease like syphilis, one may say "sexually transmitted disease," "STD," "social disease," or "venereal disease." Semantic shift is the substitution of the whole for the specific part, such as *rear end* for *buttock*. Metaphor compares things and offers up *blemish* for *pimple*. There is also something called phonetic distortion for words that we dare not speak. This involves other types of word formation: abbreviation, elimination of a final syllable, initialism, conversion, back-formation, reduplication, blending, and creation of diminutives, as in baby talk (see the chapter on **Baby Talk**). Examples are: *ladies* for *ladies room*, *vamp* for *vampire* ("a seductive woman"), *JC* for *Jesus Christ*, *burgle* from *burglar*, *peepee* for *piss*, *heinie* for *hind end*, and the list goes on. Words can also undergo elevation or degradation and become euphemistic. A forbidden or taboo meaning of a word may drive out its acceptable or general definition. When *gay* started being substituted for *homosexual,* then it became rarely used in its original sense of "happy" or "vivacious." So there are many ways in which euphemisms are formed, and the motives for generating them are as diverse and universal as the range of human emotions.

functional shift or conversion:

how words become parts of speech

Take a look at the following pairs of sentences in which the same words appear in different "functions" (parts of speech):

You committed a *major* oversight.
She graduated with a *major* in philosophy.
She *majored* in philosophy.

Your *account* is overdrawn
Can you *account* for where the money went?

She gave a *blanket* to the homeless man.
They *blanketed* the area with leaflets.

He is a *master* in the game of chess.
He has *mastered* the game of chess.

The ship dropped *anchor* at midnight.

The ship *anchored* at midnight.

The noun, verb, and adjective look alike and sound alike but their function in each sentence is different. In the first example, the adjective *major* is shown to have shifted in function to a noun, and the noun to have shifted into a verb. The second example is trickier; the noun *account* and the verb *account* were actually taken in the same Middle English period from Old French; so as far as we know no shifting of function took place. In the other examples, however, the verbs were derived from the nouns. Can we consider these verbs new additions to the language? Are *major*, adjective, noun, and verb, three words or just a single word? We will talk about this later in the chapter.

FUNCTIONAL SHIFTS

Dictionaries identify every entry word by labeling the part of speech to indicate the function or functions the word has. However, as the language is applied to describe the changes in social attitudes or supply the needs of science and technology, words constantly shift in grammatical function. *Functional shift* (or *functional change* or *conversion*) is the word-formation process by which words change parts of speech without the addition of an affix; for example, *soldier on*, a verb, is derived from *soldier*, a noun. Other examples include the change of noun to verb in *carpet*, or the change of *must* from auxiliary verb ("You *must* read this book") to noun ("This book is a *must* for any student of language"), and from noun to adjective ("This book is a *must* read"). So a word formerly used as a noun can be used as a verb, an adjective can be used as a noun, and so on. A functional shift is usually shown in a dictionary as a separate entry, or noted in an etymology, or occasionally discussed in a usage note.

Functional shift dates back to the Middle English period. Any number of our older words will show at least verb and noun meanings and often others. They have been gradually added to the language as time passed. The most common functional shift is from noun to verb, for example, when *a bottle* becomes *to bottle*. Technical language uses this device as the source of new expressions: *to access, to jeté, to lesion,* and *to polygraph* became verbs from nouns. Other common nouns, like *service,* are also converted from nouns to verbs.

Changes from verb to noun occur less frequently, possibly because nouns can easily be formed from verbs by derivation, through the addition of *-ation, -ment,* and so forth. However, verb phrases underlie numerous compound nouns: *buyout, giveback, setup, turnover* were derived from the verb phrases *buy out, give back, set up, turn over.* Noun phrases can become verbs, often first used with a hyphen, as in *to blue-shift* from *blue shift,* but frequently dropping the hyphen to become solid compounds with increasing use, for example, *to carpool, to daycare, to redline.*

Adjective/adverb pairs are common, the adverb usually deriving from the adjective, as in *clear, near, smooth,* and many more. Nouns derived from adjectives are also fairly common, including such nouns as *intellectual, juvenile, moderate, progressive,* and *rustic.* They also occur in words ending with *-ic,* such as *acrylic,* and various medical nouns, for example, *autistic, geriatric,* and *psychotic.* The appearance of such shifts can be explained by analogy with established noun use, such as *alcoholic, critic,* and *fanatic.*

Adjectives derived from nouns, such as *animal* ("animal furs"), *brute* ("brute creatures"), *capsule* ("capsule format"), *dwarf* ("dwarf stars"), *mammoth* ("a mammoth structure"), *model* ("a model house"), and *slave* ("slave labor"), do not assume comparative and superlative forms (*-er, -est*), and do not form adverbs with *-ly* nor abstract nouns with *-ness.* However, the shift from a noun to an adjective is not always clear. A reason for this is that nouns share one of the adjective's characteristic uses, that of appearing in the attributive position to another noun, such as *psychology* in *psychology journal*. Noun phrases and compounds include nouns used attributively, as *throw* in *throw weight* and *tube* in *tube sock*. Often the identification of a functional shift depends on the context in which the word appears.

Sometimes functional shifts are difficult to determine because new words appear almost simultaneously in several parts of speech, such as *de-accession* (noun, verb), *uplink* (noun, verb), and *upmarket* (adjective, adverb). There are really two categories of change: change to a base word (*to drive* becoming *a drive*) and change of compounds (*sandpaper* becoming *to sandpaper*). In English, verbs derived from nouns are particularly productive: *to bicycle, to stamp;* less productive are nouns derived from verbs, like *buy, hit,* and verbs derived from adjectives, *to tidy.*

Functional shift has for centuries been a common means of extending the resources of English, and the process is extremely productive today. There do not appear to be restrictions on the forms that can undergo conversion, so that acronyms, blends, clipped forms, compounds, and derivatives are all acceptable inputs to the conversion process. All parts of speech seem to be able to undergo conversion, and conversion seems able to produce words of almost any part of speech. The only partial restriction is that derived nouns rarely undergo conversion and particularly not to verbs. The derived noun *arrival* will not be converted into a verb if that verb means exactly the same as *arrive,* from which *arrival* is derived.

Functional shift may also involve a change within the same word class, as in a change from one type of noun to another or one type of verb to another. An example is the use of uncountable nouns as countable and vice versa. Thus, "some beer/coffee/sugar/tea" are examples of uncountable nouns, whereas "two beers/coffees/sugars/teas" show how these words can be used as countable. Similarly, intransitive verbs are often used as transitive verbs: "How long can the bird fly non-stop?" and "Can you fly a kite?" But shifts most often involve a change from one part of speech to another.

Many words have undergone functional shift, but not in all their senses. For example, the noun *paper* has several meanings, such as "newspaper," "wallpaper," and "academic article." The verb *to paper* relates only to the "wallpaper" sense. The process has been described as derivation without a change of form (zero derivation).

TOTAL AND PARTIAL CONVERSIONS

Let's get back to the question whether we are dealing here really with a word-formation process. Is the result of functional shift two words, one derived from the other, or one word with extended functions? Well, "conversion" is often subdivided into "total conversion" and "partial conversion." Total conversion is a derivation process and is considered a true word-formation pattern. Partial conversion is considered to be a matter of phrase or sentence structure.

Total conversion is talked about by linguists as "zero derivation" since "conversion" implies that one word has somehow been turned into another, thereby losing its former identity (this happens in just a few cases where, over a long period of time, the first word falls into disuse). Instances of total conversion are the noun *chemical*, derived from the adjective, the verb *bottle* from the noun *bottle*, and the noun *find* from the verb *find*. An example of partial conversion is the word *poor* in *the poor exist in every town*. Is this a noun, an adjective acting as a noun, or must we say that it really belongs to two parts of speech?

Total conversion tends to be sporadic and unpredictable and

it involves marked changes of meaning between the base word and the derived forms. However, we do not care too much about "total" or "partial" but rather recognize that English gains many words—arguably, word senses—via functional shift. There are many clear cases of conversion, with the major kinds being a noun shifting to verb (*to badger, to bottle, to bridge, to commission, to mail, to mushroom, to network, to skin, to trash, to vacation*), verb shifting to noun (*a call, a command, a commute, a dump, a guess, an interrupt, a spy*), adjective shifting to noun (*a crazy, a daily, a double, a dyslexic, a gay, a given, a nasty, the poor, a regular, a roast*), and adjective shifting to verb (*to better, to dirty, to empty, to faint, to open, to right, to total*). Prepositions, conjunctions, adverbs, and interjections can all act as the bases for conversion as shown in *to up, the hereafter, to heave-ho*, and *a maxi*. Moreover, one part of speech can undergo conversion into more than one part of speech. So, for our purposes, we do not care about a detailed analysis of the categories or linguists' issues with conversion. We can clearly see this as an important word-formation process. Apart from the more obvious possibility of creating new words with the help of prefixes, suffixes, and combining forms, conversion is probably the most productive word-formation process in modern English.

CHAPTER 16

generalization:

extending the particular
to the general

Academus was a Greek hero of the Trojan War
who lived near Athens in a fabulous estate lined with beautiful
trees and statues. The estate, which was named after him as the
Academia, eventually became a park, and it was in a grove in that
park that Plato formed a school and taught his students. In Latin,
the word *academia* came to be applied to any school or place of instruction, and this word entered French, Italian, and other languages. It was also, in the 1500s, the source of English *academy*.
Thus, the particular name of Plato's school was generalized to
any school. The change from the name of a particular person,
place, or thing to an entire class of people, places, or things is a
form of *generalization*, the process of extending or widening the
meaning of a word, name, or phrase.

Interestingly, by the 1700s the meaning of *academy* was narrowed from a general to a particular meaning, namely, a society or organization dedicated to the promotion of the arts and sciences, such as the Academy of Motion Picture Arts and Sciences, which bestows annually the Academy Awards. This narrowing of meaning is an example of *specialization*, the flip side of the coin of generalization.

Many famous proper names have undergone generalization. To mention a few, the mythical titan Atlas, whose picture appeared in medieval books of maps, gave his name to today's atlases of the world; the German physicist Gabriel D. Fahrenheit proposed in 1714 the temperature scale we now refer to in such phrases as "70 degrees Fahrenheit"; and a Belgian instrument maker by the name of Antoine Joseph Sax invented, circa 1840, the musical instrument that became known as the saxophone. For other examples, see the chapter on **Eponyms.**

AWESOME GENERALIZATIONS

That which is true of proper names is all the more true of ordinary words, which regularly undergo changes in meaning, including generalization and specialization, and at times a combination of both. The adjective *awesome* meant originally "awe-inspiring, causing an overwhelming feeling of fear, reverence, wonder, etc.," and was used in such phrases as *an awesome sight, an awesome experience.* Today, a teenager might remark after seeing a popular movie, "Wow, it was awesome," meaning it was very good. This change from a specific, literal meaning to a generalized term of approval followed a pattern seen earlier in words like *awful, horrible,* and *terrible.* These three words lost their original, literal meanings of "inspiring awe, horror, or terror" and took on the generalized meaning of "very bad or unpleasant," as in *an awful day, horrible weather, I had a terrible time.* The original meanings of these words have practically disappeared. The synonyms *horrid* and *horrendous* followed the same pattern. Similarly, the adjective *fantastic*, which originally meant "based on fantasy," has become generalized to mean "extremely good," and *incredible*, which literally means "unbelievable," is now commonly used in the sense of "very good, excellent," as in *an incredible speaker*. The process of generalization is different with nouns, in which meanings widen gradually as circumstances change and tend to remain within the compass of the original sense. In the 1600s, a *manuscript* denoted a handwritten document (from Latin *manū scrīptus*, "written by hand"), but with the invention of typewriters and computers, the word has been generalized to mean "any text before it is printed." Likewise, to *manufacture* no longer means "to make by hand," and we assume today that any manufactured product was machine-made. When first acquired from Latin, *virtue* was a desirable male quality, manliness (Latin *vir*, "man"), but over time it was extended to mean "moral excellence" in any person, whether man or woman.

But it may not be so simple and the categories are not always distinguishable. For example, the word *pigeon* meant originally any young chirping bird; later it was specialized to mean only a young dove. Then it went through generalization from "young dove" to all dovelike birds.

VICTIMS OF GENERALIZATION

arena generalized from "sandy floor of a Roman amphitheater" to any central area used for sports or other activities, and figuratively to "any area of combat or action"

bread generalized from "bit, piece, morsel" to "piece of bread," then "bread" (In Old English, the common word for bread was *hlāf*, which survives as English *loaf*) *companion* generalized from those who ate bread together (Latin *com-* "together" + *pānis* "bread") to any associate or partner

construct generalized from "piling up together," as in stones to make a house, to meanings like "piling up words to make a sentence"

culminate generalized from "reach the top of a hill" to "reach a decisive point after struggling"

dependent generalized from "hanging from something" to "supported financially by someone else"

doctrine, novice, office generalized from their original religious meanings to more general secular meanings

fanatic generalized from "excessively zealous over religious beliefs" to "excessively enthusiastic," as in *fanatic over sports*

glamour generalized from "magic, enchantment, spell" to "alluring charm or beauty" and figuratively "exciting activity," as in *the glamour of mountain climbing*

illustrate generalized from "to light up, clear up" to "make clear by pictures, examples, and so on, demonstrate visually or by reasoning"

nausea generalized from "seasickness" to "any sick feeling resembling seasickness"

pain generalized from "punishment, penalty" to "severe distress, suffering"

pants generalized from "men's wide breeches extending from waist to ankle" to more broadly defined garments for either sex

sail once meant specifically "to travel on a ship with sails," later "to travel on any ship" and figuratively "to go through effortlessly," as in *to sail through the exam*

slogan generalized from a battle cry of Celtic troops to "a motto or catchphrase used by a political or other group, or in advertising a product"

Other words that have been generalized are ordinary words like *article, business, picture,* and *thing.*

⁂

A SHORT HISTORY OF "THING"

The everyday word thing *has a remarkable history that serves to illustrate the power of generalization. In Old English,* thing *meant "an assembly or meeting of people, such as a law court or parliament," a meaning shared by related Germanic words such as Dutch* dinc, *German* ding *(in modern German,* Ding), *and Norwegian, Danish, and Swedish* ting. *After several centuries, the word's original meaning became narrowed down in all of these languages to "matter before an assembly or law court, lawsuit." This meaning, in turn, was gradually generalized to "any matter, any thing." Curiously, a similar development occurred in languages derived from Latin: The Latin word* causa *"legal matter, case, cause" was generalized in French* chose *and Italian and Spanish* cosa *to mean "matter, thing."*

NEW MEANING BY ANALOGY

Mostly, generalization is carried out by analogy. Analogy involves the perception of similarity between some object or process with some other concept or process. The basic meaning of a word is related to another word's meaning in such a way that by analogy there can be an extension of meaning from one to the other. For example, if someone is the *head* of a department, the relationship of the *head* to the body—the literal sense—is being used in an extended or figurative sense, in which there is an analogy of *head* is to *body* as *head* (= leader) is to *department*. If you say, "The population of Vermont is mushrooming," you are comparing the rapid growth in population to the rapid growth of mushrooms.

Virtually any perceived similarity can be the basis of analogical change and the source of a new meaning. An abstract concept or process can be linked to a concrete object or process and vice versa. The analogy can be quite remote and even unlikely, but if it catches on with a group of people, it may easily stick in the language. The mind looks for concrete ways of representing abstract concepts and the concrete meanings clarify the intended abstract relationship. Analogy is often said to be the most frequent and important source of semantic enrichment in the English language.

Why generalization? Many of us reach for a broader, more general word, even though our English teachers continually ask us to be more specific and provide details. They do not offer enough instruction on how to find the right word for the meaning we have in mind. So, because many of us have no particular talent for words, we choose the more general meaning, especially in everyday speech and writing. This tendency shows up historically when words acquire more general meanings. For example, *docile*, based on the same root as *doctor*, originally meant "teachable" but was generalized to "easily handled." *Guys* used to mean males of strange appearance, then it was broadened to mean any males, and now it is generalized even further to any group of people, including a group of females.

What happens when there is a new category that we need a word for? One possibility is to invent an entirely new word, but this does not happen frequently. More often, an existing word is extended in meaning to include the new category. When the meaning of a word is extended, it is done on the basis of some kind of relationship between the old meaning and the new. This is a conceptual relation. The general situation involved in extending the meaning of a word is semantic extension.

Say you are familiar with domestic cats and have a word for them; for simplicity, let's say it is the English word *cat*. Then you discover tigers and leopards. Each of these new categories gets its own noun, but in becoming familiar with these new animals, you see their similarities with domestic cats and develop a new category that encompasses all three categories of animals. How do you refer to this new category, that is, to the more general category of cats, what zoologists refer to as members of the family Felidae? One possibility, the one used by many English speakers, is to refer to this category using the same word used for its most familiar subcategory, that is, *cat*. Note that the word *cat* now has two related meanings. The extension of *cat* to include a new sense seems reasonable because the two senses are closely related. Words may extend their meanings on the basis of the generalization relation. The noun *cat* came to mean not only "domestic cat," but also "cats in general." Here is another example. The noun *chicken* can refer both to a particular kind of bird (an object) and to a kind of meat made from this bird (a mass). Notice the two senses in the following sentences:

There is a *chicken* walking around in the back yard.
There is some *chicken* in the freezer.

Flip through the dictionary and look at random for a word with four or more meanings, preferably a word you think you know. Chances are you will find that it has an unlikely hodgepodge of meanings, at least one of which will surprise you. What is the main reason for this? Well, generalization. It is the use of a word in a broader realm of meaning than it originally possessed, often referring to all items in a class rather than one specific item. For instance, *place* derives from Latin *platea*, "broad street," but its meaning grew broader than the street, to include "a particular city," "a business office," "an area dedicated to a specific purpose," before broadening even more to mean "area." In the process, the word *place* displaced the Old English words *stow* and *stede* (which survives in *stead, steadfast, steady,* and *instead*). Generalization is a natural process, especially in situations where the speaker has a limited vocabulary.

THREE FLAVORS OF GENERALIZATION

There are three types of generalization: metonymy, metaphor (covered in the next chapter), and radiation.

Metonymy is a figure of speech in which one word is substituted for a related word; the relationship might be that of cause and effect, container and contained, part and whole. For instance, in Shakespeare's *Much Ado About Nothing*, Benedick, hearing the sound of harp music, exclaims, "Now, divine air! . . . Is it not strange that sheep's guts should hale souls out of men's bodies?" Here "sheep's guts" substitutes metonymically for harp strings.

Metonymy occurs in many languages. The Greek word *dóma* originally meant "roof." Since the Greeks frequently used *dóma* to refer to "house," it became the standard meaning of the word. (In the same way English speakers sometimes use *roof* to mean house, as in the phrase *to have a roof over one's head*.) The Russian word *vinograd*, "vineyard," was so frequently used to refer to grapes, as in "Let's have a taste of the vineyard," that it has come to mean "grapes." Similar associations occur with names.

When we say *the White House*, we can mean the building in Washington, D.C. that serves as the residence of the president of the United States or the president of the United States and his staff. Metonymy can also cover extension in meaning resulting from other associations such as part and whole, for example, "drink the whole bottle" or "give me a hand."

Metaphor is the extension of a word's meaning by adding a figurative sense to the word's concrete or literal meaning. A metaphorical meaning of both *circus* and *zoo* is "any noisy, confusing place or activity," as in *The convention was a circus* and *During rush hour, the subway station turns into a zoo.*

Radiation is metaphorical extension on a grander scale, with new meanings radiating from a central semantic core to embrace many related ideas. The word *head* originally referred to that part of the human body above the rest. Since the top of a nail, pin, or screw is, like the human head, the top of a slim outline, that sense has become included in the meaning of head. Since the bulb of a cabbage or lettuce is round like the human head, that sense has become included in the meaning of *head*. The meaning of the word *head* has radiated out to include the head of a coin (the side picturing the human head), the head of the list (the top item in the list), the head of a table, the head of the family, a head of cattle, or $50 a head. Other words that have similarly radiated meanings outward from a central core include *heart*, *root*, and *sun*.

Radiation is sometimes described by the word *polysemy*. The name comes from Greek *polý*, "many," and *sēmos* "pertaining to meaning." This happens when a word acquires a wider range of meanings. For example, *paper* comes from Latin *papyrus*, which originally referred to writing material made from the papyrus reeds of the Nile. English *paper* referred to other writing materials, as those made from pulp or rags, and later extended the meaning to things like government documents, scientific reports, family archives, or newspapers.

Lexicographers distinguish between different meanings or uses of the same word, defining them in either a single dictionary entry or in separate entries based on part of speech. Such polysemous or multidefinition words differ from homonyms (words having the same pronunciation and spelling but different meanings), such as *fluke*, "barbed head of an anchor," *fluke*, "stroke of good luck," or *fluke*, "kind of flounder," which have multiple meanings *and* different etymologies, and are therefore separate dictionary entries.

CHAPTER 17

metaphor:
soaring from the literal
to the figurative

The importance of metaphor in the life of language cannot be overestimated. Not only does metaphor affect all speech and writing; it deeply influences the way we think and behave. In *Metaphor and Social Beliefs* (1983), the American scholar Weller Embler examined several current metaphors that have influenced modern social behavior. Among them is one that describes New York's subway system as the city's "main veins and arteries, distributing her human corpuscles throughout the municipal body twenty-four-hours of the day." Another common metaphor refers to large cities as jungles, and still another, used by the German philosopher Oswald Spengler in *Decline of the West*, likens a civilization to a living creature that is born, grows, and decays. And in our everyday thinking we often conceive of the human body as a machine, with the brain imagined as a complex apparatus run by cogs and wheels.

Yet another influential metaphor cited by Embler is the analogy of the myth of Sisyphus with contemporary experience. Sisyphus was the mortal whom the gods punished for his sins by condemning him to roll a stone to the top of a mountain. Each time the stone reaches the top, it falls back down the mountain and Sisyphus must roll it to the top again. In *The Myth of Sisyphus*, the French novelist Albert Camus says about this endless toil: "The gods thought with some reason that there was no punishment more awful than useless and hopeless labor." And he adds, "The worker of today labors every day of his life at the same tasks and his destiny is no less absurd."

As a last example of the influence of metaphor on our thinking and behavior, Embler turns to the popularized psychology of Sigmund Freud, especially Freud's description of the subconscious. He writes: "Freud's diagram of the Id, the Ego, and the Super Ego is a schema which is a metaphor useful merely in discussion. In *An Autobiographical Study* Freud warned against taking this schematic representation literally. 'But many readers will take the image of the subconscious literally.'"

We see from these examples that metaphors can be powerful tools of propaganda rather than mere ornamentation. If one refers to human beings as ants, as the Nazi character does in Arthur Koestler's novel *Arrival and Departure*, we know that in the speaker's mind there is no difference between men and ants and one can squash a human being as one squashes an ant by stepping on it.

From a linguistic standpoint, the importance of metaphor lies in the large numbers of meanings that can be created through its use. Simply defined, a metaphor is a figure of speech that compares two seemingly unrelated objects, transferring a characteristic of one to the other. The transferred meaning is either added to the original meaning (e.g., *pansy* "flower" comes to mean in slang "effeminate male") or it displaces the old meaning partially or completely (*blank* originally meant "white," *corn* referred to grain in general).

WHEN METAPHORS KICK THE BUCKET

There are thousands of words and phrases that are obvious metaphors because their literal and figurative senses are still current and we do not have to strain to see the analogies they draw. But English also includes hundreds of "lost" or "dead" metaphors—words and phrases we still use figuratively, but whose original, literal senses have fallen into obscurity. When we speak of a *sunny* disposition, a *cloudy* demeanor, or *starry eyes*, we don't think of the words *sunny*, *cloudy*, and *starry* literally, though we are vaguely aware of their literal meanings. But in other cases, we have no such perception. Though *aftermath* once meant the grass that grew after a farmer mowed a field, the word is no longer used this way. Many metaphors derive from events or legends that are not familiar to us or are forgotten. Few people know the Bible enough to understand that the origin of the word *sodomy* is found in the Biblical story of the destruction of the sin-filled city of Sodom; few know the Greek myth that explains *Achilles' heel*. Some metaphors are more obscure because their original literal sense was lost even before the metaphors became English; they were borrowed from other languages in which they were already used figuratively. You might say that when a "dead" or "lost" metaphor is unrecognized as such, the word or meaning has succeeded in becoming common. But then, some metaphors, especially idioms, become "frozen." Frozen metaphors tend to lose their vividness, and speakers and writers often lose sight of their metaphorical origins. For example, the metaphorical origin of *kick the bucket* "to die" is not readily apparent to most (and its actual origin is also uncertain).

Besides dead metaphors, there are other types classified by writers on rhetoric. Among them are "dormant metaphors" (not quite dead ones) and "mixed metaphors." A mixed metaphor is one in which incongruous metaphors are combined. Jeffrey McQuain, in his book *Power Language* (1996), warns readers that mixed metaphors "will hurt the message (many also fall into the pit of clichés) and perhaps even embarrass the word user." He gives over a dozen examples of mixed metaphors, including: "That's just gravy on the cake" (mixing "That's just pure gravy" and "That's just icing on the cake"). "That's a whole new ball of worms" (mixing "can of worms" with "ball of wax"). "They found themselves on the heels of a dilemma" (mixing "Achilles heel" with "horns of a dilemma").

ORIGINS OF THE METAPHOR

The term *metaphor* is taken from ancient rhetoric (Greek *metaphora*, "transference"). All figures of speech that achieve their effect through association, comparison, or resemblance—like antithesis, hyperbole, metonymy, and simile—are species of metaphor. Aristotle first described the metaphor in his *Poetics* (322 B.C.E.). He had a formula, a ratio (he called *análogon*) that "as A is to B, so X is to Y," exemplified as "As old age is to life, so is evening to day." Aristotle even said, "The greatest thing by far is to have a command of metaphors . . . since a good metaphor implies a sharp eye for resemblance." The association between disparate words can be illuminating, as when one says "The clouds are crying," to mean "It is raining." Less startling are common examples like *bull's eye,* "center of the target," *sharp criticism,* "strong criticism," *to peel one's eyes,* "to watch out for something."

We should point out that metaphor is not considered to be a word-formation process by some linguists because it is technically merely a change in the meaning and use of an "already existing" word. But, for purposes of this book, since metaphor enlarges and enriches the language, we *do* consider it a word-formation process. Furthermore, figurative meanings may actually result in new words and word combinations. *Brainstorm,* "a sudden inspiration or idea," *cliffhanger,* "suspenseful melodrama," *diehard,* "one who obstinately resists change," *goldbrick,* "to loaf on the job," *highbrow,* "an intellectual," *iron curtain,* "barrier to understanding between countries," *turtleneck,* "high, close-fitting collar," and *wiggle room,* "freedom to maneuver, latitude" all clearly exemplify the ability of metaphors to enlarge and enrich our vocabulary.

Metaphors usually add new meanings to old words. A special meaning is created by linking two unlike words to form a compound, such as *blackball, greenhouse,* and *redcoat.* With metaphor, the linkage is implicit. There are very few words that have not had figurative meanings added to literal ones. Think about *drill* ("a fire drill"), *film* ("a Hollywood film"), *hurdle* ("overcoming hurdles"), *nestle* ("nestling in a chair"), and *summit* ("a meeting at the summit"). Sometimes the figurative meaning is so strong that it comes to mind more quickly than the basic or literal meaning.

Metaphors also provide many of our idioms, jargon, and slang, as well as sayings, like proverbs: *A stitch in time saves nine, Don't count your chickens before they're hatched, Look before you leap.* While we also see many metaphors used in advertising, journalism, politics, and religion, metaphor is of great significance in everyday conversation, too. We argue with each other using terms of battle. We talk about countries as if they were people. We discuss economics in terms of health. The metaphors of war are used in politics, in sports, in medicine, in drama, and in violent crime. Metaphor plays a major role in structuring the way we think and talk about the world. We live in a time when the visual image is a powerful influence on our attitude and thoughts, and the images we see on television and in movies show up in the metaphors we add to our language. It is the "spice" of the language.

Metaphors often convey shades of meaning more succinctly than ordinary words and phrases. Sometimes proper names of well-known people and places acquire a metaphorical meaning. Examples include *Cassandra* (one who prophesies disaster), *Gibraltar* (an impregnable fortress), *Hercules* (an exceptionally strong man), *Jonah* (one who brings bad luck), and *Rubicon* (a decisive, irrevocable step). Some animal names or derivatives carry metaphorical meanings: "He *wolfed* down his chicken nuggets."

Many of us, though, view metaphor as a skill—as something beyond our use or understanding. Most people use metaphors regularly without realizing that they do. Daily, and without thinking about it, we use such expressions as *eyes* of a potato, the *head* of a hammer, and the *foot* of a hill. You could argue about whether such terms are metaphors now, but they once definitely were.

THE SPICE OF LANGUAGE

Here is a list of metaphors from everyday speech, alphabetized by keyword (e.g., *apple, back burner, ballpark figure, curve,* etc.):

>   compare apples and oranges "compare unlike things"
>   put on the back burner "defer"

give a ballpark figure "give an approximate estimate"
throw a curve "take by surprise, usually suddenly or uncomfortably"
be in deep water "be in serious trouble"
march to a different drummer "follow a course different from the ordinary"
walk on eggs "act with extreme caution"
apply elbow grease to "put hard work into"
see eye to eye "agree"
something smells fishy "something looks suspicious"
put one's foot in one's mouth "commit a clumsy verbal blunder"
add fuel to the fire "aggravate a bad situation"
between a rock and a hard place "between two bad alternatives"
go on a wild goose chase "go on a senseless chase or pursuit"
raise someone's hackles "make someone angry"
go haywire "go out of control"
the jury is still out "no decision has been made yet"
tie the knot "get married"
light a fire under someone "provoke someone into action"
be out to lunch "be out of touch with reality"
put through the mill "put through a difficult ordeal"
throw a monkey wrench into "interfere with the normal operation of"
keep one's nose clean "stay out of trouble"
be over the hill "be past the prime of life"
leave a paper trail "leave a written record, especially of incriminating activities"
make a quantum leap "make a sudden and significant advance"

pull a rabbit out of a hat "perform a magic trick"

raise a red flag "give a warning or danger signal"

run a tight ship "exercise strict control over a business, etc."

turn tail "run away out of fear"

come unglued "become nervous or unstable"

with one voice "unanimously"

under someone's wing "under someone's protection or patronage"

throw someone to the wolves "victimize someone for selfish gain"

have X-ray vision "able to see through bodies, like Superman"

So, whether colloquial or poetic, simple or complex, a metaphor compares two unlike ideas or objects and highlights the similarities between them. It accomplishes in a word or phrase what would likely take many more words to express. The metaphor sets up the comparison to evoke a mental picture. We know that poetry would suffer or not exist without metaphor, but so would much of our daily language.

CHAPTER 18

specialization:

mice, viruses, worms, and a parliament of owls

When Douglas Engelbart, who invented the computer mouse in 1963, was asked how he came up with the name *mouse* (plural *mice*) for the device that controls the movement of the pointer on a computer screen, he said he couldn't remember. It was just something that occurred to him when he saw the connecting cord "trailing out the back like that, sitting there, just its funny little shape." And so, almost inevitably, he named this particular electromechanical device after the familiar long-tailed little mammal that it resembled. In this incidental manner, the word *mouse* acquired a specialized meaning it never had before.

This is one of the ways in which words change in meaning: They become specialized. Consider the word *computer*. In the 1600s, it meant a person who computes or calculates mathematically. Then, when a calculating machine was invented in the late 1800s, it was naturally called a computer. It did not take a leap of imagination to apply this word in the 1940s to an electronic calculator. But it's a far cry from this simple machine to today's complex electronic and digital programmable machine—still, we call it a computer. As this example shows, specialization is a process by which the scope of a word's meaning is narrowed or reduced.

TECHNO TERMS

Computer usage has introduced into the language a number of other specialized meanings for old words. Here are a few:

ADDRESS: Not the name of the street or city where you live, but the name under which you get your e-mail.

HARDWARE: Not metal supplies, like nails, nuts, and bolts, but the hard parts of a computer, like the keyboard, printer, disk drives, and microchips.

MEMORY: Not the part of the brain where remembrances are stored, but the part of a computer where data are stored.

MENU: Not the list of dishes in a restaurant, but a list of options that pops up on your computer screen.

WINDOW: Not the opening in a house for light and air, but the rectangular area on a computer screen where programs are displayed.

VIRUS: Not the infective agent that multiplies in the body to cause illness, but a man-made code that replicates itself in a computer to cause damage.

WORM: Not the tiny, squirming creature in your garden, but a special kind of virus that worms itself into a program to destroy data.

But specialization is hardly limited to computer or other high-tech usage. It occurs in all areas of life. Take, for example, the common word *chatter*. It ordinarily means the babble of a child or the patter of people chatting casually. But in the realm of electronic intelligence it has taken on the sinister specialized meaning of signals of a possible terrorist attack picked up by secret listening devices. So when you hear or read about some chatter reported by homeland security, you can't dismiss it as mere babble. Or consider the word *wrap*, which formerly evoked the image of some kind of clothing wrapped around a person, like a shawl or scarf. But in the world of catering and party planning, a wrap has the specialized meaning of a tortilla or other thin bread wrapped around a filling of vegetables, tuna, cheese, and so on—the sort of food also known as a burrito, a crepe, an egg roll, and the like.

Specialization is the opposite of generalization and is found early on in English. In the Middle English period, for example, Chaucer's *Canterbury Tales* (about 1385–1400) abounds in words whose meanings became specialized over time. The following lines from Chaucer contain some of these words:

For catel hadde they ynough and rente (For cattle had they enough and rent).

In this line, *catel* ("cattle") means "property" (from Middle Latin *capitale*). Since the most common form of property was bovine animals, like cows and steers, eventually the word *cattle* took on the specific meaning that it has today. This specialized meaning is first recorded in 1555. In the same Chaucerian line, *rent*, meaning "income from property" (from Old French), came to mean periodical payment by a tenant to a landlord as early as the 1300s.

He was also a lerned man, a clerk. Here the word *clerk* doesn't mean a shop assistant, but a scholar. As far back as the Old English period, scholarship was limited to clergymen, hence Old English *cleric*, "clergyman" (later spelled *clerk*), came to mean a scholar. Scholars often functioned as secretaries, bookkeepers, and other assistants, so they were called clerks (a usage still found in the "law clerks" of Supreme Court justices and judges of lower courts). The specialized sense of a shop or store *clerk* made its debut in the early 1500s.

And bathed every veyne in swich licour (And bathed every vein in such liquor).

Here *licour* has the general meaning of "liquid" (from Old French). Early in the 1300s the word was applied to a drink, as of water or wine, from which arose the specialized sense of an alcoholic drink, the way the word is mostly used today.

Of his complexioun he was sangywn (Of his complexion he was sanguine).

By *sangwyn* Chaucer meant "reddish, ruddy." The word came from Latin *sanguineus*, meaning "bloody" or "blood-red." The modern specialized meaning of *sanguine*, "cheerful, confident," first encountered in the early 1500s, derives from the association of a ruddy complexion with excessive blood in the veins, blood being one of the four humors (choler, phlegm, and black bile are the others) that in medieval times were thought to determine a person's temperament. Thus a ruddy individual was considered temperamentally cheerful and optimistic, as opposed to others who were choleric, phlegmatic, or melancholic.

Ye, sterve he shal . . . The poysoun is so strong and violent (Yes, starve he shall . . . The poison is so strong and violent). The Middle

English verb *sterven* (Old English *steorfan*) meant "to die," and Chaucer is saying in this line that the poisoned individual was going to die. Both German *sterben* and Dutch *sterven*, closely related to the English word, mean "to die." But in English the word became specialized. By about 1530 it had the narrow meaning, "to die of hunger." Thomas Pyles and John Algeo, in *The Origins and Development of the English Language*, point out that the common expression "to starve to death" would in earlier times have the senseless meaning of "to die to death," and when people now say "I'm starving," they only mean that they're very hungry, not that they're dying of hunger. This is a good example of how profoundly specialization alters the meaning of a word.

SPECIALIZATION BY NECESSITY

Students of language have offered various explanations for the narrowing of meanings. One of them is cultural necessity. The word *screen* originally meant a covered frame for protection from cold, heat, and other threats. When movies were invented, a word was needed to describe the frame with a flat surface on which pictures were projected, and *screen* seemed appropriate. Then television brought with it the display *screen* on the TV set. The computer *screen* followed. Cultural need brought about these changes. In an earlier farming and hunting culture, interest in animal life caused speakers to develop popular names for animal groups, a number of which still exist. There were close to fifty such names, among them a *bale* of turtles, a *bevy* of quail, a *drove* of oxen, an *exaltation* of larks, a *flock* of birds or sheep, and, somewhat satirically, a *parliament* of owls.

Another reason is the existence of words having the same or similar meanings. When synonyms exist side by side in the language, speakers try to distinguish between them. Gradually, each word takes on a specific meaning. This is what happened in Middle English when the native word *deer*, which meant "animal," came to clash with two newer synonyms, *animal*, borrowed from Latin, and *beast*, borrowed from Old French. As *beast* became widespread, the meaning of *deer* narrowed in scope and began to be applied specifically to animals of the deer family, since deer were highly prized by hunters. Later, when *animal* became the general word, *beast* took on the specialized sense of "a lower, brutish type of animal." All three words were thus retained in English. Similarly, in Middle English the word *boy* had a synonym, *knave*, and a near-synonym, *girl*, which meant "a child of either sex." When *boy* became the common word for "a male child," *knave* took on the specific meaning of "a male servant," while *girl* came to fill the empty slot of "a female child." Obviously no need was felt for a word meaning "a child of either sex," since *child* covered that meaning satisfactorily.

A third impetus toward specialization is the loss or disappearance of a word's original meaning. An *undertaker* was originally one who undertook any task; once this general meaning went out of use, only the specific sense of a funeral director remained. The basic meaning of *disease* was the literal "lack of ease, discomfort." But as this general sense waned, the specific meaning of "illness" took its place.

Often specialization involves a degradation of meaning. The word *knave*, which in Middle English meant "boy, male servant," was degraded in Modern English to "rascal, rogue." *Doom*, which originally meant "judgment" (still found in *doomsday*, "judgment day"), came to mean "adverse fate, bad end, ruin," as in *The Dictator finally met his doom*. The word *silly* has gone from its original highly favorable meaning, "happy, blessed," to an increasingly unfavorable set of meanings, including "innocent, weak, pitiful, unfortunate," culminating in "simple, ignorant," and finally "foolish."

Words known popularly as Janus words (from *Janus,* the Roman god of doorways who faces two ways) have two contradictory meanings, one of which is favorable, the other not. Some examples are: *oversight,* meaning either "vigilant or responsible care" or "inadvertent or careless omission"; *sanction,* meaning either "approval, permission" or "punitive measure." Janus words bear watching to determine whether they will follow the pattern of other words in which a favorable meaning loses out over its opposite.

generation:
many ways of growing words

INTRODUCTION

In *Gulliver's Travels*, Jonathan Swift (1667–1745) describes the language of the Houyhnhnms, a race of horses endowed with reason, as having no word to express something evil except by referring to the brutish Yahoos. "Thus," writes Swift, "they denote the folly of a servant, . . . a stone that cuts their feet, a continuance of foul or unseasonable weather, and the like, by adding to each the epithet of *Yahoo*." By contrast with the limited vocabulary of the Houyhnhnms, the vocabulary of English in Swift's time may have been too large for him. He had a strong dislike for new words, especially words he regarded as vulgar or slangy, such as *mob* and *phiz*. Yet even as Swift declared an end to good English after the Civil War of 1642, his contemporary, Benjamin Franklin, listed in his

Drinker's Dictionary (1733) no less than 228 terms for drunkenness (this number has grown since to 2,231, according to the word collector Paul Dickson).

The creation of new words is hardly new in English. It actually goes back to Anglo-Saxon times. Speakers of Old English routinely made up words to fill gaps in the language, usually by combining existing words into compounds like *palm-aeppel* (a date), *sweordbora* (swordbearer), and *godspel* (gospel, literally, "good talk"). The English of Geoffrey Chaucer (1343?–1400) abounded in compounds like *bake-mete* (pie), *marybones* (marrowbones), and *coverchief* (head covering). And Shakespeare, who coined such common words as *birthplace* and *eyeball*, was perhaps the most prolific of word inventors. According to Jeffrey McQuain and Stanley Malless, authors of *Coined by Shakespeare* (1998), the Bard probably added as many as 1,500 words to the English language, including many words we think of as modern or contemporary: *addiction, investment, premeditated, undervalue, well-behaved.*

While there is no limit to the number of new words that can be generated in a language, English is foremost, both in the size of its vocabulary (estimates have run from half a million to over a million words) and the rate at which it produces new words. In this era of globalization, English has come to be known both as an international language ("World English") and as a *default language*, that is, as the language most likely to be used in any system of communication if one does not or cannot opt for any other.

One way of measuring the expansion of the English vocabulary is by comparing the number of entries in standard dictionaries since 1755, when the first great modern dictionary, Samuel Johnson's *Dictionary of the English Language*, burst upon the world. That work contained about 50,000 terms, considered a monumental number in those days. By 1828, Noah Webster's *American Dictionary of the English Language* included about 75,000 entries. Its 1864 successor, known as "the Unabridged edition," claimed 116,000. Less than thirty years later, the 1890 *Webster's International Dictionary* boasted the extraordinary number of 175,000. In 1934, *Webster's Second New International Dictionary* claimed 600,000! Finally, the 1961 *Webster's Third*, which eliminated many of the "encyclopedic" and obsolete entries in its predecessor, was still able to claim 450,000 terms within its covers.

The reason for this great expansion is not a secret. The progress achieved since the industrial revolution in technology, science, education, business, and in all other fields of knowledge has had no precedents in history, and with every advance came a concomitant growth of vocabulary. Consider just a handful of new words generated during the past fifty years: *aerospace, antimatter, brainwashing, computerize, cryonics, laptop, liposuction, telemarketing, waitron, wannabe.* These, like a great many of the words that find a permanent place in the language, are formed in distinct patterns.

There being no limits to creativity in the formation of words, new words continue to crop up regularly in countless unexpected forms. However, the processes of generation are finite and well-defined.

CHAPTER 19

baby talk:
hush, little baby,
don't say a word

Out of the mouth of babes come . . . words.
The vocabulary of infants and young children is mostly of interest to their parents. Yet linguists have written volumes on this subject. They distinguish between *baby talk*, which they define as the utterances of young children, and *motherese* and *fatherese* (or *parentese*), which refer to the way parents (and, by extension, nannies, grandparents, and other caretakers) use baby talk when speaking to babies. A technical term for the speech patterns used by grown-ups addressing a baby is *child-directed speech*. A term used to cover a wide range of speech patterns, including those used in addressing patients or elderly dependents, is *caregiver speech*. Baby talk is not only used by parents, nannies, and other adults, but by pet owners talking to their pets (a practice that has been called *doggerel*), lovers exchanging endearments, and

anyone communicating on an infantile level. In his novel, *Seventeen* (1916), the American writer Booth Tarkington describes the way a pet owner speaks to Flopit, her dog: "Izzum's ickle heart a-beatin' so floppity! Um's own mumsy make ums all right, um's p'eshus Flopit!"

Some very common words originated in baby talk. Such words consist usually of one or two syllables that begin with a consonant. The words *babe* and *baby* evolved from an earlier word, *baban*, which was probably motherese for the repeated syllables *ba, ba* typically uttered by infants. The word *babble*, "to prattle like an infant," came apparently from the same source, and is found in other languages besides English, such as Low German *babbele*, Icelandic *babbla*, and Old French *babiller*, "to babble," and Latin *babulus*, "one who babbles." Similarly, the word *mama, mamma* for "mother" appears in many languages, as does the word *papa, pappa* for "father." The word *dad, daddy* is also represented, in somewhat different form, in Latin and Greek *tata*, Welsh *tad*, and Sanskrit *tata-s*.

Baby talk begins when an infant or toddler mispronounces the name of a person or thing and the parents repeat it when talking to the child. If, for example, the child calls the grandfather "Grampy" instead of "Grandpa," the parents and the rest of the family might begin to refer to the grandfather as "Grampy." This kind of usage is quick to spread. Indeed, a well-known *hypocorism* (technical term for a pet name or endearment, from *hypo-*, "under" + Greek *korizesthai*, "to caress") is "Granny" or "Gammy" for "Grandma." The diminutive ending *-y* (and its variant, *-ie*) is one of the commonest forms of baby talk in English, found in words like *doggie, ducky, birdie, kiddie, cutie, kitty*, and in names like *Betsy, Jackie, Ronnie, Margie, Danny*, and *Benny*.

Clipped words or names often result from baby talk. Such short forms as *chick, chimp, mom, pop, Meg, Peg* (nicknames for *Mar-*

garet), and *Dot, Doll* (for *Dorothy*) originated in baby talk. Words imitating sounds may have started as baby talk. Typical words in this class are *baa* (of sheep), *bowwow* (of dogs), *cheep* or *tweet* (of birds), *meow* (of cats), *moo* (of cows), *oink* (of hogs), and *quack* (of ducks and geese).

BABY BABBLE

Baby talk is concerned with the limited activities of babies, much of which involve simple physical processes. The following is a list of words common in baby talk:

BEDDY-BYE: The time for a baby or very young child to go to bed.

BINKIE: A pacifier. From *Binky*, a brand of pacifier.

BLANKIE: A baby's blanket.

BOO-BOO: A minor injury. A reduplication of *boo*, as in boo-hoo, "noisy weeping."

BUDDY: Chum, pal, brother. Baby talk for *brother*.

BUNNY: A rabbit. From *bun*, a word for a rabbit's tail.

BYE-BYE: Good-bye.

CHOO-CHOO: A railroad train. Alteration and reduplication of *tr-* of *train* in imitation of the sound of a train in motion.

DA-DA: Father.

DIN-DIN: Dinner.

DO, DOO, DOO-DOO, or **DOODY:** 1. Feces. 2. defecation. Perhaps alteration of *dirty*.

ICKY: Sticky; disgusting.

JAMMIES: Pajamas.

MAMA: Mother.

NANA: Grandma.

OOPSY-DAISY!: Said on tossing a baby up and down. Probably from *upside-down.*

OWIE: A minor injury; a boo-boo. From *ow*, a cry of pain.

PEE or **PEE-PEE:** 1. Urine. 2. To urinate. (baby talk for *piss*) 3. A penis.

PIGGIE: A baby's finger or toe. From the game "This little piggy went to market."

POOP or **POO-POO:** Feces; defecation. Probably from a reduplication of *pooh*, an exclamation of dislike or disgust.

POTTY: Toilet-training pot or chair.

TEDDY: A stuffed toy bear. Named in cartoons after President *Teddy* Roosevelt, famous for hunting bears.

TEENY-WEENY, TEENIE-WEENIE, TEENSY-WEENSY, or **TEENTSY-WEENTSY:** Very small; tiny. Alteration and reduplication of *teeny*, itself a blend of *tiny* and *wee.*

TINKLE: A urinating.

TUMMY: Stomach. Alteration of *stomach* + diminutive ending *-y.*

TUSH, TUSHIE: Buttocks. Alteration of Yiddish *tukhes.*

WAWA: Water.

WEE-WEE: A urinating.

YUCKY: Same as **icky.**

YUM, YUMMY, or **YUM-YUM:** Pleasing to the taste; delicious.

Baby talk is a universal feature of language, with a distinctive vocabulary in most languages. For example, in French, a boo-boo is *bobo*, yum-yum is *miam-miam*, pee-pee is *pipi*, and milkie is *le lolo*. The baby talk of more than thirty languages has been recorded. See also the chapters on **Nonsense Words** and **Onomatopoeia.**

CHAPTER 20

blends or portmanteau words:

the frabjous utility of beautility

In 1976, the linguist Margaret M. Bryant wrote an article in the journal *American Speech* entitled "Blends Are Increasing." In it she pointed out that before the 19th century *blends*, or two words combined to form a new word, were rather uncommon and did not become a widespread formation until the 20th century. There is little doubt that the impulse to telescope words together comes from the modern need to speed things up, to save time, to do things quickly. Blending is a form of abbreviation or contraction, as evinced by the fondness headline-writers have for them. An extreme example of "headline-ese" is TEX-MEX'S POP SPANGLISH JARGOT (translation: the Texan-Mexican dialect is a popular Spanish-English jargon or argot). Perhaps the most notorious blender in the last century was *Time* magazine, which created *Timese* or *Timespeak*, a style of writing marked by the use of such blends as *cinemactress, guesstimate, slanguage, cinemogul,* all blends that include letters or sounds that the two words have in common (cinem*a* + *a*ctress, gu*ess* + *ess*timate, s*lang* + *lang*uage, cinem(a) + *m*ogul).

PORTMANTEAU WORDS

Blends are also called *blend words, amalgams, fusions, hybrids,* and, notably, *portmanteau words.* A portmanteau is a trunk or suitcase that opens into two hinged halves. It's a British word borrowed from a French blend of *porter,* "to carry," and *manteau,* "a cloak." The term *portmanteau word* was popularized by Lewis Carroll's *Through the Looking-Glass* (1872), in which Humpty Dumpty explains the word *slithy* in the nonsense poem "Jabberwocky":

> ". . . slithy means 'lithe and slimy.' 'Lithe' is the same as 'active.' You see it's like a portmanteau—there are two meanings packed into one word." Further on he says: " 'Mimsy' is 'flimsy and miserable' (there's another portmanteau for you)."

Carroll's portmanteaus were not the usual blends of two words with a common sound in the middle, but clever fusions of two words, several of which have become part of the language. Among them are *chortle* (blend of *chuckle* and *snort*), *galumph* (blend of *gallop* and *triumph*), *frabjous* (irregular blend of *fabulous* and *joyous*), and *frumious* (blend of *fuming* and *furious*). These coinages are meant to suggest the action they describe: to *galumph* is to gallop triumphantly; a *frabjous* day is fabulous and joyous.

English portmanteau words were not invented by Carroll. Various short, expressive words, often imitative of sounds, are found earlier in the language and appear to be blends. Among them is the verb *slosh,* "to splash through mud or slush," used since the early 1800s, and apparently a blend of the earlier words *slop* and *slush.* Similarly, the verb *smash,* "to break into pieces," known since the early 1700s, seems to be a blend of the earlier *smack* and *mash.* And *splatter,* "to splash and scatter," attested since the 1770s, is probably a blend of *splash* and *spatter.* Another expressive word, *squiggle,* known since the early 1800s, originated as a blend of *squirm* and *wriggle.*

A famous early American example of a blend is *gerrymander,* coined in 1812, and referring to the act or practice of dividing a county or state along political lines to allow the party in power to retain a majority. The term was derived from the name of Massachusetts governor Elbridge *Gerry,* who signed a bill in 1811 that redrew the representative districts so as to favor his own Democratic party. History or legend has it that a drawing of the redistricted map of Essex County, Massachusetts, caused the painter Gilbert Stuart to tell the editor of a Boston paper that it resembled a salamander. "A salamander?" the editor said. "Call it a Gerrymander!" The term, a blend of *Gerry* and (sala)*mander,* quickly caught on; caricatures of the salamander-like map were widely publicized, and the verb *to gerrymander* became part of American English. In *Safire's New Political Dictionary,* William Safire writes:

> Governor Gerry, a signer of the Declaration of Independence and later one of James Madison's Vice Presidents, has become— thanks to linguistics—one of the villains of American history. Actually, he never sponsored the redistricting bill and is said to have signed it reluctantly.

SCUZZY ORIGINS

Blends are sometimes so successful as single words that their origin remains obscure or uncertain. The slang word *scuzzy*, meaning "dirty or grimy," is such a word. It may be a blend of *scummy* and *fuzzy*, but perhaps it's an alteration of *disgusting*; its actual origin remains uncertain. H. L. Mencken, in *The American Language*, takes a stab at several such words. He writes: "*Boost* (*boom* + *hoist*) is a typical American blend. I have a notion that *blurb* is a blend also. So, perhaps, is *flunk*; Dr. Louise Pound says that it may be from *fail* and *funk*." Current dictionaries disagree. The origin of *boost* is deemed unknown; *blurb*, coined by Gelett Burgess (see chapter on **Coinages**), was not acknowledged by the coiner as a blend; and *flunk*, according to *Webster's New Collegiate Dictionary*, is perhaps a blend of *flinch* and *funk*. Mencken also guesses that *blurt*, "to utter abruptly," is a blend of *blare* and *spurt*, and that *dumbfound* is a blend of *dumb* and *confound*, but only the latter has been confirmed by lexicographers.

Mencken was not alone among language mavens to conjure up unverified blends. Bergen and Cornelia Evans, in their *Dictionary of Contemporary American Usage* (1957), assert that *dandle*, "to move (a baby, etc.) up and down," is a blend of *dance* and *handle*. This is pure conjecture, since *dandle* has been in English since the 1500s, long before blends of this kind were ever formed.

What motivates people to create blends? A prime impulse seems to be a wish to shorten a phrase that seems too long or clumsy. Thus, an *exercise bicycle* is transformed into an *exercycle*, *aviation electronics* is turned into *avionics*, a *croissant sandwich* becomes a *croissandwich*, and a *simultaneous broadcast* is more felicitously rendered as a *simulcast*. This process of collapsing two or more words into one is especially popular in commerce and industry, as in *Breathalyzer* (for *breath analyzer*), *Instamatic* (blend of *Instant*

and *automatic*), *Sunoco* (for *Sun Oil Company*), *Lescol* (for *less choles-*
terol), and in place names, such as *Chunnel* (for *Channel Tunnel*),
Oxbridge (for *Oxford* and *Cambridge*), *Pakistan* (from the initials of
Punjab, Afghania, Kashmir + the ending *-istan,* as in *Baluchis-*
tan), *Eurasia* (blend of *Europe* and *Asia*), and *Malaysia* (blend of
Malay and *Asia*).

A blend is perhaps most appropriate when it names something that is itself a blend or hybrid. Some examples of such
words are: *tiglon* or *tigon* (blend of *tiger* and *lion*), the hybrid offspring of a male tiger and female lion, and *liger* (blend of *lion*
and *tiger*), the hybrid offspring of a male lion and female tiger;
zedonk (male *zebra* and female *donkey*) and *zonkey* (female *zebra* and
male *donkey*); *yakow* (blend of *yak* and *cow*) and *beefalo* (blend of
beef cattle and *buffalo*).

Language hybrids make for similarly perfect blends. Among
them are *Frenglish* (blend of *French* and *English*), which is English
containing many French words, by contrast with *franglais* (blend
of *français* and *anglais*), which is French containing many English
words. The term *franglais* was popularized by René Etiemble, a
professor of comparative languages at the Sorbonne. In a book,
Parlez-vous franglais?, published in 1964, he criticized the inordi-
nate influence of English words, especially Americanisms, on
the French language, urging the excision of such anglicisms as *le*
planning et research, le weekend, and *le country.* To stop what he considered a misuse of the French language, he proposed French
equivalents to anglicisms, such as *roquette* for *rocket* and *métingue*
for *meeting.*

Other well-known language mixtures include *Hindlish* or
Hinglish (blend of *Hindi* and *English*); *Japlish* or *Janglish* (blend of
Japanese and *English*); *Spanglish* (blend of *Spanish* and *English*); *Yinglish*
(blend of *Yiddish* and *English*); *Chinglish* (blend of *Chinese* and *Eng-*
lish). All of these, as well as *Singlish* (Singapore English), *Italglish,*

Russlish, and *Taglish* (Tagalog English), are informal names, often regarded as inferior forms of the base languages.

The most useful blends are those that supply names for new things or ideas. *Smog* was coined to designate the mixture of *smoke* and *fog,* and *smaze,* the mixture of *smoke* and *haze,* that pollute the atmosphere. A *brunch* is the perfect name for a meal between *breakfast* and *lunch.* A *pulsar,* or pulsating star, is a blend of *puls*(ating) (st)*ar,* and a *pixel,* the smallest element in a picture, is a blend of *pix* (= pics) and *el*(ement). *Medicare* and *Medicaid* are blends, respectively, of *Medic*(al) + *care,* and *Medica*(al) + *aid.* In the 1970s, when the blend *beautility,* for a combination of beauty and utility, made its debut, both the American William Safire and the British Bernard Levin chose this word to illustrate the perfect blend.

Safire: "The best new word that fills a gap in the language was minted by architectural writer Ada Louise Huxtable to describe a happy marriage of form and function: 'beautility.'"

Levin: "A survey of what Lewis Carroll called portmanteaus— words created by a kind of linguistic dialectic from two other words, [includes] the now accepted *beautility.*"

Many blends have no utility and are formed playfully or for the nonce. Time magazine's *yumptious* (blend of *yummy* and *scrumptious*) died aborning. Other miscarriages of recent decades were: *faction* (blend of *fact* and *fiction*), not bad per se but clashing with the standard word *faction,* and *oilonnaire* (blend of *oil* and *millionaire*).

As for the question, are blends increasing? it appears that they are, but mostly in commercial names. In *The Oxford Companion to the English Language* (1992), its editor, Tom McArthur, writes: "... blending is increasing because of the need for compact scientific and technical names such as *amatol* from *ammonium nitrate* and *trinitrotoluene*, and for ... quasi-blends such as *Mentadent*, a toothpaste flavoured with menthol ... *Atomergic Chemetals* is the portmanteau name for a company with varied interests."

coinages:
the art of minting new words

"Young schollers not halfe well studied...
seeme to coign fine words out of Latin," wrote Richard Puttenham in 1589 in *The Arte of English Poesie*. The comparison of new
words to coins newly minted seems to have been well-established in Puttenham's Elizabethan English. To coin new words
means to make them up, the way the government manufactures
shining new coins by stamping metal. We also speak of *minting*
words and even *borrowing* them (see Part 6, **Borrowing**), as if
they were coins of the realm. If words were worth their weight
in money, we'd all be rich. Still, it has become customary to
speak of new or invented words as *coinages*.

Coinages that name new concepts are rarely completely new
creations. Even the classic example of *googol* cannot be said to be
a totally new invention. *Googol*, a word meaning the number 1

followed by 100 zeros (10 to the 100th power), was coined in 1940 by Milton Sirotta, a boy of nine who was the nephew of the U.S. mathematician Edward Kasner. In the book *Mathematics and the Imagination*, written with James Newman, Kasner relates that, when he asked his young nephew to name a very large number, larger than the number of elementary particles in the entire universe (estimated to be 10 to the 80th power), Milton thought a moment, then exclaimed, "a googol!" A new word, no doubt, but being a child's invention, it may have been easily influenced by the name of the then very popular comic-strip character Barney *Google*.

Despite its whimsical derivation, *googol* became important in advanced mathematics, spawning other new technical terms, such as *googolplex* (1 followed by a googol of zeros), *googolpolygon* (a polygon with a googol sides), and *googolhedron* (a polyhedron with a googol faces). And it should tickle the fancy of Internet users to learn that the most popular search engine in the world, *Google*, was named by its inventors, Larry Page and Sergey Brin, as a play on the word *googol*. Their use of this term was meant to reflect Google's objective: to organize the immense amount of information on the World Wide Web to googol-like numbers. Not in his wildest fantasies could little Milton Sirotta have imagined that his spontaneous coinage would one day be carried into the outer reaches of cyberspace.

MINTING NEW WORDS

Another classic coinage is the word *gas*, attributed to the 17th-century Flemish chemist Van Helmont, who invented it to denote a chemical principle present in all bodies. A century later, the word was adopted to describe any fluid substance, like air, that tends to expand indefinitely, and soon afterward it was applied to a flammable gas mixture. How did Van Helmont stumble on this mysterious word? It is generally believed that in coining *gas* he was influenced by the similar-sounding Greek word *cháos*, "a chasm or empty space," which the Swiss physician and alchemist Paracelsus had earlier (1500s) used to refer to a certain element in spirits. Though it would have been fitting, punwise or otherwise, had Van Helmont coined *gas* out of thin air, it appears that he did not.

A modern example of an obscure coinage that has been traced to an equally obscure source is the word *quark*. A quark is a fundamental nuclear particle from which protons and other subatomic particles are composed. *Quark* was coined in 1961 by an American particle physicist, Murray Gell-Mann, who took the word from the line "Three quarks from Muster Mark!" in James Joyce's masterpiece *Finnegans Wake* (1939). The line reflected Gell-Mann's theory that there are three types of quarks (named *down quark, up quark,* and *strange quark*) that combine in various ways to make up all subatomic particles. As to where Joyce got the word, it has been suggested that he borrowed it from the German slang term *Quark*, meaning a trifling thing, trash, rubbish.

Unlike *googol, gas,* and *quark,* most coinages are made up of the stock of existing words. In his 1949 novel, *Nineteen Eighty-Four,* George Orwell coined the word *Newspeak* (for a language designed to distort the truth) by combining the adjective *new* with the verb *speak.* Orwell's coinage became the model for other new words ending in *-speak,* such as *adspeak* (the language of ads), *businesspeak* (the jargon of business), and *kiddiespeak* (children's language). But let's not assume that words can never be minted out of thin air. English words are made up of syllables, and it has been estimated that the number of syllables that can be used in English to form new words runs into the hundreds of thousands. Consider *-bir-*, *-gub-*, *-zas-*, or *-ig*, *-ud*, *-loob*, and *-moob*. All such syllables can be used singly or in combination to form unique new words.

A master of such coinages was Frank Gelett Burgess (1866–1951), an American illustrator, poet, and humorist whose early books of humor (*Goops & How to Be Them, Are You a Bromide?, Maxims of Methuselah in Regard to Women, Burgess Unabridged: A New Dictionary of Words You Have Always Needed*) are still in print. As a coiner, he is best known for having invented the word *blurb* to describe the exaggerated and effusive recommendations found on the dust jackets of books.

COINAGES **OUT OF** CIRCULATION

A glance at *Burgess Unabridged* reveals many other strange, mysterious, funny, and deserving coinages that have unfortunately never caught on. Here are a few:

OOFLE, *noun.* A person whose name you cannot remember: *There goes, uh, you know, Mrs. Oofle!* *-verb.* To try to find out a person's name without asking.

PAWDLE, *noun.* A person of mediocre ability, raised to undeserved prominence: *The company's new CEO is a nice guy but a pawdle.*

VOIP, *noun.* Food that gives no gastronomic pleasure; any provender that is filling, but tasteless. *-verb.* To eat hurriedly, without tasting: *Stop voiping your food!*

These and similar "Burgessisms" are akin to the category of *Sniglets*, words that should be part of the standard dictionary but aren't. They are not nonsense words, since they actually "mean" something (see the chapter on **Non-**

sense Words). Nor are they nonce words, since they are intended, however unrealistically, to be used in speech and writing (see the chapter on **Nonce Words**).

⁜

COINAGES **IN** CIRCULATION

Successful coinages by individuals are relatively rare, though certain words known to have been coined by particular people have succeeded in making their way into dictionaries. Here are a few:

DONTOPEDALOGY: A propensity for putting one's foot in one's mouth; a tendency to say something inappropriate or indiscreet. Coined by Prince Philip, the Duke of Edinburgh, from *donto-* (from Greek *odóntos,* "tooth") + *pedal* (from Latin *ped-,* "foot") + *-logy* ("science, study"). Prince Philip applied the word humorously to himself. Its popularity, such as it is, is due more to its having been coined by a celebrated royal than to its aptness as an encapsulation of the expression "to put one's foot in one's mouth."

ECDYSIAST: A stripteaser. Coined by the writer and social critic H. L. Mencken (1880–1956) from *ecdysis,* the technical term for the shedding of the outer skin by a reptile or insect + the ending *-ast* in *enthusiast.* Mencken, author of *The American Language* (1921), coined the word with tongue in cheek as a euphemism for moralists who found the word "stripteaser" too racy.

FACTOID: An unsubstantiated statement, account, or report published as if it were factual. Coined by the novelist Norman Mailer from *fact* + *-oid* (as in *android,* *humanoid*), in reference to his fictionalized biography of Marilyn Monroe, *Marilyn: A Biography* (1973), in which he treated his subject novelistically.

PSYCHEDELIC: Any of a class of drugs that alter one's perception of reality. Coined in the late 1950s by Humphry Osmond, a British psychiatrist who researched the effects of mescaline and LSD, from a Greek word for "mind-revealing" or "mind-manifesting." The term is still used by believers in the curative powers of mind-altering chemicals, such as LSD, psilocybin, DMT, and others. Nonbelievers refer to psychedelic drugs as hallucinogens.

SERENDIPITY: An aptitude for making unexpected discoveries by accident. Coined by the English author Horace Walpole (1717-97) from *Serendip*, a former name of Sri Lanka (Ceylon) + the suffix *-ity*. In a letter dated January 28, 1754, Walpole explains that he coined the word after the title of "a silly fairy-tale, called *The Three Princes of Serendip*; as their highnesses travelled, they were always making discoveries, by accidents and sagacity, of things they were not in quest of." The *Oxford English Dictionary* points out that the word was formerly rare, but it gained wide currency in the 20th century.

WORKAHOLIC: A person addicted to work, obsessed with one's job, or having a compulsive need to work constantly. Coined in the late 1960s by Wayne Oates, an American pastoral counselor, from *work* + a(lco)*holic*. The word spawned the combining forms *-aholic* and *-oholic*. (See the chapter on **Combining Forms**.)

Another author by the name of Burgess (no relation to Gelett), the British novelist Anthony Burgess (1917–93), was also a noted coiner of words, but of a different kind. His futuristic novel, *A Clockwork Orange* (1962), is written almost entirely in a mixture of English and coined words based chiefly on Russian. Many of the words come directly from Russian, such as *devotchka*, "girl," *govorett*, "to talk to," *malchick*, "boy," *moloko*, "milk," and *platch*, "to cry." Some are anglicizations of Russian words, such as *horrorshow*, "good" (Russian *khorosho*) and *rabbit*, "work" (Russian *rabot*). Others are coinages based on various patterns of English word formation. For example, *chumble*, "to mumble" (blend of *chat* and *mumble*), *sarky* (short for *sarcastic*), *sinny* (shortening and alteration of *cinema*), and *charles* (alteration of *chaplain*). A considerable number of words are whimsical inventions worthy of Gelett Burgess. They include:

appy polly loggy: An apology

drencrom, synthemesc, vellocet: Names of various drugs

gulliwuts: Guts

pee and em: Pa and Ma

skolliwoll: School

TECHNO-TERMS

Most coinages are anonymous creations that insinuate themselves into the language gradually, almost always by one of the processes of word formation discussed in this book, such as compounding, derivation, and back-formation. But whatever form these coinages take, the common denominator among them is that they describe something new that cries out to be named. The *Internet* was such a coinage. The name, formed from *inter*(national) + (Arpa)*net*, first popped up in 1974 as a descendant of Arpanet, a U.S. government information network (the Advanced Research Projects Agency network) that was created in 1968 to keep up with Soviet advances in aerospace and nuclear science. In 1992, when the World Wide Web was launched, the Internet became a global commercial network connecting millions of computers. Soon it became known informally as "the Net," with the World Wide Web being dubbed "the Web."

The Internet quickly produced new coinages, the two most prominent being the adjective *dot-com* and the noun and verb *blog*. As computer-related companies proliferated in the 1990s, they started to be called "dot-com firms" or "dot-com companies," after the ".com" in their names. Every such name also contains the "at" symbol @. What is this symbol called? The American National Standards Institute has called it "commercial at." Others call it the "at sign" or "at symbol." Informally, it has been nicknamed a *snail, twist, curl, whorl, gizmo,* and *shmitshik.* At this writing, a new, seemingly authoritative name for the ubiquitous @ is *atmark.*

An endlessly fascinating new coinage in the world of cyberspace is *blog,* formed by contraction of *Web log.* A *blog* is essentially an online personal diary or journal available to the public on a Web site. There are countless blogs on the Web, and new ones appear every day. Its vocabulary is likewise expanding: *to blog* means "to post blogs"; *blogging* or *blogrolling* is "the act of posting or updating one's blog"; the author of a blog is a *blogger;* *blogophiles* are "blog-lovers"; the *blogosphere* is the realm of bloggers and blogging; and a *nom de blog* is "the pseudonym of a blogger." Standard dictionaries are having great difficulty keeping up with the Brobdingnagian explosion of blogisms. *Time* magazine has even instituted a *Blogwatch* column, featuring reports such as the following:

... there are an estimated 100,000 active Iranian blogs, so that Persian now ties with French as the second most used language in the blogosphere.

Blog has engendered offspring like *vlogs*, "blogs that includes video clips," run by *vloggers*; *phlogs* "blogs that include photos," run by *phloggers*; and *splogs* "spam blogs," which are nonsense texts linked to sites that *sploggers* are trying to promote.

TRADEMARKS

The best-known coinages by far are trademarks, the names of thousands of products and services repeated endlessly in television and radio commercials. Ironically, the most popular ones tend to become generic and, to the chagrin of their owners, in danger of losing their status as legally protected brand names. Few of us would guess that such common words as *aspirin, band-aid, cellophane, cornflakes, escalator, granola, kerosene, linoleum, nylon,* and *zipper* were formerly trademarks. Companies spend millions to create memorable trade names, and more millions trying to defend them from infringement by competitors. Their coinages have to be original and distinctive, fall trippingly from the tongue, and be easy to remember. Think of *Kleenex, Xerox, Frisbee, Mr. Clean,* and *Coke.* To pick on the least obvious coinage in this group, the saucer-shaped plastic disk called *Frisbee* was invented in 1957 by an American, Fred Morrison, and its name was registered as a trademark in 1959. The plastic disk was named as an alteration of "Frisbie," after the lightweight tins in which Mrs. *Frisbie's* pies were baked at the Frisbie bakery in Bridgeport, Connecticut.

Three of the dangers facing trademarks are: (1) their being spelled in lower-case, like common words, (2) changing their part of speech, usually noun to verb, and (3) losing their literalness and becoming figurative or metaphorical. When people begin to say "He xeroxed me a copy," or "I fedexed him the package," the capitalized trademarks *Xerox* and *FedEx* are on their way to becoming generic. When people speak of their mayor or governor as "Mr. Clean," they are no longer referring to a liquid cleanser but to a politician of spotless reputation. When Internet users talk about "googling for information" on a search engine, the verb use is a tribute to *Google's* popularity but also a warning that the name's days as a trademark may be numbered.

POLITICAL COINAGES

A prime motive for coining words is social and political change. Opponents of legalized abortion needed a positive term to designate their movement, as they deplored the negative sound of *antiabortion* and *antiabortionist*. To turn things around, they chose to promote themselves as "right-to-life" and "pro-life," implying thereby that those who favored abortions were against life. Not to be outdone, the "proabortion" movement or "proabortionists," deciding that the emphasis on abortion in their names had negative overtones, went on to coin the names "pro-choice" and "pro-choicer" for themselves, implying that they are not against "life" but rather in favor of everyone's right to choose to have an abortion if necessary.

Animal-rights groups had a similar problem: how to describe concisely and effectively the mistreatment and exploitation by human beings of various animal species. The term "antivivisection," referring to the movement opposing medical experimentation with animals, was old-fashioned, negative, and too restricted in meaning. A new coinage was called for. An American psychologist, Richard D. Ryder, heeded the call and came up with the term *speciesism*, modeled on such terms as *racism, sexism,* and *ageism.* Defined as the act or practice of discriminating against certain species of animals, such as rabbits, hamsters, and even dogs and cats, *speciesism* is condemned as inflicting needless pain and depriving animal species of the same rights that human beings have. Opponents of speciesism tend to be of various stripes, some animal liberationists who disapprove of holding animals captive in zoos, some who would object strenuously if the residents of zoos were transported back to the wilds of the Amazon or the Kalahari desert.

The above and many other social and political coinages are euphemisms, created deliberately to avoid sounding too blunt, negative, or offensive. (See the chapter on **Euphemism.**)

CHAPTER 22

combining forms:

a dictionary invention

One of the goals of the women's-rights movement of the 1970s was to purge the language of sexism. A part of the program was the elimination of the sex-specific word *man* in occupational titles which was seen as negating the role of women in the workplace. To avoid reference to gender, new terms were created: *mail carrier, camera operator,* and *chair* or *chairperson,* replacing *mailman, cameraman,* and *chairman.* These and many similar new terms were codified in the 1977 *Government's Dictionary of Occupational Titles.* Alongside such changes in the vocabulary as the use of *flight attendant* in place of *stewardess* and *steward,* and the adoption of *Ms.* as an optional form of address by the Government Printing Office, was the conversion of the word *person* into a combining form, spelled as *-person.*

Though a few compounds ending in *-person* had been in English formerly, for example, *salesperson* (1920s) and *tradesperson* (1880s), the use of the combining form became quickly a vogue in many walks of life: For example:

Politics: *chairperson, congressperson, councilperson, select-person, statesperson*

Sports: *fisherperson, marksperson, first-baseperson, track-person, yachtsperson*

Law: *foreperson, juryperson*

Workplace: *repairperson, policeperson, workperson*

Media: *anchorperson, sideperson, weatherperson*

Religion: *churchperson, layperson*

Business: *businessperson, committeeperson, spokesperson*

Home: *houseperson*

The proliferation of *-person* was of particular interest in that it ran counter to the long-held assumption that combining forms, by definition, could be used only in combinations and not stand alone as independent words. This was clearly not the case with *-person*.

A PRACTICAL DEVICE

What, then, is a combining form and where did the term come from?

Back in the late 19th century, the editor of the monumental *Oxford English Dictionary* (*OED*), Sir James Murray, proposed that a word that occurs only in combination with other words should be called a *combining form*, to distinguish it from traditional suffixes and prefixes, which are grammatical forms of words. (See the chapter on **Prefixes and Suffixes**.) Murray chose not to use the label *affix* since this was an umbrella term for prefixes and suffixes, and he felt that a combining form and a prefix/suffix were different things, even though there is some connection between them. Following the *OED*'s lead, every modern English dictionary has since adopted the *OED* style, featuring many entries labeled *combining form* or *comb. form*. Yet you are not likely to find the term or label *combining form* in most English-language textbooks or books on style and grammar, which tend to lump combining forms under affixes.

A *combining form* is a dictionary invention (and some would say convention). It is a practical invention, since dictionaries save a lot of space by covering many words formed with a combining form under a single combining-form entry. For example, the combining form *-graphy* not only covers old words taken from Greek like *biography* and *geography*, but any word formed in English with *-graphy*, like, say, *photography*, *radiography*, and *mammography*.

Originally, Murray and his subeditors applied the term to the first element in classical or learned compounds, such as *acantho-*, described in the *OED* as "the combining form of Greek *ákantha*, 'thorn.'" Later the *OED* applied the term *combining form* to all forms that combine with a word or part of a word to make a new one. Thus, *acoustico-* was described as a combining form of the English word *acoustic*, and *acuto-*, as a combining form of English *acute*. The *OED* also applied the label to classical endings like *-onym*, meaning "word" or "name" (derived from Greek *ónyma*, *ónoma*, "name"), in words like *acronym*, *antonym*, and *toponym*. Though these words seem to have come entirely from Greek or Latin, they were actually formed in English using the combining form *-onym*:

acronym, "a word formed from the initial letters of a name
or phrase, such as *radar* (radio detection and ranging),"
coined in the 1940s from the combining forms *acr(o)-,*
"tip, point" + *-onym.*

antonym, "a word that is the opposite of another," coined in
the 1860s from the combining forms *ant(i)-,* "opposed to"
+ *-onym,* on the model of the classically-derived *synonym.*

toponym, "a place name," coined in the 1890s from the combining forms *top(o)-* (from Greek *tópos,* "place") + *-onym.*

James Murray's assumption that combining forms could
only occur in combinations, never as actual words, was generally
justified during the 19th century. Initial combining forms like
aero- (*aerogram*), *astro-* (*astrology*), *electro-* (*electromagnet*), *geo-* (*geology*),
or terminal ones like *-graphy* (*choreography*), *-logy* (*psychology*), *-onym*
(*pseudonym*), *-philia* (*acidophilia*) did not exist as free-standing
words. This state of affairs changed in the 20th century, when
many common words were turned into combining forms, so
that it was no longer possible to say that combining forms only
existed in combinations. The reason for the proliferation of
combining forms is clear: combining forms are space-saving
and time-saving substitutes for lengthy explanations. Besides,
they are productive forms, useful in creating new words.

THE MOTIVATIONS BEHIND COMBINATIONS

The impetus behind the creation of a combining form is varied.
The combining form *-cast,* derived from *broadcast* and forming
such terms as *telecast, simulcast,* and *podcast* ("a recording posted on
a Web site and downloaded to an iPod or other player"), was a

by-product of the growth of telecommunications. A combining form like -*proof*, meaning "resistant or impervious to (someone or something)," resulted from practical advances in commerce and industry. As a noun, *proof* has many meanings, such as *proof* of a crime, *proof* of an arithmetical operation, a photographic *proof*, the page *proofs* of a book. As an adjective it means "resistant," as in *proof against leaks*. It is this adjective that was turned into a combining form in words like *foolproof, rainproof, childproof, waterproof*, and *leakproof* when products were invented that were invulnerable to damage, even when tampered with.

Another motive for extracting a combining form from a word is to duplicate or reproduce the idea contained in the word. This is how the combining form -*speak* came about. The template for -*speak* was the word *Newspeak*, coined by the novelist George Orwell (1903–50) in his 1949 classic, *Nineteen Eighty-Four*. Newspeak was an artificial language designed to express only politically correct thoughts. It replaced *Oldspeak*, which had words for subversive ideas.

In the same book, Orwell coined words like *crimethink* (subversive political thinking), *oldthink* (politically incorrect thinking), and *doublethink* (contradictory thinking, such as "War is Peace," "Freedom is Slavery"). While -*think* never took off as a word-forming element, -*speak* did. Many words ending in -*speak* have sprouted since the 1960s, most meaning "a group's or profession's jargon or lingo," for example, *adspeak* (advertising jargon), *artspeak, businessspeak, computerspeak, femspeak* (feminist jargon), *gayspeak, technospeak* (technological jargon), *videospeak* (television jargon). Other words in -*speak* refer to one's style of speaking or writing, for example, *doublespeak* (ambiguous or misleading speech or writing), *bureaucratspeak, litcritspeak* (literary criticism writing). Most uses are for the nonce (see the chapter on **Nonce Words**), such as *discospeak, Freudspeak, Olympspeak, Pentagonspeak.*

There is a somewhat disparaging tinge attached to all of these words, reflecting the association of *-speak* with the original *Newspeak*, an artificial language with a limited and self-serving vocabulary.

Sometimes the reverse occurs, and a free-standing word is extracted from a combining form. The combining form *mini-*, clipped from *miniature*, had been used sporadically in Great Britain since the 1930s. But its use exploded in the 1960s, spurred by the popularity of smaller-than-average motor vehicles called *minicars, minicabs,* and *minibuses*. Suddenly *mini-* got attached to anything small, short, or minor, for example,

Small: *minicalculator, minicomputer, minifestival, mininuke, minipark, minitank*

Short: *minicourse, minilecture, minidress, miniseries, miniskirt, miniwear*

Minor: *miniboom, minibudget, miniplanet, minirevolution, ministate*

In due course, words like *minidress* and *miniskirt* were shortened to *mini* ("girls wearing minis"), as were *minicars, minicameras,* and anything small or miniature. The word served also as an adjective: *a mini musical, a mini stove.*

Mini- was inevitably followed by something even smaller, and that was the combining form *micro-*, meaning "very small." Attached to countless words, many of which have become part of the standard vocabulary, *micro-* gave us *microchip, microcircuit, microprobe, microprocessor, microwave,* and many others. It has been also used as a noun and adjective. As nouns and adjectives, both *mini* and *micro* were vogue words, bound to go out of fashion eventually (although as the name for small cars, *mini* is still popular).

But the combining forms *mini-* and *micro-*, though no longer as productive as they were in the latter part of the 20th century, have remained entrenched in English technical vocabulary. They are used especially in product names and trademarks, as *Minimouse* (for a computer mouse), *Minibook, Mini-Edition, Micro-world, Micro-Mark,* and *Micro-Star.*

CYBERSPEAK

Combining forms often reflect the interests and obsessions of the society that spawns them. The development of high-speed electronic computers sparked the creation of *cyber-*, a combining form abstracted from *cybernetics*. This was a word coined in 1947 by the U.S. mathematician Norbert Wiener (1894–1964) to describe a new discipline, the study of the operation of complex electronic and other systems. Wiener formed the word from a Latinate form of Greek *kybernétēs*, "steersman" + the English suffix *-ics*. As the use of computers became widespread, *cyber-* came into popular use to describe anything made possible by computers. One of the first words formed with *cyber-* was *cyberphobia*, meaning "a fear or dislike of computers." When new computer models were introduced, many users were said to suffer *cyberphobic* reactions, whose typical symptoms were nausea, vertigo, cold sweats, and sometimes hysteria. Such individuals were called *cyberphobes*.

Among other new words formed with *cyber-* were *cybertalk, cyberart, cyberfashion*, all referring to computers. A genre of science fiction having to do with computers was called *cyberpunk*, a name also applied to a computer hacker. Sexual activity involving e-mails and Web sites was named *cybersex*, and the business of buying Internet domain names in order to sell them to companies for a profit came to be known as *cybersquatting*, its practitioners being dubbed *cybersquatters*. But by far the most important *cyber-* word had to be *cyberspace*, coined on the model of *aerospace* to describe the vast realm of online computer systems, including e-mail, graphics, files, and Internet browsing.

Some well-known combining forms had their origin in a word. *Marathon* is one such word. The modern 26-mile footraces called marathons in which thousands participate every year had their beginning in 1896, when the Olympic Games of ancient Greece were revived in Athens. The race was named after the plain of *Marathon*, situated some 25 miles northeast of Athens, where in 490 B.C.E. the Athenians defeated the Persians in a decisive battle. According to legend, news of the victory was carried to Athens by a young courier, Pheidippides, who ran all the way without stopping and fell dead as soon as he delivered the good news. The long-distance foot race was established to commemorate this young runner's feat.

The word *marathon* has also been used since the early 1900s in the extended sense of any prolonged contest, event, or other activity involving endurance, such as *a dance marathon, a chess marathon, a marathon Congressional session.* The combining forms *-athon* and *-thon* were generated from both the literal and extended senses of *marathon*. A *bikeathon*, for example, is a long-distance bicycle race, usually organized as a fundraising event, as is the extended discussion called a *talkathon*, the long-distance walking race advertised as a *walkathon*, and the popular television broadcast to raise money for a charitable cause, known as a *telethon*. Other words formed with *-athon* or *-thon* have tended to be coined for the nonce. For example, *discothon* ("a competition among disk jockeys"), *quiltathon* ("a quilt-making contest"), *radiothon* ("a radio fundraising broadcast"), and *Bachathon* ("a series of Bach concerts").

Another combining form inspired by a word is *-aholic* or *-holic*. That word was *workaholic*, meaning "a compulsive or obsessive worker," coined in the late 1960s by Wayne Oates, an American pastoral counselor, by blending *work* and *alcoholic*. The concept of a workaholic having the addictive and compulsive personality of an alcoholic caught the public's imagination, and soon a spate of new words ending in *-(a)holic* began popping up everywhere. There were *beefaholics, carboholics* ("carbohydrate addicts"), *chocoholics* ("chocolate addicts"), *colaholics, computerholics, golfaholics, sexaholics, spendaholics, sweetaholics,* and so on.

Combining forms that are least likely to endure are those triggered by a particular event, usually in politics. A prime example of this is the combining form *-gate*, derived from *Watergate* and widely applied in the media to any scandal resembling or suggesting the Watergate scandal, which erupted during the administration of President Richard Nixon and led to his resignation in 1974. Innumerable words ending in *-gate* flooded the media all through the 1970s and a good part of the 1980s. Every scandalous political event or situation (and nonpolitical one as well) was tagged with the combining form: Cattlegate, Dallasgate, Hollywoodgate, Irangate, Koreagate, Nannygate, Oilgate, Quakergate, Sewergate. As memories of Watergate faded, the combining form that it engendered faded as well.

On the other hand, the political combining form *-nomics,* which was engendered by *Nixonomics,* referring to President Nixon's economic policies, seemed to have a longer life, though destined to recur only after the election of a new U.S. president whose name ends with an *n*. While the awkward *Carternomics* and *Fordonomics* never caught on, *Reaganomics* and *Clintonomics* had long and successful runs in the media. We have not heard so far of *Bushonomics*.

The most likely combining forms to last are scientific, technological, and commercial ones, many of which have classical Latin and Greek roots. For example:

agri- or *agro-* "agricultural" (from Latin *agrī-, ager*, "field"), as in *agrichemical, agriproduct, agrobusiness, agroecosystem, agroindustry.*

flexi- or *flex-*, "flexible" (by shortening), as in *flexibacteria, flexinomics* (flexible economics), *flexiroof, flextime* or *flexitime* (flexible time in the workplace).

petro-, "petroleum" and, by extension, "oil-rich" (from Greek *pétra*, "rock"), as in *petrocrat* (an oil-rich country bureaucrat), *petrodollars* (surplus dollars of oil-exporting countries), *petrobillions, petromoney, petropolitics, petropower.*

syn-, "synthetic" (by shortening), as in *syncrude* (oil), *synfuel, syngas, synjet, synoil, synthane* (synthetic methane), *synzyme* (synthetic enzyme).

A distinctive quality of technical and scientific combining forms is the ease with which they cross language lines. Combining forms like *tele-, hydro-, electro-, -meter, -phone, -graph,* and so on, are not restricted to English but common to many languages such as French, German, Spanish, and Russian. In the 1950s, during the preparation of the 1961 *Webster's Third New International Dictionary* (*W3*), its etymologists could not always determine the language in which many scientific terms, such as *electroencephalogram* and *telethermometer*, were first used, since so many languages shared the combining forms that made up the terms. To solve the problem, the editor of *Webster's Third*, Philip Gove, decided to adopt a descriptive umbrella term, "International Scientific Vocabulary" (ISV), for scientific terms made up of combining forms whose language of origin was unknown. Consequently, thousands of entries in that dictionary carry the label ISV.

But just as it's doubtful that we will find a reference to that great invention, the combining form, in current language textbooks or stylebooks, so we're not likely to find in the same sources any mention of that other important innovation, the ISV label. If there is any moral to be learned from this, it is that teachers of language arts who urge their students to "look it up in the dictionary" should themselves spend some time studying its contents.

CHAPTER 23

compounding:
making new words out
of old ones

The practice of forming compounds in English is of ancient origin. "The English," writes Robert Clairborne in *Our Marvelous Native Tongue* (1983), "retained the old Indo-European habit of making new words out of old ones: joining two words ... to yield a new meaning." Old English abounded in compounds like *grindetothum*, "molar" (literally, 'grinding tooth'), *ælmihtig*, "all-mighty," *sweordbora*, "sword-bearer," *heortsēoc*, "heart-sick," and was especially prolific in poetic compounds called kennings, a word of Old Norse origin related to English *ken*. Typical kennings were compounds like *hwælrad*, "whale-road," for the sea, and *mere-hengest*, "sea stallion," for a ship, images that influenced various English poets across the centuries. The English poet Gerard Manley Hopkins (1844–89) was famous for kennings like "dapple-drawn-dawn

Falcon" in his poem *The Windhover,* and "fresh-firecoal chestnut-falls" in the poem *Pied Beauty.*

There is great freedom—one might almost say license—in creating compounds. English is hardly alone in compounding; other languages indulge in it as well. Among standard Spanish words are closed compounds like *cumpleaños,* "birthday" (literally, "reach-years"), *parabrisas,* "windshield" (literally, "stop-breezes"), *ciempiés,* "centipede" (literally, "hundred feet"). Italian compounds include closed ones like *ferrovìa,* "railway," and *arcobaleno* "rainbow," and open ones, like *parola chiave,* "keyword." In German, which forms mainly closed compounds, an employment agency is called by the mouthful *Stellenvermittlungsbüro,* literally, "employment mediation bureau." French prefers open compounds like *poudre à canon,* "gunpowder," and hyphenated ones like *pot-au-feu,* "beef and vegetable stew" (literally, "pot on the fire"). And it was Greek that gave English the valuable compound *oxymoron* for a figure of speech in which two or more words are contradictory in meaning (e.g., "cruel kindness"). Greek *oxýmōron* is a compound formed from *oxýs,* "sharp" and *mōrós,* "dull."

NEWSPEAK

In an appendix to his 1949 novel, *Nineteen Eighty-Four,* George Orwell describes in detail the official language, *Newspeak,* of a future totalitarian society in the fictitious country of Oceania. He divides the vocabulary of Newspeak into three parts, A, B, and C. The A vocabulary consisted of simple, common words like *hit, run, dog, tree, sugar, house, field.* The C vocabulary consisted entirely of scientific and technical terms. It was the B vocabulary that played the greatest role in influencing the thinking of the people of Oceania. That was because the words were deliberately constructed to "impose a desirable mental attitude upon the person using them."

"The B words," writes Orwell, "were in all cases compound words. They consisted of two or more words, or portions of words, welded together in an easily pronounceable form." He cites as examples the words *goodthink*, meaning roughly "orthodoxy, conformity," *crimethink*, "thought-crime," *bellyfeel*, "a blind, enthusiastic acceptance," *sex-crime*, "sexual immorality," *goodsex*, "chastity," *joycamp*, "forced-labor camp," and *duckspeak*, "to quack like a duck." The latter, writes Orwell, "implied nothing but praise, and when the *Times* referred to one of the orators of the Party as *doubleplusgood duckspeaker* it was paying a warm and valued compliment."

In making compound words central to his artificial language, Orwell showed a deep understanding of the power of compounding words. Half-a-century-and-change later, compounds are the fastest-growing and, to critics of this productive linguistic process, among the most insidious elements in the present-day English vocabulary. The previous sentence, incidentally, includes a compound noun created ad hoc, *half-a-century-and-change*, and two compound adjectives, *fastest-growing* and *present-day*.

THE POWER OF COMPOUNDING

A casual check of a few recent newspaper and magazine issues unearthed the following sentences, in which we have italicized the compounds:

Perhaps the most noticeable trend this fall is the *full-fledged* arrival of *round-toed, high-heeled* shoes. (*New York Times*)

She had shown him a '*backdoor*' way to gain access to his *software* without a *password*. (*New York Times*)

Call him what you will—*househusband, stay-at-home* dad, *domestic engineer*. (*Reader's Digest*)

So, in the *fast-paced* and *ever-changing* world of *offshore outsourcing*, some entrepreneurs in Russia have launched . . . *denial-of-service* cyberattacks on the *Web sites* of *online* gambling companies. (*Information Week*)

The sixteen italicized compounds in these four quotations illustrate the wide variety characterizing this type of formation. They include the closed compounds *backdoor, software, password, househusband, offshore, outsourcing,* and *online*; the hyphenated compounds *full-fledged, round-toed, high-heeled, fast-paced, ever-changing, stay-at-home,* and *denial-of-service*; and the open compounds *domestic engineer* and *Web site*. Notice that the closed compounds tend to be nouns, while the hyphenated ones tend to be adjectives. As for the open compounds, they too tend to be nouns, like the closed ones. That is why many write *Web site* as a closed compound, *Website* or *website*. Nobody, however, would write *domestic engineer* as a closed compound, simply because it would be too long a word. As a rule, a closed compound consists of two short words combined to form a solid unit, as if it were a single word, for example, *steamboat, roughneck, bookworm*.

Granted that there may be an overuse of compounds, there is no denying their power in expressing complex ideas in a succinct and often memorable way. Take the compound verb *stonewall*, meaning "to obstruct (an investigation, etc.)," which emerged in 1973–74 during the Watergate hearings. The image of a stone wall far more effectively conveys the idea of a solid obstruction than the word *obstruction* does. Just as a picture is worth a thousand words, a picturesque word or phrase is worth a dozen trite ones. Similarly, the informal compound *no-brainer* manages to impart tersely the idea that *this is something that requires little thought or effort to understand or do*, so that, barring repeated use, *no-brainer* serves a useful purpose in communication.

One might ask, on the other hand, what possible service is rendered by many nonce or ad-hoc compounds, as in the following excerpts from an issue of *eWeek*, a weekly newsmagazine:

> The TestView suite includes Web-testing components and provides enterprise-level test management capabilities.
>
> Numerous products are available . . . , ranging from free-standing overlay defensive networks to single-point-in-time-and-space detection programs.

These sentences are technical and intended for professionals in the field of electronics. Still, one questions the necessity of complex collocations like "enterprise-level test management capabilities" and "free-standing overlay defensive networks," not to mention "single-point-in-time-and-space detection programs," a specification that Einstein might find hard to swallow, if not to fathom.

There is a pattern in the development of compounds. Compound nouns usually begin life as two single-syllable words separated by a space, then are joined by a hyphen, and finally coalesce into one word, thus: *boy friend, boy-friend, boyfriend; loan word, loan-word, loanword.* There is a span of time in which all three forms may coexist uneasily, a situation that is known to have driven many a dictionary maker to distraction. Generally, though, at least in American English, compound nouns consisting of two short words eventually close up and become one, as we see in words like *bathroom, blackboard, footstool, typewriter,* and *girlfriend.* By contrast, compound nouns made up of three or more words will tend to remain hyphenated: *son-in-law, daughter-in-law, mother-of-pearl, attorney-at-law, happy-go-lucky.* Finally, there are many compound nouns that remain open, such as *ice cream, high school, legal aid, patrol car, post office, maid of honor, editor in chief,* and *glove compartment,* either because they consist of more than two syllables, or simply by convention. (In defiance of convention, some have taken to changing open compounds to closed or hyphenated ones, writing them *highschool, icecream, editor-in-chief, maid-of-honor.*) If you are uncertain whether a compound is closed, hyphenated, or open, you are advised to consult a current dictionary.

HOW TO MAKE A COMPOUND WORD

Some scholars have categorized compounds as being of two types, either native formations, like *coffeehouse, livingroom,* and *steamboat,* or formed on Latin and Greek patterns, as *agriculture, horticulture, neurology,* and *photography.* We think this is a mistake. The subject of compounds is complicated enough without compounding—if you excuse the pun—its difficulty by including in it words made up of affixes and combining forms, like *biology* and *orthography.* These so-called classical forms are best treated as derivatives (and will be discussed in the appropriate chapter). Our definition of a compound is that of a word whose parts are themselves words, and not parts of words.

So, let's say you wish to form a new compound. The first thing to know is that you can join words from just about any part of speech to create a compound:

from a noun and a noun: *football, sunscreen, blood test*

a noun and an adjective: *airtight, age-old, camera-shy*

a noun and a participle: *heartbroken, earsplitting, dog-eared*

a noun and a verb: *browbeat, sidestep, force-feed*

an adjective and a noun: *redcap, first-class, solar wind*

an adjective and a verb: *highlight, fine-tune, quick-freeze*

a verb and a noun: *blowtorch, flashlight, password*

a verb and an adverb: *breakup, dugout, drive-by*

an adverb and a verb: *bypass, download, outcome, upkeep*

an adverb and an adjective: *evergreen, outspoken, upswept*

And so on.

There are two kinds of compounds: those that are self-explanatory, such as *armchair, footrest, barbed wire, science fiction, businessman;* and those whose meanings are opaque or obscure and require explanation. Among the latter are such compounds as *greenhouse*, "place for cultivating plants" (not the same as a *green house*), *holiday* (not the same as a *holy day*), *comeback*, "clever retort" (not the same as *come back*, "return"), *red tape*, "bureaucratic routine" (not *a red-colored tape*), *real estate*, "property" (not *an estate that is real*). In speech, understanding the meaning of a compound often depends on where the stress is placed. In a compound, the stress usually falls on the first word: GREENhouse, COMEback, RED tape, REAL estate. Where the two words are not intended as a unit, the stress will be relatively even: compare the compound *Lookout Cliff*, a place name, pronounced LOOKout Cliff, with the phrase *Look out! Cliff!*, pronounced LOOK OUT! CLIFF!

The ease with which compounds enter the language also facilitates their exit. Unless they are truly essential, most compounds last a short time, perhaps a few years, and quietly slip out of usage. Every decade or so, dictionary editors make a clean sweep of old and abandoned compounds in order to make room for new ones. The following compounds, formed in the 1960s, have gone out of use and are no longer included in standard dictionaries:

blue movie A pornographic movie

cushioncraft A craft that rides on a cushion of air

dataphone A telephone that transmits data

education park A group of schools built on a park

feedforward The control of feedback at the input end

granny dress A loose, long-sleeved, ankle-long dress

Hong Kong flu A form of Asian flu

incinderjell An incendiary gel used in flamethrowers

jet-hop To travel by jet aircraft

This sampling of dated compounds can be multiplied as one goes back in time. As fashions, interests, and situations change, compounds are among the first elements in the vocabulary to vanish and be replaced by newer compounds, which in turn might one day also face extinction. That fate is true, to some extent, of most words (except the basic function words) and, of course, of most living things.

derivation:

forming many words from a single word

Toward the end of the last century, the English language was infected by a rash of *iveitis*. Words ending in *-ive* began showing up everywhere, especially in self-help articles and books: *preventive, supportive, assertive, coercive,* and so forth. The author William Safire, in *What's the Good Word?* (1982), called it punningly "an outbreak of *ives*," adding that about 2,000 words ended in *-ive*, four-fifths of them in the form *-tive*. Why the outbreak? One answer seemed to be that, unlike other adjectives (*a helpful spouse, a strong attitude, a forceful manner*), words ending in *-ive* (*a supportive spouse, an assertive attitude, a coercive manner*) imply a permanent or habitual quality, something that professionals in the social sciences, who like to sound definitive or conclusive, find highly attractive and, yes, positive. (The last four are adjectives in *-ive*, as the word *adjective* itself is, that's how entrenched the usage is.)

VERY ADDICTIVE DERIVATIVES

What this little history tells us is that words, like viruses, are catching, contagious. They are literally communicable. People afflicted with *ives* will always choose the words *addictive, causative, evaluative, executive, permissive, preemptive, proactive, procreative, preventative, preventive,* and so on, over other alternatives, *alternative* being one of them. There are many examples of this form of verbal contagion. One that has created considerable controversy is the group of verbs ending in *-ize.* Sometime in the last century, words in *-ize* became especially productive, and, as they multiplied, many of them were bitterly condemned by critics. While some of the new coinages were so peculiar that they disappeared almost overnight (*friendlyize, picturize, uniformize, reflectorize*), a good many took up full-time residence in the language, words like *accessorize, burglarize, glamorize, moisturize,* and *personalize.* Yet even a word like *jeopardize,* which had been in the language since the 1640s, took the brunt of censure. Here's what J. Lesslie Hall, who defended the word, wrote in his book, *English Usage,* in 1917:

> Some rhetorical scholars and many purists will not tolerate *jeopardize*; but say we must use *jeopard*. T. L. K. Oliphant calls it 'barbarous.' Quackenbos calls it 'a monstrosity,' and says we might as well say 'walkize,' 'singize'. . . . William Cullen Bryant put it on his forbidden list.

Yet this was nothing compared to the virulent attacks leveled at *finalize* and *prioritize.* The former, in particular, was widely condemned after its inclusion in the newly published *Webster's Third New International Dictionary* in 1961. *Prioritize,* too, received its share of obloquy and ridicule, as in this parody of social-science jargon published by the critic Edwin Newman in *The*

New York Times (January 16, 1977) under the title "My College Essay": "I do have a special interest, based on what I hope is a creative self-perception. It is to upgrade my potential. When I prioritize my goals/objectives, that comes first."

If one doesn't hear much public criticism these days of *finalize* and kindred words, it's probably because they no longer raise the hackles of editors and English teachers. It seems that ultimately no amount of criticism can halt the spread of new coinages formed by analogy; even as *prioritize* was being ridiculed, new verbs in *-ize* were making their debut: *strategize* ("to devise strategies"), *suboptimize* ("to make optimal use of subsystems"), *colorize* ("to enhance with color by computer"), and so on.

The coinage of many new words in *-ive* and *-ize* is typical of the process of derivation, which is the most productive process of word formation. Words like *rightly, rightness, righteous, righteously, righteousness,* all extensions of the word *right,* are traditionally called *derivatives,* a term that comes from Latin *derivare,* meaning literally "to draw off from a stream" (from *rivus,* "stream"), since the longer words are *derived* or drawn off the short word like water from a stream.

Some linguists prefer to use the fancier word *paronym* instead of *derivative* for such a word (from Greek *paronymon,* "side name"). The trouble is that they define a paronym kind of circuitously as "a word related to another by derivation, as *derivation* and *derivative* are derived from *derive,* thus being paronyms of *derive.*" And as if this were not confusing enough, some prefer calling derivatives by still another name, "conjugate words." We choose to stick to the traditional term *derivation* for the process of forming words like *beautiful, beautify, beauteous,* and *beautician* from the simple word *beauty.* By the same token, *beautifully* can be called a derivative of *beautiful,* and *beautifier* and *beautification* can be viewed as derivatives of *beautify.*

Almost every part of speech is involved in derivation. Through derivation, adjectives are formed from nouns (*lovable* from *love*), nouns from verbs (*computer* from *compute*), adjectives from verbs (*conceivable* from *conceive*), nouns from nouns (*indexation* from *index*), and verbs from nouns (*prioritize* from *priority*). Derivation is also involved in processes like **back-formation, functional shift,** and the formation of **diminutives.**

HOW TO MAKE DERIVATIVES

Derivation consists chiefly of adding suffixes or prefixes to base words. The words *personal, personally, personality, personalize* were derived from *person* by attaching the suffixes *-al, -ly, -ity,* and *-ize.* The words *nonachiever, nonevent, nonhuman,* and *nonstandard* were derived from *achiever, event, human,* and *standard* by attaching to them the prefix *non-.* The sesquipedalian word *antidisestablishmentarianism* (meaning, seriously, "opposition to those who oppose establishment of a state religion") was derived from the noun *establishment* (itself derived from the verb *establish* and the suffix *-ment*) through the addition of the prefixes *anti-* and *dis-* and the suffixes *-arian* and *-ism.*

Some linguists include under derivation the process of inflection, which refers to the grammatical changes that a word undergoes to indicate number, person, or tense. In this process, the suffixes *-ed* and *-ing* attach to a verb to form the past tense and the present participle (*brewed, brewing*); the suffix *-s* or *-es* attaches to a noun to form the plural (*books, dresses*); the suffixes *-er, -est* attach to an adjective to indicate the comparative and superlative forms (*smaller, smallest*). Others take note of basic differences between the two processes and prefer to keep inflection separate from derivation.

Derivatives sometimes differ in meaning substantially from their base words. The terms *gentrify* and *gentrification,* denoting the practice of upgrading a poor, run-down property or neighborhood to raise its value, were derived from *gentry*, a word referring to aristocracy or nobility, neither of which have much to do with poor, neglected urban areas. Indeed, the terms, coined by real-estate developers, were criticized at first as pretentious and snobbish, but for want of better ones, they stuck. Likewise the terms *destabilize* and *destabilization*, coined by government intelligence agencies, did not mean to render something unstable, but to topple a foreign government by covert actions. These derivatives are also examples of **euphemisms.**

The term *desertification*, by contrast, designates a serious and straightforward problem in various countries, Spain being the latest among them. There is no verb *desertify*; *desertification* was derived from *desert* by addition of the suffix *-ification*, on the analogy of such words as *ossification* ("conversion into bone") and *petrification* ("conversion into stone"), and it denotes the process by which fertile land turns barren as a nearby desert gradually intrudes.

Similar to *-ification*, the suffix *-ization* became specialized as an attachment to the names of various countries. Originally this double suffix (from *-ize* and *-ation*) meant the act or process of becoming (American, English, etc.), as in *Americanization, anglicization*. But with the end of colonialism in many countries, the suffix took on several new meanings: (1) "the transfer of political power and authority to the native peoples of (a country)," as in *Indianization, Jordanization, Moroccanization*; (2) "the act or practice of nationalizing foreign possessions in (a country)," as in *Egyptianizton, Algerianization, Nigerianization*; (3) "the transfer of the conduct of a war to native forces of (a country)," as in *Vietnamization, Iraqization.*

Derivatives of proper names appear in a variety of forms. Among them are those that end in:

-(i)an: *Bartokian, Bellovian (Saul Bellow), Chaucerian, Churchillian, Darwinian, Dickensian, Freudian, Nabokovian, Orwellian, Shakespearian, Shavian (George Bernard Shaw), Tolstoyan, Wagnerian, Wordsworthian;*

-esque: *Chaplinesque, Dantesque, Fanonesque, Haydenesque, Kafkaesque;*

-ism/-ist: *Calvinism/Calvinist, Darwinism/Darwinist, Marxism/Marxist;*

-ite: *Clintonite, McCarthyite, Nixonite, Reaganite, Trotskyite.*

An interesting example of the derivational possibilities in proper names is found in the writings of the American neurologist Oliver Sacks about Tourette's syndrome, a neurological condition marked by tics and involuntary noises and movements. In several of his books and articles (e.g., *New Yorker*, August 23, 2004), he employs various derivative forms of the syndrome's name. He shortens the name to *Tourette's* ("Some people with Tourette's are able to catch flies on the wing"). He employs the lowercase synonym *tourettism* for the name ("Not just the speed but the quality of movement and thought is altered in tourettism..."). He uses the lowercase adjective *tourettic* ("My tourettic patient Ray... Tourettic or post-encephalitic speed goes with disinhibition"). In *The Oxford Companion to the English Language,* Tom McArthur adds to this list some rare derivatives, such as the adverbs *Tourettically* and *Tourettishly,* the informal adjectives *Touretty* and *Tourettish,* and the noun *Touretter,* for someone who has the syndrome. This has been done with other disorders, for example, *parkinsonism* (for *Parkinson's disease*) and *parkinsonian,* but perhaps not as extensively.

Advances in science, commerce, and technology stimulate

the creation of derivatives. Interest in the environment and ecology made the prefix *eco-*, "ecological" productive, leading to the formation of derivatives like *ecocatastrophe, ecodevelopment, ecodoom, ecodoomster* ("a predictor of ecodoom"), *ecofreak* (slang for "an ardent environmentalist"), *ecomone* ("an ecological hormone"), *econiche, econut* (slang synonym of *ecofreak*), *ecopolitics, ecotage* ("sabotage of environmental polluters"), and so on. Science contributed many new derivatives, especially in physics. The American physicist Olexa-Myron Bilaniuk coined the term *tardyon* (from *tardy*, "late") for a subatomic particle that moves slower than the speed of light, modeling it on *tachyon* (from Greek *tachys*, "swift"), a hypothetical particle that moves faster than the speed of light.

Since the invention of the Internet, the most common derivative terms are produced in cyberspace through the merger of commerce and technology. The formative element *e-* or *E-* (abbreviation of *electronic*) has produced innumerable coinages that are instantly recognized by Web site surfers and we are not just referring to *e-mail* or *email*. Examples of *e-* and *E-* words include *eBay* (electronic buy-by-bidding), *E-commerce* (and its variant, *E-business*), *E*Trade* ("electronic stock trading"), *E-cards* (what used to be called greeting cards), *eNature* ("online field guides"), *eMedicine* ("online medical journals"), *e-financing, e-gold, E-mentoring, e-library, ePALS* (classroom exchange), *eMusic, eMuseum,* and even *eHow* (instructions on how to do everything).

A close competitor of the *e-* or *E-* prefix is the *i-* or *I-* prefix (abbreviation of *Internet*), featured in the names of enterprises like *iTools* (Internet tools), *iTunes* (digital jukebox), *Ifilm* (popular movies), and *iVillage* (a search engine). Some of the names bear more than a slight hint of the influence of the first-person singular *I*, as for example a search engine for cash prizes called *iWon.* Another goes a step further by attaching the *i-* prefix to an appropriate acronym for Education and Resource Network, thereby coming up with the irresistible name *iEarn.* (See the chapters on **Abbreviations and Acronyms** and **Prefixes and Suffixes.**)

CHAPTER 25

eponyms:

what's in a name? sometimes
a word or a phrase

An eponym (from Greek *eponymos*, "named for") is a word or phrase derived from a name. The name may be real, imaginary, literary, biblical, or mythical. It may be the name of a person (usually the surname), such as *Ampere, Caesar, Lynch, Maverick,* or the name of a place, such as *Babel, Cologne, Java, Limerick.* The words derived from the names may be nouns, such as *boycott, cardigan, leotard, sandwich;* or they may be adjectives, such as *herculean, platonic, saturnine,* and *venereal;* or they may be verbs, such as *mesmerize, pasteurize, shanghai, tantalize,* and *vulcanize.*

Eponyms may also be **clippings** like *dunce* (a term of ridicule clipped from the name of the medieval scholar John *Duns* Scotus) and *tawdry* "cheap and showy" (clipped from Saint *Audrey's lace*), **blends** like *gerrymander* and *Eurasia,* and **compounds** like *Doberman pinscher, Molotov cocktail,* and *Heimlich maneuver.* Eponyms have contributed thousands of words to the language.

One use of eponyms is figurative or symbolic. When someone says "That child is destined to be an Einstein," we know exactly what the speaker means, even though there is no dictionary entry that defines "Einstein" as "a genius." The speaker is making a comparison or allusion to Albert Einstein, who was regarded as the foremost genius of the last century. Likewise, one might refer to an extremely wealthy person as "a Rockefeller," after the famous American family of oil magnates; or call a talented singer "a Caruso," after the great operatic tenor Enrico Caruso. The name *Webster* or *Webster's* (after Noah Webster, who published in 1828 the first American dictionary) has been a synonym for a dictionary since 1928. It is not uncommon to overhear a customer in a bookstore asking for a "Webster," or for a schoolteacher to tell pupils that "Webster doesn't approve" of such-and-such a usage. In all these cases, the names are capitalized, and the speakers or writers are aware, however vaguely, of alluding to real people or their works. Eponyms like these hover on the border between proper names and common nouns. The works of artists and fashion designers are also commonly called by the name of their creators. For example, "The museum owns three Van Goghs and two Gauguins." "She wore a Chanel to the Oscars, a Dior to the Emmys, and a Donna Karan to the Tonys."

Allusive eponyms often come from the Bible or from literature. Examples include such epithets as *a doubting Thomas, a Jezebel* (a wicked woman), *a Solomon* (a very wise man), *a Nimrod* (a skilled hunter), *a Judas* (a traitor), *a Shylock* (a vengeful moneylender), *a Pollyanna* (an eternal optimist), *a Mrs. Grundy* (a narrow-minded person who is critical of every breach of convention). One might describe a man as a *Casanova,* in allusion to Giovanni Casanova, an Italian writer of the 1700s noted for his amorous adventures. Similar types have been called a *Don Juan* (after a legendary Spanish lover called Don Juan Tenorio), a *Lothario* (after a young seducer in a popular play of the 1700s, *The Fair Penitent*), or a *Romeo* (after the romantic lover in Shakespeare's *Romeo and Juliet*).

Close to allusive eponyms are the names of many diseases and disorders. Most derive from the names of the physicians who discovered or described them (e.g., *Alzheimer's disease, Hodgkin's disease, Down syndrome, Tourette's syndrome*), though sometimes they are named after a famous sufferer (*Lou Gehrig's disease*). Medical eponyms also include names of body parts, symptoms, and surgical procedures (e.g., *Meckel's ligament, Still's rash, Babinski reflex, Cockett and Dodd operation*). Some collectors have recorded over 7,000 medical eponyms. All of them spell the eponymous name with an initial capital. In a few cases, a common noun is derived from the name of the medical condition or disease, *parkinsonism*, derived from *Parkinson's disease, tourettism*, derived from *Tourette's syndrome*. (See the chapter on **Derivation**.)

UNCAPITALIZED EPONYMS

The best-known eponyms are those that function as common nouns and are not capitalized within a sentence. They are no longer connected in the minds of users with the proper names from which they originated and are treated like everyday words. Early examples of such eponyms include *bedlam, guy, pander, pandemonium*, and *tawdry*. Pronunciation changes obscured the origin of *bedlam*, denoting "a scene of commotion and confusion, a virtual madhouse." The word was a figurative use of the name *Bedlam*, used in the 1600s as a short name for (*St. Mary of*) *Bethlehem*, an insane asylum in London, England. *Bethlehem* was pronounced *Bedlam* before the name began to be used figuratively.

The word *guy* originated in England in the 1800s as the name of a somewhat tattered effigy of *Guy Fawkes* (1570–1606), who led the failed "Gunpowder Plot" to blow up the British monarch and Parliament in 1605. Effigies of Guy Fawkes were carried in a procession and burned on November 5, the anniversary of the discovery of the Gunpowder Plot. The word was used in England to refer to a figure of ridicule, but in the United States it became a colloquial term for any man or fellow.

The verb *pander*, meaning "to act as a go-between or procurer," is found in Chaucer's *Troilus and Criseyde* and in Shakespeare's *Merry Wives of Windsor*, originally as a noun meaning "a go-between, a procurer." The noun was derived from *Pandarus*, the name of Cressida's uncle, who acted as a go-between for Troilus to procure Cressida's love for him. The verb was derived from the noun.

The noun *pandemonium*, meaning "a chaotic uproar or tumult," or "a place of such tumult," is a figurative use of *Pandemonium*, coined by John Milton in *Paradise Lost* as the name of Satan's palace rising out of Chaos to become the center or capital of Hell. Milton coined the name from Greek *pan-*, "all" + Latin *daemonium*, "evil spirit, demon."

Most modern eponyms tend to be the names of people noted for something and turned into common nouns without any other change in the spelling than loss of the initial capital letter. The most famous among such terms is *boycott* ("to boycott a business, a product, etc."; "a boycott against a store"), since it was adopted by many languages to refer to any organized campaign to refuse to deal with someone or something (French *boycott, boycotter*; German *Boykott, boykottieren*; Spanish *boicoteo, boicotear*). The English term (both as verb and noun) came from the name of Captain Charles C. *Boycott* (1832–97), an English land agent who refused to lower the rents of Irish tenant farmers and was consequently subjected to a "boycott" by the tenants.

Running neck and neck with *boycott* in international use is *sandwich*, named after the Earl of *Sandwich* (1718–92), in allusion to his habit of consuming nothing but some slices of meat between slices of bread while spending long hours at gaming tables. His actual name was John Montagu, and had that been well-known, we might be eating "montagus" instead of sandwiches.

An American eponym that also attained international renown is the verb *lynch*, meaning "to put someone to death without a lawful trial," especially by a mob. Originally (1830s) the term meant to whip or otherwise punish corporeally an accused person without a lawful trial, and was derived from *Lynch law*, in allusion to William *Lynch* (1742–1820), a Virginian who in 1780 organized a vigilante committee to punish those accused of committing crimes in his county. Over the years the term came to mean passing and carrying out a sentence of death, usually by hanging, without subjecting the accused to a lawful trial.

Other notable words derived from names include:

atlas, a book or collection of maps; so called from the picture of Atlas, the Titan, supporting the heavens or the world on the front cover of early collections of maps. The mythical Atlas fought an unsuccessful war against Zeus, who condemned him to bear the heavens (usually depicted as the terrestrial globe) on his shoulders.

Babbitt or **babbitt**, a complacent, conventional middle-class businessman; named after George F. *Babbitt*, the main character in the novel *Babbitt* (1922) by the American novelist Sinclair Lewis. The word *Babbittry* was derived from the eponym.

blarney, smooth-talking flattery; named after the *Blarney Stone*, an inscribed stone in a position difficult to reach inside the Castle of Blarney, a village near Cork, Ireland. According to popular legend, anyone who manages to gain access to the stone and to kiss it is supposed to have thereafter a cajoling tongue and the ability to flatter and tell lies effortlessly. Lady Blarney, a smooth-talking fine lady in Oliver Goldsmith's *The Vicar of Wakefield*, was named in allusion to the Blarney Stone.

bunk, empty talk, humbug, nonsense; a shortening of *bunkum*, named after the county of *Buncombe*, North Carolina, originally in the phrase "to talk for Buncombe (or Bunkum)," meaning "to make a long, meaningless speech." The phrase originated in a long, dull speech made in 1820 before the U.S. Congress by Congressman Felix Walker, who represented a district that included Buncombe County. When he was repeatedly interrupted by his colleagues, Walker explained apologetically that he was compelled to "talk for Buncombe." The verb *debunk*, "to expose humbug," was coined in 1923. The term *hokum*, a synonym of *bunk*, was formed about the same time by blending *hocus-(pocus)* and *bunkum*.

cardigan, a sweater or jacket that opens down the front; named after the 7th Earl of *Cardigan* (J. T. Brudnell), 1797–1868, who wore such a jacket when he led the heroic Charge of the Light Brigade (Sept. 26, 1854) during the Crimean War. Compare *raglan*.

cashmere, a fine wool; named for *Cashmere* (now *Kashmir*), a region in the Himalayas where this wool is obtained from the long-haired goats bred there.

chauvinism, exaggerated, militant patriotism; so called (through French *chauvinisme*) from the name of Nicholas

Chauvin, a wounded French veteran of the Napoleonic wars famed for his unconditional devotion to Napoleon and the Empire, who was at first admired, but, after Napoleon's downfall, ridiculed for his excessive patriotism, especially as his name was popularized in a famous 1831 vaudeville, *La Cocarde Tricolore* ("The Three-colored Cockade").

derby, a stiff felt hat with rounded crown and narrow brim; named for the *Derby*, the most important annual horse race in England, at which men wore this kind of hat. The Derby was founded by the 12th Earl of *Derby* in 1780, after the county of this name in central England.

derrick, a crane for lifting heavy weights; originally, a structure for hanging someone, a gallows, named after *Derick*, surname of a noted hangman of the Tyburn gallows in London during the 1600s.

dunce, a stupid person; originally spelled *Duns*, clipped from the name of John *Duns* Scotus (c. 1265–1308), a teacher of theology and philosophy at Oxford who challenged the basic teachings of Thomas Aquinas. Followers of Aquinas attacked the disciples of Scotus, calling the "Dunsmen" or "Dunses" nitpicking sophists, and finally equating them with fools and blockheads, which led to the word's present meaning.

guillotine, a device with a large blade for beheading people; named (through French) for Joseph Ignace *Guillotin* (1738–1814), a French physician who was a member of the Constituent Assembly in 1789 when he proposed that those condemned to death should be beheaded by a machine, which would be quicker and more humane than the methods used until then by executioners. Though the machine he recommended was not invented until 1791, it was named after him as though he had been its inventor.

hector, to bully; from earlier noun *Hector*, any of a gang of bullies roaming the streets of London during the 1600s, named for *Hector*, the champion of Troy in *The Iliad*, who fought the Greeks in a bullying fashion.

malapropism, a ridiculously inappropriate use of words; derived from *Mrs. Malaprop*, a character in Richard Sheridan's comedy *The Rivals* (1775), who regularly misapplies long words by replacing the intended word with one that merely sounds like it, as in "as headstrong as an allegory on the banks of the Nile." The name was coined by Sheridan from the adverb *malapropos* "inappropriately," borrowed from French *mal à propos*, (literally) "badly for the purpose."

maverick, an individualist, a political independent; (originally) an animal unmarked with a brand; named after Samuel A. *Maverick* (1803–70), a Texas rancher who refused to brand his cattle, saying that branding was a cruel practice. His neighbors accused him of lying, since not branding allowed Maverick to claim any unbranded cattle on the range as his. This led to long-term fighting between Maverick and his neighbors. By the turn of the century, *maverick* had taken on the meaning of someone independent and unconventional, especially a politician who breaks away from his party to run on an independent ticket.

mentor, a trusted guide and advisor; named after *Mentor*, the faithful friend of Ulysses in Homer's *Odyssey*. When

Telemachus, the son of Ulysses, sets out in search of his father at the end of the Trojan War, the goddess Athene assumes the form of Mentor when she accompanies Telemachus as guide and adviser in his search.

morphine, a drug extracted from opium; derived (through French and German) after *Morpheus*, the Roman god of dreams, son of the god of sleep. The name *Morpheus* was coined by Ovid from Greek *morphe*, "form," in allusion to the shapes visualized in dreams. The drug was named in reference to its sleep-inducing properties.

pompadour, an upswept style of hair; named after the Marquise de *Pompadour* (Jeanne-Antoinette Poisson, 1721–64), the mistress of Louis XV of France, who wore her hair in this style. A noted patroness of art and literature, not only her hairdo but the fashions and colors she exhibited were named after her and widely imitated. It was she who made the oft-quoted remark, *Apres nous le déluge!* "After us, the deluge!"

raglan, a loose overcoat with sleeves extending to the collar; named after Lord *Raglan* (1788–1855), a British field marshal who wore such a coat during the Crimean War. Compare *cardigan*.

silhouette, a portrait made by tracing the outline of a profile, figure, and so on; named after Étienne de *Silhouette* (1709–67), the controller of finances in France in 1759. Calling an outline portrait a *silhouette* was supposed to ridicule the petty economies introduced by Silhouette, since it was a cheap way of making a portrait instead of having it painted by an artist. Another account takes the portrait name to be a sarcastic reference to Silhouette's short tenure of eight months in office. Still another explanation for the name is that Silhouette himself decorated the walls of his chateau with outline portraits instead of spending money on paintings.

Other interesting eponyms are *limousine, macadam, mackintosh, masochism, maudlin, mayonnaise, meander, nemesis, oxford, panama, pullman, shrapnel, sodomy, spaniel, spartan, turkey, tuxedo, worsted,* and *zeppelin.*

Words derived from names of scientists include *ampere, angstrom, celsius, fahrenheit, farad, faraday, joule, ohm, volt,* and *watt.*

Plant names derived from the names of persons include *begonia, bougainvillea, camellia, dahlia, poinciana, poinsettia, wisteria,* and *zinnia.*

Words derived from the names of famous authors include *Chaucerian, Dantesque, Kafkaesque, Machiavellian, Nabokovian, Orwellian, Rabelaisian, Shakespearian, Shavian, Swiftian, Tolstoyan.*

Words derived from place names include *bikini, calico, canter, champagne, cologne, damask, denim, gauze, jeans, sardonic, shanghai, sherry,* and *stygian.*

MODERN EPONYMS

ARCHIE BUNKER, a type of working-class bigot; from the name of a television character in the sitcom series *All in the Family,* which premiered in January 1971.

BORK, a verb meaning to attack a political candidate, especially in the media; named after Judge Robert H. *Bork,* whose nomination to the Supreme Court in 1987 was rejected by the Senate after an extensive media attack by his opponents.

QUISLING, a traitor who cooperates with the enemy;

named after Major Vidkun *Quisling,* who headed Norway's puppet government under the Nazis in World War II and was executed for treason in 1945.

SOLON, a lawgiver (often used in headlines instead of "legislator" to save space); named for *Solon* (ab. 638–558 B.C.E.), an Athenian statesman and lawgiver.

STRANGELOVE, a military strategist who plans large-scale nuclear warfare; named after Dr. *Strangelove,* a mad military planner in the 1964 motion picture "Dr. Strangelove or: How I Learned to Stop Worrying and Love the Bomb," directed by Stanley Kubrick.

WATERGATE, a major political scandal; named for the *Watergate* building complex in Washington, D.C., where an attempt to break into the offices of the Democratic National Committee in 1972 led to a political scandal in President Richard Nixon's administration.

To list and explain all the eponyms that have come into English would take up an entire book. Indeed, a number of dictionaries of eponyms, listing thousands of names that have become part of the language, have been published. Recent ones include: *A New Dictionary of Eponyms,* by Morton S. Freeman (Oxford University Press, 1997), *Elsevier's Dictionary of Eponyms,* by Rogerio A. Latuse (Elsevier Science Ltd, 2001), and *Chambers Dictionary of Eponyms,* by Martin Manser (Chambers Harrap Publishers Ltd, 2004).

CHAPTER 26

neologisms:
how long does a new word remain new?

A neologism (from French *néologisme*, formed from Greek *néos*, "new," and *lógos* "word") is a technical term for what we ordinarily call a new word. When a neologism first appears in speech or writing, it may startle and puzzle because of its strangeness. You wonder what it means, where it came from, how it is pronounced, and whether it is acceptable in Standard English or merely a voguish or slangy usage. Many technical and semitechnical terms are considered neologisms for a long time. A scientific term like *graviton* ("the unit of gravitational force") sounds like a new word, but it has been used in physics since the 1940s. The term *twigloo* (a blend of *twig* and *igloo*), a kind of temporary shelter made of twigs by environmentalists protecting forests, is a 1990s term that still seems new because of its relative rareness.

True neologisms are either words taken from another language, such as the sing-along entertainment *karaoke* (from Japanese) and the popular dessert *tiramisu* (from Italian), or pure coinages like *kludge*, "any clumsily improvised system" and the number *googol* (see the chapter on **Coinages**). Most neologisms, however, are based on some earlier word or words. In the 1970s, the word collector Willard R. Espy coined the word *semordnilap* for words that spell another word in reverse, such as *doom*, *straw*, and *repaid*. He made up his new word by simply reversing the spelling of *palindromes*, which is the term for words or phrases that spell the same word or phrase forward and backward, such as the words *level* and *noon*, the name *Eve*, the sentence *Madam, I'm Adam*, and the language name *Malayalam*.

A more recent example of a neologism is *phishing*. A front-page article in *The New York Times* of March 24, 2004, informed the reader that *phishing*, defined as identity theft through fake e-mail messages and Web sites, "got its name a decade ago when America Online charged users by the hour. Teenagers sent e-mail and instant messages pretending to be AOL customer service agents in order to fish—or phish—for account identification and passwords they could use to stay online at someone else's expense." At first glance, it would seem that the word was coined by blending the phrase *phony fishing* into *phishing*. But probably a broader influence was the practice in American slang of whimsically changing initial *f* to *ph*, as in *phat* "great, wonderful" (altered from *fat* in the 1960s), *phone phreak*, "one who uses electronic devices to place long-distance calls," (common in the 1970s), and *phooey*, a variant of *fooey*, popularized in the 1920s. *Phishing* and the derivative *phisher*, for one who *phishes* or sends fraudulent e-mails, are neologisms bound to become commonplace as Internet servers warn their customers to beware of phishers disguised as official messages and asking for personal information.

THE BACKLASH

Words like *semordnilap*, *twigloo*, and *phishing* are technical coinages used within narrow or specialized contexts and therefore bother no one. There are, however, neologisms that raise the hackles of people who find them pretentious, ungrammatical, unnecessary, or offensive blots on the language. These neologisms tend to be common, everyday words one finds in a daily paper or hears on a radio or TV show, and people who cannot bear seeing or hearing them are usually language conservatives who wish to keep the mother tongue free of contamination and impurity. It might surprise many speakers today that standard words like *accountable*, *donate*, *enthused*, *practitioner*, *presidential*, and *reliable* were roundly condemned and ridiculed by influential critics of the late 19th and early 20th centuries. For many years, the verbs *finalize* and *prioritize*, the adjective *preventative*, and the sentence-modifying adverb *hopefully* were criticized and condemned by language purists. These words were eventually accepted by most users of English and incorporated in standard dictionaries, although from time to time someone raises an objection to using *finalize*, *legitimize*, or some other word ending in *-ize*.

Since neologisms generally remain "new" for a relatively short time, dictionaries of neologisms tend to be short-lived. A great many of the neologisms recorded in the three volumes of the *Barnhart Dictionary of New English* (1973, 1980, 1990) found their way into standard dictionaries and can no longer be considered "new words." The same can be said of a more recent work, *The Oxford Dictionary of New Words*, second edition, published in 1997. Since the original edition appeared in 1991, many of its entries, such as *cyber-*, *e-mail*, *hip-hop*, *outsource*, and *sleazebag*, have made their way into college-level dictionaries and can hardly be regarded as "new."

TRACKING NEOLOGISMS

For those interested in keeping track of neologisms, there are periodicals and Web sites that provide information on the latest entries into the language. A useful source is the bimonthly *Copy Editor*, which not only comments frequently on neologisms, but features a regular "Dictionary Update" column, edited by Jesse Sheidlower, which presents in dictionary format current neologisms culled from the files of the *Oxford English Dictionary*. The April–May 2005 column, for example, lists among others the terms *baby tee*, "A tight-fitting, esp. cropped T-shirt, intended to be worn by adult women," *krumping*, "A form of fast dancing associated with hip-hop culture, usually performed competitively," and *vlog*, "A blog that incorporates video clips." These entries are illustrated by citations from various newspapers and magazines such as *Vanity Fair*, *Los Angeles Times*, *Rolling Stone*, *Time*, and *Business Week*.

TIRED AND EXPIRED

An amusing example from *Copy Editor* is a boxed listing of what it calls Internet clichés, which appeared in its December 2001–January 2002 issue. The list purports to show how quickly neologisms become trite from overuse:

E- Short for *electronic*, this was named Word of the Year in 1998 by the American Dialect Society. But, oh, how soon it became a cliché, in *e-commerce*, *e-business*, *e-payments*, *e-tailing* and, of course, the names of businesses like *eBay*, *E*Trade*, and *eSchwab*.

META- From the Greek for "after" or "beyond," this combining form showed up everywhere, from science fiction (Neil Stephenson's *metaverse*) to the Web (*meta tags*).

SMART It's not fresh, and it's certainly not smart. Forget *smart transmitters, smart phones,* and *smart appliances.*

ÜBER- The days for this German prefix are, literally, over. Bury *übergeek, überhip,* and *übercool.* [Not quite over, we fear. From *The New York Times Book Review* of October 17, 2004: "Stephen King . . . has folded in characters from his non 'Dark Tower' novels, turning this into an über-narrative that, he suggests, is the keystone to his other work."]

WEB- Copy editors are still arguing over whether *Web site* should be two words and initial-capped, but most agree that the combining form should be curbed, whether *webhead, webzine,* or *webonomics.*

Since 1990, the American Dialect Society (ADS) has been selecting annually the new words and phrases that best typify the year just passed. Based on its membership's nominations and votes, winners are selected and a "Word of the Year" is announced. In addition, it lists various categories of words and phrases, such as "the most useful," "the most creative," "the most euphemistic," "the most original," "the most outrageous," "the most likely to succeed," "the most unnecessary," and occasionally, "the best revival of an old term." The ADS emphasizes that its selections reflect the concerns and preoccupations of the year gone by, and that the words need not be new but they are usually newly prominent. (A list of the winners and losers can be found on the ADS Web site, *www.americandialect.org.*)

The Words of the Year so far have been:

1990 *bushlips* "insincere political rhetoric." Runners-up included *notebook PC* "a portable personal computer weighing 4–8 pounds," and *rightsizing* "adjusting the size of a staff by laying off employees." Most amazing: *bungee jumping* "jumping from a high platform with elastic cables on the feet."

1991 *mother of all* "greatest," as in *the mother of all bosses.* Most likely to succeed: *rollerblade* "skate with rollers in a single row." Most successful: *in your face* "aggressive, confrontational." Most original: *pharming* "genetically modifying farm animals to produce human proteins for pharmaceutical use."

1992 *Not!* "an expression of disagreement." Most likely to succeed: *snail mail* or *s-mail* "mail that is physically delivered, as opposed to e-mail." Most amazing: *Munchausen's syndrome by proxy* "illness fabricated to evoke sympathy for the caregiver." Most original: *Franken-* "genetically altered." Most outrageous: *ethnic cleansing* "purging of ethnic minorities."

1993 *information superhighway* "the large-scale communications network created by computers." Most amazing: *cybersex* "sexual stimulation through the computer." Most imaginative: *McJob* "a generic, unstimulating, low-paying job."

1994 a tie between the combining form *cyber-* and the verb *morph* "to change form." Most trendy: *dress down day* or *casual day* "a workday when employees are allowed to dress casually." Most euphemistic: *challenged* "indicating an undesirable or unappealing condition."

1995 *World Wide Web*, and its variants *Web, WWW, W3*.
Most useful: *E.Q.* for "emotional quotient, or the ability to
manage one's emotions, seen as a factor in achievement."
Most original: *go postal* "act irrationally, often violently,
from stress at work."

1996 *mom*, as in *soccer mom, minivan mom, waitress mom,
single mom*. Most useful: *dot*, used instead of "period" in
e-mail addresses. Most original: *prebuttal*, "preemptive
rebuttal." Most controversial: *Ebonics* "African-American
vernacular English" (blend of *ebony* and *phonics*).

1997 *millennium bug* "the bug predicted to affect detrimen-
tally all computers at the start of the millennium," later
called *Y2K*. Most likely to succeed: *DVD* "Digital Versatile
Disk, optical disk expected to replace CDs." Most useful
(tie): *-[r]azzi* "an aggressive pursuer" and the derisive in-
terjection *duh* to express someone else's ignorance or
stupidity.

1998 the ubiquitous *e-* prefix. Most euphemistic: *senior moment* "momentary lapse of memory due to age."

1999 *Y2K* (see *millennium bug*). Most useful: *dot-com* "a company operating on the Web." Most original: *cybersquat*
"to register a Web address intending to sell it at a profit."

2000 *chad*, the notorious scrap of paper torn off a ballot
that invalidated it and upset the presidential election.
The word elbowed out *muggle*, the Harry Potter term for
a nonwizard or any plain, unimaginative person. It also
beat *civil union*, meaning a legal same-sex marriage. Most
creative: *dot bomb* "a failed dot-com." Most euphemistic:
courtesy call "an uninvited call from a telemarketer."

2001 *9-11* or *9/11* "the terrorist attacks on September 11, 2001." Most useful (tie): *facial profiling* "using video 'faceprints' to identify terrorists and criminals," and *second-hand speech* "overheard cell-phone conversation in public places."

2002 *weapons of mass destruction* or *WMD*, sought for in Iraq. Most likely to succeed: *blog* "weblog, a Web site of personal events, comments, and links." Most useful: *google, v.* "to search the Web using the search engine Google."

2003 *metrosexual* "a fashion-conscious heterosexual male." Most useful: *flexitarian* "vegetarian who occasionally eats meat." Most creative: *freegan* "person who eats only free food" (patterned on *vegan*). Other candidates included *embed, v.* "to place journalists with troops or a political campaign," the virus *SARS* (Severe Acute Respiratory Syndrome), the combining form *-shoring,* "indicating the location of jobs or businesses, for example, *offshoring,* moving them out of the country, *nearshoring,* moving them to Canada." *text, v.* "to send a text message," and *tanorexia,* "the condition of being addicted to tanning" (a play on *anorexia*).

2004 *red state* "a state whose residents favor conservative Republicans in the political map of the United States"; *blue state* "a state whose residents favor liberal Democrats; *purple state* "a state whose residents are undecided; a swing state." Most useful: *phish* "to induce someone to reveal private information by means of deceptive e-mail." Most unnecessary: *stalkette* "a female stalker." Most euphemistic: *badly sourced* "false." Other candidates in-

cluded the euphemism *wardrobe malfunction* "unantici-
pated exposure of bodily parts" (referring to such an exposure on television) and *flip-flopper* "a political
candidate who repeatedly reverses positions on important issues."

2005 The surprise Word of the Year was *truthiness* "the
quality of stating concepts or facts one wishes or be-
lieves to be true, rather than known to be true." Runners-
up were *podcast* "a digital feed containing audio or video
files for downloading to a portable MP3 player" and *intel-
ligent design* or *ID* "the theory that life could only have
been created by a sentient being (promoted by propo-
nents of creation science as a necessary part of school
curricula alongside explanations of evolution)." Most creative: *muffin top* "the bulge of flesh hanging over the top
of low-rider jeans." Most euphemistic: *holiday tree*
"Christmas tree." Most likely to succeed: *sudoku* "a number puzzle in which numbers 1 through 9 must be placed
into a grid of cells so that each row or column contains
only one of each."

Back in 2000, the ADS not only named the Word of the Year
but chose also the Word of the Decade, the Word of the Century, and the Word of the Millennium. The Word of the Decade
was the *Web*, which beat among others the prefix *e-*, the combining form *Franken-*, *ethnic cleansing*, *senior moment*, and the slangy *way*,
"very" (as in *way cool*). The Word of the Century was *jazz*, an interesting choice, considering that it outmatched such weighty
terms as *DNA*, *media*, *melting pot*, *modern*, and *World War*, though it
certainly deserved to rout the other, rather lightweight nomi-
nees, *cool*, *teenager*, *T-shirt*, and *teddy bear*. The Word of the Millen-

nium was the pronoun *she,* which did not exist before the year 1000 (it replaced *heo,* which was too often confused with *he*). A close runner-up was *science.*

VARIETIES OF NEOLOGISMS

As the ADS choices show, it's not easy to determine which new word or phrase will leave a permanent mark on the language. But once a word or phrase becomes part of everyday usage, it ceases to remain new for long. Call it an axiom: Most new words either disappear quickly or become old quickly. Though we may not be sure if a word is new (unless we study its history), we may be sure that it won't be new for very long. Internet terms that seemed novel just a few years ago—*browser, cookie, dot-com, e-mail, emoticon, home page, search engine, surfing the Net*—are surprisingly familiar and commonplace. So all we can say about neologisms is that most of them are created to express something new, are formed by various established processes of word formation, and can be categorized under certain names, such as:

abbreviations and acronyms. Examples: *CIO* (Chief Information Officer), *DVR* (Digital Video Recorder), *GMO* (Genetically Modified Organism), *SARS* (Severe Acute Respiratory Syndrome).

back-formations. Examples: *weaponize,* "to equip with weapons" (a back-formation from *weaponization*) and *Iraqify* "to make someone or something Iraqi" (a back-formation from *Iraqification*). A current example of a new back-formed word comes from Great Britain. It is *celeb,* a vogue verb derived from *celebrity,* meaning "to include celebrities at a social affair, especially to promote a cause," as in *The party was successfully celebed with*

*show-biz personalities. Celebing for a fashionable cause
can draw a big crowd.*

blends. Examples: *cinevangelism*, "the use of movies to
spread evangelism," a Time magazine coinage (Aug. 16,
2004); *Juneteenth* (a blend of *June nineteenth*), "an
African-American holiday celebrating the anniversary of
the Emancipation"; *eatertainment*, "dining combined with
entertainment"; *nutraceutical*, "food that is thought to
provide health benefits," a blend of *nutr(ient)* and
(pharm)aceutical.

borrowings. Examples: (from Brazilian Portuguese) *capoeira*,
a popular martial art, exercise, and dance; (from Mexican
Spanish) *chalupa*, a bowl-shaped tortilla dish filled with
vegetables and cheese; (from the Persian word for wool)
pashmina, a fine cashmere wool from the wild goat of the
Himalayas; (from Japanese) *unami*, the rich, savory taste
of many Asian foods, regarded as a basic flavor distinct
from salty, sweet, sour, and bitter.

clippings. Examples: *brane*, from *membrane* (a four-dimen-
sional space in string theory); *enviro* (an environmentalist); the slang term *props*, "praise, credit, respects" (a
clipping of *propers*).

coinages. Examples: *blings*, "shiny jewelry"; *dubs*, "automobile wheels"; *mouse potato* "person who spends too
much time on the computer" (patterned on *couch
potato*); *decarcerate*, "to release from prison," as in *The
goal is to decarcerate nonviolent drug offenders*; *DNA*,
verb, "to check the DNA of (an accused person)," as in
*I'm impressed that defendants in a criminal case are
being DNA'd*; *counterfactuality*, "speculation about how

the past might have unfolded under different circumstances," and *counterfactual history,* "alternate history."

combining forms. Examples: *-ista,* as in *barista,* "a server or waiter at a bar," and *fashionista,* "a follower of fashions or one involved in the fashion industry"; *-erati,* as in *digerati,* "a devotee of digital computers"; *glitterati,* "ostentatiously wealthy people," and *soccerati,* "soccer stars and fans"; *-think,* as in *groupthink, newthink, sickthink.*

compounds. Examples: *eldercare,* "organized care of elderly people"; *spider hole,* "an underground hideout"; *backstory,* "historical background of a story"; *wakeboard,* "a short board on which a rider is towed across a motorboat's wake."

derivatives. Examples: *jiggy,* "exciting, stylish"; *spendy,* "given to spending, extravagant"; *volumize,* "to add volume to (one's hair, etc.)"; *letteracy,* "the use of initial capitals to indicate words, as C for *cancer, L* for *liberal* (often as *C-word, L-word,* etc.)"; *smoothie,* "a thick drink made of fruit puréed in a blender with yogurt, juice, and other ingredients."

euphemisms. Examples: *companion animal* (instead of *pet*), *guardian* (instead of *owner*), *abortion-rights advocate* (instead of *pro-choice* or *abortionist*), *abortion-rights opponent* (instead of *pro-life* or *anti-abortionist*), *nonbeliever* (instead of *atheist*).

Many more examples of neologisms are found in various chapters of this book, though by the time you read this they may no longer be considered new!

CHAPTER 27

nonce words:
words serving a need
of the moment

Nonce words should not be confused with nonwords or nonsense words. A *nonword*, as defined in the *Random House Webster's College Dictionary* (1997), is "a meaningless word that is not recognized or accepted as legitimate." In *Garner's Modern American Usage* (2003), Bryan Garner lists a series of words that were labeled nonwords about a hundred years ago by the critic Richard Grant White, including words like *enthused, experimentalize, preventative, doubtlessly,* and *irregardless.* Whatever he may think of these words, Garner wouldn't label them *nonwords.* Nor would we. In fact, we think that there is no such thing as a nonword. As Gertrude Stein might have said, a word is a word is a word.

A *nonsense word* is, of course, a word. It may not have a precise meaning, or any meaning for that matter. It is coined to create a particular effect, and if that effect works well, the nonsense word becomes a permanent fixture in the language, like *chortle* and *frabjous*. (See the chapter on **Nonsense Words**, for examples.)

ORIGINS OF NONCE WORDS

What, then, is a *nonce word*? In *The King's English* (3d ed., 1930), H. W. and F. G. Fowler describe it as follows:

> A 'nonce-word' (and the use might be extended to 'nonce-phrase' and 'nonce-sense'—the latter not necessarily, though it may be sometimes, equivalent to nonsense) is one that is constructed to serve a need of the moment. The writer is not seriously putting forward his word as one that is for the future to have an independent existence; he merely has a fancy to it for this once. The motive may be laziness, avoidance of the obvious, love of precision, or desire for a brevity or pregnancy that the language as at present constituted does not seem to him to admit of.

Among the examples the authors cite (and correct parenthetically) are *remindful* (mindful), *insuccess* (failure), *deplacement* (displacement), *correctitude* (correctness), *briskened* (quickened), and *unquiet* (unrest). The Fowlers admit that these may have been mere slips of the pen; but they chastise the writers for being careless, or, at worst, capricious in their use of words.

The word *nonce*, meaning "a particular purpose or occasion," is used especially in the phrase *for the nonce*. This phrase was an alteration of the Middle English phrase *for the nanes*, which was a misdivision of *for then anes*, "for the ones" (meaning the one time, occasion, etc.). In 1884, during the preparation of the

Oxford English Dictionary (*OED*), the editor, James Murray, coined the term *nonce-word* to label words that appeared to have been used only once or "for the nonce." In addition to *nonce-word*, the *OED* introduced terms like *nonce-form*, *nonce-meaning*, and *nonce-use* to label lexical items that seemed to have occurred only once in its files.

NONCE-WORDS

The *OED* has over a thousand entries labeled *nonce-wd.* Here are some examples:

TOUCH-ME-NOT-ISHNESS (nonce-wd.). Cf. stand-off-ish. 1837 Dickens Pickw. [*The Pickwick Papers*] viii. There was a dignity in the air, a touch-me-not-ishness in the walk, a majesty in the eye of the spinster aunt.

TRICHOMANIAC (nonce-wd.) a hair fetishist. 1949 R. Graves Common Asphodel 303. From descriptions in his poems it is clear that the first thing that he [sc. Milton] saw in a woman was … her hair. He was, in fact, a trichomaniac.

TWI-THOUGHT (nonce-wd. after twilight). 1885 G. Meredith Diana xxiv. Diana saw herself through the haze she conjured up. 'Am I worse than other women?' was a piercing twi-thought.

Most nonce words are transparent, formed from established words, and their meanings grasped at a glance. Here are some examples (with the nonce words italicized):

"The beloved author had a stage presence that was *belovable*" (Daniel A. Rose, *The New York Observer*, Nov. 29, 2004)

"Beefy, brash, styled like a *gangstermobile*, it [a Chrysler 300C sedan] is resonating with urban hipsters" (Daren Fonda, *Time*, Aug. 16, 2004)

" '. . . it's difficult to establish a reputation.' Ah, the *R-word*. Call it rep, call it *cred*, call it whatever you want" (*ESPN*, July 18, 2004)

RECOGNIZING NONCE WORDS

It's not easy to recognize a nonce word and to brand it as such. Many words that appear to have been formed for the nonce turn out, upon further investigation, to have been used before. To take one example, in an essay (*New York Times Book Review*, Sept. 19, 2004), the novelist Philip Roth wrote this about his latest work, *The Plot against America*: "Orwell . . . imagined a dystopia, I imagined a uchronia." A survey of current dictionaries showed no entry for *uchronia*. What did Roth mean by that word? It *seemed* to be a nonce word, but the fact that it registered no meaning suggested that it was more likely a rare word, not picked up by lexicographers. An Internet search proved this to be true. *Uchronia* was coined circa 1991 as a short name for the "Usenet Alternate History List"—formed from *U*(senet) + *chron-* "time" + *(utop)ia*—and by 1997 it was used as a synonym for the terms *alternate history, allohistory,* and *counterfactual history,* all referring to novels, short stories, or other works that offer alternative versions of historical events. In Roth's novel, the *uchronia* he describes is one in which the pro-Nazi aviation ace Charles Lindbergh wins the 1940 presidential election instead of Franklin Roosevelt and decides to keep the United States out of World War II. The novel depicts the profound effect of this decision on the lives of American Jews, as typified by Roth's Newark family.

WHEN NONCE WORDS CATCH ON

As has happened a century ago with many so-called nonwords, coinages that appear to be nonce words sometimes catch on with the public and become fashionable. In a chapter entitled "Nonce Words" in his book *On Language* (1980), William Safire introduces the subject as "a guide to those currently 'in' phrases that make up our transient-talk," in effect equating many nonce words with "vogue words." Among the items on his list are: *biggie* (as in "Hollywood biggie"), *slimdown* looks, *glitch*, *-aholic*, *condomania* (in housing), *glitterati*, and *whatsisface*. These may have begun life as nonce words, but have grown into half- if not full-fledged members of the English lexicon.

Nonce words are often playful, humorous, or fanciful coinages, many of them puns. Some typical examples are *herstory* (a feminist play on *history*), *petishism* (a pun formed from *pet* and *fetishism*), *smotherlove* (a pun on *mother love*), and *yumptious* (a blend of *yummy* and *scrumptious*). In *What's the Good Word?* (1982), Safire enumerates some of his own coinages: "I have denounced trendy alienation as 'anomietooism,' warned of 'future schlock,' and, in a Schadenfreudian slip hailed 'urbane renewal.'" The piece, entitled "A Barrel of Puns," elicited a barrel of letters, one of which includes the following letter by Marie Borroff, of Yale University:

> I learned the term 'wideawake hat' from A. A. Milne's poem 'The Alchemist' (the alchemist is said to put on a big wide-awake hat at night and sit in his writing room, writing). I always thought it was a nonce word, a jocular opposite of 'nightcap.'

But then I came across it again in a British book and looked it up, and found . . . that a wideawake hat is a broad-brimmed felt hat, said to be so called because it has no nap.

Among the most prolific creators of nonce words are poets. Gerald Manley Hopkins's famous short poem "Pied Beauty" contains the nonce words *couple-color, rose-moles, fresh-firecoal, chestnut-falls,* and *fathers-forth.* In his poem "To Autumn," John Keats describes the season with such evocative nonce phrases as "bosom-friend of the maturing sun," "hair soft-lifted," "the soft-dying day," and "stubble plains." The Irish poet Seamus Heaney, winner of the 1995 Nobel Prize in Literature, wrote a poem entitled "Nonce Words," whose last stanza reads:

And blessed myself
in the name of the nonce
and happenstance,
the *Who knows*
the *What nexts*
and *So be its.*

JOYCIAN NONCE

No writer in English has shown greater inventiveness in coining words for the nonce than another Irishman, James Joyce (1882-1941), the author of *Ulysses* and *Finnegans Wake.* Most of Joyce's nonce words are designed to convey the stream of consciousness or interior monologue of his characters. Here are typical examples from *Ulysses,* from Chapter 8 of part 2: *hoofirons, steelringing, fifenote, longindying, clappyclap, fernfoils, bronzelydia,* and *oceangreen.* The meanings of these compounds can be understood with relative ease. But it is in *Finnegans Wake* that Joyce pulls out all stops. The work is so thick with invented words that it requires a skeleton key to decipher its contents, to say nothing of its plot, which is impenetrable and has been subjected to many questionable interpretations and theories. Chapter 1, which is comparatively straightforward, begins this way:

riverrun, past Eve and Adam's, from swerve of shore to bend of bay, brings us by a commodius vicus of recirculation back to Howth Castle and Environs. Sir Tristram, violer d'amores, fr'over the short sea, had passen-core rearrived from North Armorica on this side the scraggy isthmus of Europe Minor to wielderfight his penisolate war: nor had topsawyer's rock by the stream Oconee exaggerated themselse to Laurens County's gorgios while they went doublin their mumper all the time. . . .

It's safe to say that Joyce carried the idea of nonce formations to extremes. Another writer given to coining words, Anthony Burgess (see the chapter on **Coinages**) paid homage to Joyce by coining a verb from Joyce's book's title in this sentence from the novel *Inside Mr. Enderby* (1963): "The intermittent drone was finneganswaked by lightly sleeping Enderby into a parachronic lullaby chronicle." The verb *to finneganswake*, both allusive and suggestive, is a prime example of a nonce word.

SEPARATING NONCE FROM NEOLOGISM

Can we call a nonce word a neologism? Yes and no. Loosely, any nonce word *is* a new word, though coined for a particular occasion. *DNA* used as a verb, as in the sentence "The prisoners are

DNA'd these days," may have been used only once by a speaker or writer, but it is a genuine neologism. Another nonce coinage, *to catastrophize*, "to tend to look at things as catastrophes," can be easily viewed as a neologism. Strictly speaking, however, a neologism is a new word that has attained widespread use, even if for a relatively short time. A verb like *downhold*, as in the sentence "The administration has decided to downhold non-defense spending," becomes a neologism when it infiltrates bureaucratic jargon. *Frankenfood*, which appeared in the early 1990s to describe in a pejorative way food that has been genetically modified, seemed at first to be a nonce word. But once it caught on, and even spawned a combining form, *Franken-* (as in *Frankenbean* and *Frankensalmon*), the word was categorized as a neologism and promptly entered in several dictionaries. What these examples show is that time has to pass before we can call a newly coined word either a nonce word or a neologism.

In his book *Words About Words* (1983), David Grambs defines *nonce word* as "A word devised for one occasion or publication and usually short-lived, as contrasted with a neologism; makeshift or convenient term, such as one invented by a novelist for a special usage or meaning."

What is the difference between a nonce word and a hapax legomenon? A hapax legomenon (from Greek, "once said") is a literary term for any word or phrase that occurs only once in a document, in the works of an author, or in the literature of a language. For example, Shakespeare used the word *birthplace* only once, in *Coriolanus*, who says "My birthplace hate I," referring to Rome, where he was born. In this play, then, as in all of Shakespeare's works, *birthplace* is a hapax legomenon. But it is the kind of word that Shakespeare might have used many times but, for whatever reason, did not. By contrast, a nonce word is one made up deliberately for a particular purpose or effect, and therefore unlikely to appear again, as exemplified above in the poems of Hopkins and Keats.

Nonce words are common both in writing and speech, but they are noted chiefly in print, where they stand out, which, of course, is their purpose. Writers create such words to lend flavor and variety to a description, narrative, or commentary. For this reason alone they are worth noticing.

CHAPTER 28

nonsense words:

grammarithemetic and lots of things beside

If you think that nonsense words are too non-sensical to be considered words, think again. Nonsense words may be devoid of conventional meaning, but often, and especially when they are inspired inventions, they have a catchy, humorous, satirical, and endearing quality that makes them memorable and endows them with a sense that surpasses everyday meaning. It is to this quality that nonsense words owe their popularity. The most beloved children's verses, rhymes, and stories are known for the nonsense words, phrases, and sentences in them. And nonsense can be useful. Teachers use nonsense syllables (*glump, trib, donk*) to teach sound–spelling correspondence to young pupils. Cryptographers are known to send important coded messages by prefacing and closing crucial details with nonsense words.

Nonsense words have had a long history in English literature. Perhaps the most famous word regarded as nonsensical is *honorificabilitudinitatibus* in Shakespeare's *Love's Labour's Lost*. The word crops up in the play in this exchange between the page Moth and the clown Costard, as both slyly criticize the word-swallowing pedantry of Moth's master Don Armado and the schoolmaster Holofernes:

MOTH [aside to Costard]: They have been at a great feast of languages, and stolen the scraps.

COSTARD: O, they have lived long on the alms-basket of words, I marvel thy master hath not eaten thee for a word; for thou art not so long by the head as honorificabilitudinitatibus: thou art easier swallowed than a flap-dragon.

This long word, considered the longest in English literature, has an interesting history. It is not only found in Shakespeare, but in the private notebooks of his contemporary, Sir Francis Bacon. Believers in the theory that Bacon wrote the plays ascribed to Shakespeare have for centuries claimed that this was a nonsense word written into the play by Bacon as an anagram revealing his authorship. The anagram is the Latin "hi ludi, F. Baconis nati, tuiti orbi," meaning "these plays, born of F. Bacon, are preserved for the world."

But, as the critic Amanda Mabillard comments, "While this is an interesting coincidence, one must be careful not to take the anagram too seriously. The word "honorificabilitudinitatibus" is not a nonsense word at all, but rather it is the dative singular conjugation of a real medieval Latin word. Dante actually used it more than once, as did other writers of the period. A translation of it would be "the state of being able to achieve honors."

FOREIGN OR NONSENSE?

As we can see from this, foreign words are easily thought of as nonsense. *Hocus-pocus,* the formula used in performing magic tricks, is one such word. It first appeared in the 1630s as a mock-Latin incantation used by conjurers. In a 1655 book, *A Candle in the Dark; or, a Treatise Concerning the Nature of Witches and Witchcraft,* the author writes, "I will speak of one man ... who called himself The Kings Majesties most excellent Hocus Pocus, and so was called, because at the playing of every Trick, he used to say, *Hocus Pocus, tontus talontus, vade celeriter jubeo. ...*" A subsequent theory, that the term was a perversion of a phrase in the Latin communion service, *Hoc est corpus meum,* "This is my body," is accepted by some etymologists and doubted by others. The *Oxford Dictionary of English Etymology* (C. T. Onions, ed.) derives *hocus-pocus* from the mock-Latin formula *hax pax max Deus adimax,* used by beggars and street performers in the 1500s. Pseudo-Latin words were the nonsense words of the Middle Ages.

In *Gulliver's Travels,* Jonathan Swift invented nonsense words liberally to add color to his stories. Parodying the oriental style found in travel books of his day, he writes in *A Voyage to Lilliput*: "Golbasto Momarem Evlame Gurdilo Shefin, Mully Ully, Gue, most mighty emperor of Lilliput, delight and terror of the universe, whose dominions extend five thousand *blustrugs* (about twelve miles in circumference) to the extremities of the globe; monarch of all monarchs. ..." In *A Voyage to Brobdingnag,* he writes: "She gave me the name of *Grildrig.* ... The word imports what the Latins call *nanunculus,* the Italians *homunceletino. ...* I called her my *Glumdalclitch,* or little nurse."

BORDERLINE NONSENSE WORDS

A word bordering on nonsense, but saved from extinction by its appearance in the *Journal* of Sir Walter Scott, is *floccinaucinihilipilification*, which he uses in the sense of "a devaluation or belittling." His *Journal* note of March 18, 1829, reads: "They must be taken with an air of contempt, a floccinaucinihilipilification of all that can gratify the outward man." The word's unusual length has gained it entry in several dictionaries, as this one in the *Random House Compact Unabridged Dictionary* (1996):

> **floc.ci.nau.ci.ni.hil.i.pil.i.fi.ca.tion** (flok'sə nō'sə ni'hil ə pil'ə fī kā'shən), *n. Rare.* the estimation of something as valueless (encountered mainly as an example of one of the longest words in the English language). [1735–45; < L *flocci* + *nauci* + *nihili* + *pili* all meaning "of little or no value, trifling" + -FICATION]

In *Poplollies and Bellibones: A Celebration of Lost Words* (1997), Susan Kelz Sperling writes that the term used by Scott was coined by linking the four words *flocci, nauci, nihili,* and *pili* appearing in an Eton grammar of Latin. In the Foreword to Sperling's book, the language writer Willard R. Espy comments: "We are well rid of *floccinaucinihilipilification*, 'the habit of belittling'. . . . Surely this monster can never have entered the vernacular—except perhaps as a joke, like *supercalifragilisticexpialidocious*, popularized by Walt Disney in a motion picture a few years back." It would probably surprise Espy to learn that the above-mentioned Random House dictionary also includes the following entry:

> **su.per.cal.i.frag.i.lis.tic.ex.pi.al.i.do.cious** (sōō'pər kal'ə fraj'ə lis'tik ek'spē al'i dō'shəs), *adj.* (used as a nonsense word by children to express approval.)

Nonsense words that have a suggestive sound, no matter how hard their spelling or pronunciation, tend to take on lives of their own. In his book, *Words* (1982), Paul Dickson tells the story of three nonsense food names created by the U.S. armed forces in surveys of food preference. The nonsense names *funistrada, buttered ermal,* and *braised trake* were listed, along with 375 real foods, as controls to determine whether those taking the poll were paying attention. In a 1974 survey, *funistrada* ranked above such foods as eggplant, instant coffee, apricot pie, canned lima beans, grilled bologna, and cranberry juice. Neither of the two other nonsense names ranked as high as *funistrada,* which suggests that the soldiers *were* paying attention, but there was something about *funistrada* that, like Pavlov's bells, made the GIs salivate.

NURSERY NONSENSE

The longest-lived nonsense words are found in nursery rhymes. All languages have such rhymes, most of them very old and anonymous. Like speakers of other languages, English speakers hear them as infants and never forget them. All they need to hear is the first line or title, and they remember the rest: *Hey Diddle Diddle, Hickory Dickory Dock, Pat-a-cake Pat-a-cake, Humpty Dumpty.* Nonsensical tongue twisters learned as children are equally memorable: *Peter Piper picked a peck of pickled peppers; How much wood would a woodchuck chuck; She sells sea shells at the seashore.* Children's games and dances are also frequently accompanied by meaningless rhymes: *Eenie, meenie, miney, moe, catch a turtle by the toe; Ring-a-ring-a-roses, a pocket full of posies; All around the mulberry bush, the monkey chased the weasel.*

It's a short step from these traditional nonsense rhymes to the celebrated nonsense verses of Lewis Carroll, Edward Lear, and Dr. Seuss. Like the nursery rhymes, the nonsense verses composed by Carroll, Lear, and Dr. Seuss combine nonsense words with whimsical storytelling. The stories have readable spelling and punctuation, and the same sentence structure as regular stories, except that they are meaningless. Such stories must have inspired the American linguist Noam Chomsky, in his groundbreaking book *Syntactic Structures* (1957), to illustrate what he considered a grammatically well-formed sentence with this example:

*colorless green ideas sleep furiously.

Chomsky's sentence is pure nonsense but entirely correct grammatically. So is this verse from Edward Lear's poem "The Youthful Cove":

The first his parrient was, who taught
The cove to read and ride,
Latin, and Grammarithemetic,
And lots of things beside.

Both examples are formed in grammatically correct English. But while every word in Chomsky's nonsense sentence is a real English word, Lear combines nonsense words like *parrient* and *Grammarithemetic* with real words. A similar distinction is made in the anthology *Poetry Out Loud* (1993). Comparing the poems of Lewis Carroll with those of the modern American poet e. e. cummings, the book's editor, Robert Alden Rubin, writes:

A *nonsense verse* is like a child playing—there's usually some logic, but it doesn't follow 'grown-up' rules. Its inventions and unlikely combinations are its charm. Here [in the poem *Jabber-*

wocky], Lewis Carroll invents imaginary words, but the *sense* of English grammar is so strong he can tell a story anyway. E. E. Cummings, on the other hand, uses real words in seemingly ungrammatical and nonsensical ways. What makes Carroll's poem 'nonsense' is its lack of any serious message; Cummings's poem [*Anyone Lived in a Pretty How Town*], for all its strangeness, has a point to make.

Lewis Carroll (1832–98), the pen name of Charles Lutwidge Dodgson, is best known for his *Alice's Adventures in Wonderland* (1865) and *Through the Looking-Glass and What Alice Found There* (1872), both of which have been translated into more than eighty languages and are among the most quoted works in English. The poem *Jabberwocky* appears in *Through the Looking Glass*, and though most of its words are nonsensical, Humpty Dumpty and Alice try to make sense of the first stanza:

'Twas brillig, and the slithy toves
Did gyre and gimble in the wabe:
All mimsy were the borogroves,
And the mome raths outgrabe.

"That's enough to begin with," Humpty Dumpty interrupted: "there are plenty of hard words there. 'Brillig' means four o'-clock in the afternoon—the time when you begin *broiling* things for dinner."
"That'll do very well," said Alice: "and '*slithy*'?"
"Well, '*slithy*' means 'lithe and slimy.' 'Lithe' is the same as 'active.' You see it's like a portmanteau—there are two meanings packed into one word."
"I see it now," Alice remarked thoughtfully: "and what are '*toves*'?"

"Well, 'toves' are something like badgers—they're something like lizards—and they're something like corkscrews."

"They must be very curious-looking creatures."

"They are that," said Humpty Dumpty: "also they make their nests under sundials—also they live on cheese."

"And what's to 'gyre' and to 'gymble'?"

"To 'gyre' is to go round and round like a gyroscope. To 'gimble' is to make holes like a gimlet."

"And 'the wabe' is the grass-plot round a sundial, I suppose?" said Alice, surprised at her own ingenuity.

"Of course it is. It's called 'wabe,' you know, because it goes a long way before it, and a long way behind it—"

"And a long way beyond it on each side," Alice added.

"Exactly so. Well then, 'mimsy' is 'flimsy and miserable' (there's another portmanteau for you). And a 'borogrove' is a thin shabby-looking bird with its feathers sticking out all round—something like a live mop."

"And then 'mome raths'?" said Alice. "I'm afraid I'm giving you a great deal of trouble."

"Well, a 'rath' is a sort of green pig: but 'mome' I'm not certain about. I think it's short for 'from home'—meaning that they'd lost their way, you know."

"And what does 'outgrabe' mean?"

"Well, 'outgribing' is something between bellowing and whistling, with a kind of sneeze in the middle: however, you'll hear it done, maybe—down in the wood yonder—and when you've once heard it, you'll be *quite* content. . . ."

The poem contains many other nonsense words that Humpty Dumpty doesn't explain. Among them are several that have become a part of standard literary English and have found their way into various dictionaries, including *jabberwocky*, "gibberish, nonsense" (from the poem's title, which refers to a menacing creature called a *Jabberwock*); *bandersnatch*, "an imaginary wild and fierce animal, or a person like it"; *galumph* "to march on exultantly with clumsy bounding movements" (a blend of *gallop* and *triumphant*); *frabjous* "wonderful, superb" (a blend of *fabulous* and *joyous*); and *chortle* "to chuckle with a snort" (a blend of *chuckle* and *snort*). Carroll was a master of what came to be known as *portmanteau words*. (See more in the chapter on **Blends.**)

The English writer and artist Edward Lear (1812–88) made a career out of nonsense. He wrote *The Book of Nonsense* (1846) for the grandchildren of his patron, the earl of Derby. The book consists entirely of limericks, five-line humorous verses. Lear called them "nonsense" (the name "limerick" had not yet become known) because his verses were nonsensical. His later books, *Nonsense Songs, Stories, and Botany* (1870), and *Queery Leary Nonsense* (published posthumously in 1911), included long poems such as the above-cited "The Youthful Cove." A typical piece from the later period is "The Dong with a Luminous Nose," which includes these lines:

> The wandering Dong through the forest goes!
> The Dong! the Dong!
> The Dong with a luminous Nose!
> Long years ago
> The Dong was happy and gay,
> Till he fell in love with the Jumbly Girl
> Who came to those shores one day.
> For the Jumblies came in a sieve, they did,
> Landing at eve near the Zemmery Fidd
> Where the Oblong Oysters grow. . .

Though there are fewer nonsense words in this poem than in "Jabberwocky," there are enough in it to give the same overall effect as Carroll's poem does. The Dong is a close kin to the Jabberwock.

The most famous nonsense writer of our times is unquestionably Dr. Seuss (1904–91), a writer of children's books whose full name was Theodor Seuss Geisel. He was a prodigious coiner of nonsense words and verses. Among the beloved creatures he invented are the Cat in the Hat, the Beagle-Beaked-Bald-Headed Grinch, the Lorax, Yertle the Turtle, Horton the Elephant, and hundreds of others, from the two Biffer-Baum Birds to the Zizzer-Zazzer-Zuzz.

In a typical Dr. Seuss book, *There's a Wocket in My Pocket* (1974), a little boy imagines strange creatures lurking everywhere in his house with names that rhyme with the names of the places they're found in. He imagines seeing a *woset* in his closet, a *nink* in the sink, a *yottle* in a bottle, a *nooth grush* on his tooth brush, a *zlock* behind the clock, and so on. Dr. Seuss accompanies the text with colorful drawings in which the nonsense names are matched up with an assortment of weird-looking creatures.

RELATIVE NONSENSE

The closest relatives to nonsense words in standard English are terms for confusing, unintelligible, or meaningless speech or writing, including:

BABBLE: Going back to the 1200s, this word was formed apparently in imitation of the repetitive sounds made by babies. It is similar to *blah-blah*, and related to Latin *babulus*, "one who babbles." The word is used especially to form compounds like *psychobabble, technobabble, Eurobabble*. The widely used and pejorative term *psychobabble* was coined by the writer Richard

Rosen, who defined it as a "monotonous patois" and "psychological patter." Cyra McFadden, who wrote the best-selling novel *The Serial* (1977), which satirizes California psychobabble, has said about it, "I define it as semantic spinach, and I say the hell with it."

BAFFLEGAB: This is a pejorative term for pretentious and confusing jargon, coined in the 1950s from "gab that baffles." It is often applied to the speeches of politicians.

BOSH: Another word for "nonsense," this came from a Turkish word meaning "empty," and was popularized by the novel *Ayesha*, by J. J. Morier, a 19th-century British writer of romance novels set in countries of Asia Minor.

GIBBERISH: A word known since the 1550s, it was apparently formed from *gibber-* (representing meaningless chatter and perhaps influenced by the earlier *jabber*) and the suffix *-ish*, found in language names like *English, Spanish, Turkish*.

GOBBLEDYGOOK: The word was coined in 1944 by a Texas Congressman, Maury Maverick, to describe the pretentious and confusing jargon of bureaucrats, which he compared to the gobble of turkey cocks. When asked how he got the word, he answered: "I do not know. It must have come in a vision. Perhaps I was thinking of the old bearded turkey gobbler back in Texas, who was always gobbledy gobbling and strutting with ludicrous pomposity. At the end of this gooble was a sort of gook."

MUMBO JUMBO: This term for unintelligible, complicated, and confusing language was apparently formed in imitation of such language and was probably an alteration of *mumble-jumble*. Reduplications like this are fairly common in English: *hanky-panky, hunky-dory, walkie-talkie*. Nevertheless, some etymologists have connected *mumbo jumbo* with an African (Mandingo) name of a god, *mama dyumbo*, based on a 1738 description of a fearsome bugbear called "Mumbo-Jumbo" among African tribes. How this African name came to be used for unintelligible, confusing language has not been explained, and makes one think that this is an instance of etymological mumbo jumbo. (See also the chapter on **Reduplication**.)

We cannot in all conscience conclude this chapter without mentioning one of the commonest kinds of nonsense words concocted in English: the hybrid nonce word/nonsense word most of us seize upon when we can't for the life of us remember a word or name that's on the tip of our tongue. The most common ones are *watchamacallit, whatsitsname, whatsitsface, whoozis,* and *whoozit*. But in case you've forgotten, here is a partial list of some of the others you may have used on occasion:

dingbat, dingus

doodad, doodinkus

doohickey, doojiggers, doowhistle

gilguy, gilhoolie, gizwatch

howyacallit, hoosiedingy, hootis, hootmalalie

jigamajig, jigamaree, jigumbob

thingamabob, thingummy, thingy

whodingy, wimwom, wingdoodle

And let's also remember the high numbers: *eleventeen, xteen, gazillion, jillion, umpty-umpth,* and *zazillion.* The highest number is, of course, a *googol,* which, despite its funny look, represents a real number, no nonsense about it.

onomatopoeia:
from buzzing bees to tintinnabulating bells

One of the great questions of all time is how spoken language got started. No one knows the answer, but that hasn't stopped linguists from conjecturing. Among the theories compiled for the origin of language by Danish linguist Otto Jespersen, perhaps the most famous one is the *bow-wow theory*, which holds that language began in imitations of the sounds emitted by animals—sounds like the *bow-wow* of dogs, the *meow* of cats, the *quack-quack* of ducks, the *moo* of cows, the *oink* of pigs, the *hiss* of snakes, and so on. Not coincidentally, these are some of the first sounds learned by children from songs like *Old MacDonald Had a Farm* and *Baa Baa Black Sheep*.

Another thesis is the *ding-dong theory*, according to which language began when people named things after a sound associated with them, such as the *ding* of a bell, the *crash* of thunder, the *splash* of water. A third is the *pooh-pooh theory*, which maintains that speech arose from involuntary exclamations made in pain, disgust, fear, anger, repulsion, and the like, as *ow, ouch, aah, ugh, grr*, or *phew*. Then there is the *yo-he-ho theory*, proposing that speech arose from the rhythmic grunts and other sounds made by people working together, as in pulling, lifting, digging, and so forth.

All of these theories are based on the idea that language began with some kind of imitation of sounds, which is what *onomatopoeia* is about. This rhetorical term may be great for spelling bees but it's something of a misnomer. Though defined as "the imitation of sounds," the term came through Latin from a Greek word meaning "the making of names" (from *onóma*, "name" + *poieîn*, "to make"), which hasn't much to do with either sounds or their imitation. A more accurate term for an imitative word is *echoism* (coined by the great lexicographer Sir James Murray), since such a word literally echoes a sound. But after hundreds of years in circulation, *onomatopoeia* is the term you will find in most books.

The language-origin theories based on onomatopoeia are generally discounted for at least two reasons. First, because imitative words are in most languages relatively few, and none of the theories can adequately account for the thousands upon thousands of words that have nothing to do with sounds, words like *earth, sun, moon, sky, star,* and *tree.* Second, imitative words differ from one language to another. The bark of an English or American dog may sound like *bow-wow*, but a French dog says *gnaf-gnaf,* a Russian dog *tyaff-tyaff,* a Chinese dog *wu-wu,* a Japanese *wan-wan,* and an Israeli *hav-hav.* This is true of most other words imitative of sounds, like the *tick-tock* of a clock or the *clang-clang* of a trolley. And let's not forget that, in English, dogs sound sometimes like *arf-arf* or *woof-woof* or *ruff-ruff* besides *bow-wow*. In other words, even though animal species and falling, running, hitting, and jumping objects everywhere make the same sounds, their human imitators merely mimic the sounds but cannot reproduce them.

WHAT ARE ONOMATOPOEIC WORDS?

Onomatopoeic, echoic, or imitative words, then, are those that attempt to reproduce or suggest the myriad sounds made by animals or people, or found in nature and the environment. There are no rules governing the formation of such words. All that is necessary is that the imitative word resembles or suggests the sound. A number of conventional sound words have developed this way. They include:

1. Exclamations or Interjections

   ah!—of surprise, joy, etc.

   aha!—of triumph, surprise, etc.

   ahchoo!—of sneezing

   ahem!—throaty sound to attract attention

   bah!—of contempt

   boo—of disapproval or derision

   er—of hesitation

   fie—of disgust

   hah?—of suspicion, interrogation, etc.

   ha-ha!—of laughter

   ho-hum—of boredom

huh?—of disbelief, confusion, etc.

humph!—of disbelief

oh!—of surprise, sympathy, etc.

ouch!—of sudden pain

phew!—of disgust or exhaustion

pshaw!—of impatience or contempt

psst—unobtrusive sound to call someone's attention

sh or *shh*—of shushing

tehee—of snickering laughter

tsk-tsk—of pity or commiseration

tut-tut—of disapproval or disdain

ugh!—of aversion or horror

uh-huh—of agreement

uh-oh!—of concern or chagrin

uh-uh—of disapproval

2. Speech Sounds

babble—speak meaninglessly

blab—talk too much

blah—meaningless chatter

blah-blah-blah—continuous meaningless chatter

chatter—talk rapidly or pointlessly

gab—chat idly

hallo or *hello!*—call or answer someone

hey!—call attention; express surprise

hi—greeting

ho!—call to attract attention

holler—yell

hush!—urge to be quiet

jabber—chatter

murmur—low, indistinct speech

mutter—speak in a murmur

natter—talk on and on

prattle—chatter or babble

shush!—urge to be quiet

squeal—a sharp, shrill cry

stutter—speak spasmodically

susurrate—whisper

tattle—talk idly

whimper—speak low

whine—make a low, complaining sound

yada-yada-yada—continuous meaningless or predictable chatter

yap—talk snappishly

3. Animal Sounds

baa—of a sheep

bow-wow—of a dog

buzz—of a bee

caw—of a crow

chirp—of a bird

chirr—of a grasshopper

chirrup—of a bird

cluck—of a hen

cock-a-doodle-doo—of a rooster

coo—of a dove or pigeon

gobble—of a turkey

he-haw—of a donkey

hiss—of a snake

honk—of a goose

hoot—of an owl

meow—of a cat

moo—of a cow

neigh—of a horse

oink—of a pig

peep—of a small bird

purr—of a cat

quack—of a duck

tweet—of a small bird

whinny—of a horse

woof—of a dog

4. Sound Words

bawl	*fizz*	*rattle*	*wheeze*
belch	*flick*	*sizzle*	*whiz*
bump	*flutter*	*splatter*	*whoop*
burp	*hiss*	*squawk*	*whoosh*
chuff	*huff*	*squeal*	*whump*
chug	*hush*	*squish*	*wow*
crackle	*gargle*	*thud*	*yahoo*
crash	*gurgle*	*thump*	*yawp*
crinkle	*guzzle*	*thwack*	*yikes*
croak	*jangle*	*titter*	*yip*
croon	*jingle*	*twitter*	*yoo-hoo*
crush	*patter*	*ululate*	*zap*
drone	*putter*	*whack*	*zing*

5. Sound Effects

bang	*boing*	*boom*	*click*	*clip-clop*
beep	*boo-hoo*	*clang*	*clink*	*clunk*

ding-a-ling	gop	ploosh	swish	wham
ding-dong	grr	pow	thwang	whoom
eek	kerplunk	rat-tat-tat	tweep	yoop
glub	oof	screech	va-va-voom	youch
glug	oops	sploosh	vroom	zoom

The five lists above cover the major groups of imitative words in English. The lists are not exhaustive by any means, merely representative. Not included in the list of "Sound Words," for example, is the name of the game *tic-tac-toe*, formed in imitation of the sound made by a pen or pencil brought down on a slate while playing the game. Also omitted are words that describe animal sounds, such as *bark, bleat, bray, caterwaul, mewl*, or the names of birds formed in imitation of their call, such as the *cuckoo* and the *whippoorwill*. The list of examples under "Sound Effects" can be vastly expanded because words like these are formed arbitrarily in action cartoons and comic strips.

Closely related to imitative words are *phonesthemic* words, which are two or more words that share a speech sound and are associated with certain meanings. This phenomenon is called *phonesthesia* (from Greek *phōné*, "sound" + *aísthēsis*, "perception") or *sound symbolism*, and the speech sounds are known as *phonesthemes*. The phonestheme *gl-*, for example, is associated with the meaning "light" or "shining" in such words as *glare, gleam, glimmer, glint, glisten, gloss, glow, glower*; the cluster *fl-* is associated with "moving light" in words like *flame, flare, flash, flicker, flimmer*, and with "quick motion" in words like *flee, flip, flit, flop, flow, flurry, flutter, fly*; the cluster *-ash* suggests "violent motion" in words like *bash, clash, crash, dash, gnash, mash, slash, splash*; and the cluster *-ump* suggests a clumsy action or thing, as in *bump, dump, hump, lump, rump, slump, stump, thump.*

Phonesthemes are not necessarily clusters; they can be single sounds, like the vowel *-i-*, which suggests smallness or slightness, as in *bit, imp, kid, little, slim, slip, thin*; or the initial consonant *j-*, suggesting up-and-down motion, as in *jig, jingle, jog, jounce, juggle, jump*; or final *-p, -t, -k*, suggesting a sudden stop, in words like *clip, crack, hack, pat, rap, snip.*

An oft-noted characteristic of echoic words is their tendency to take an iterative or frequentative form, as in *itsy-bitsy, teeny-weeny, truly-uly.* These iteratives take on various forms:

(1) They repeat exactly a base form, e.g., *gobble-gobble, tweet-tweet, woof-woof;*

(2) They alter the repeated form, e.g., *bow-wow, pitter-patter, tick-tock, zigzag;*

(3) The repeated form serves as an intensifier (mostly in slang words), e.g., *jeepers-creepers, okey-dokey, teeny-weeny, tip-top;*

(4) The iterative word is an alteration of a standard phrase, e.g., *itty-bitty* (alteration of *little bit,* further altered to *itsy-bitsy*), *hokey-pokey* (alteration of *hocus-pocus*).

Poetry makes much use of onomatopoeia. Here are three excerpts from poems by Shakespeare, Rudyard Kipling, and Edgar Allan Poe:

When roasted crabs hiss in the bowl,
Then nightly sings the staring owl,
Tu-whit, tu-who! a merry note,
While greasy Joan doth keel the pot.
　　　(William Shakespeare, "Winter")

We're poor little lambs who've lost our way,
Baa! Baa! Baa!
We're little black sheep who've gone astray,
Baa—aa—aa!
                (Rudyard Kipling, "Gentlemen-Rankers")

Keeping time, time, time
In a sort of Runic rhyme,
To the tintinnabulation that so musically wells
From the bells, bells, bells, bells
Bells, bells, bells—
From the jingling and the tingling of the bells.
                (Edgar Allan Poe, "The Bells")

phrasal verbs:

getting by, down, in, off, on, over, and out

The expression most closely associated with the psychedelic era of the 1960s is "turn on, tune in, drop out." The coiner of this expression was Dr. Timothy Leary, a clinical psychologist at Harvard University, famous for his advocacy of the use of the hallucinogenic drug LSD. Leary was fired from Harvard in 1963 for experimenting with LSD and other drugs. When the communications expert Marshall McLuhan advised him to make up a "snappy" slogan to promote the use of LSD, Leary came up with "turn on, tune in, drop out," which became the clarion call of the generation of hippie acid-droppers whom he chiefly influenced. In 1965, he published a book titled *Turn on, Tune in, Drop out,* which is still in print.

Turn on, tune in, drop out are phrasal verbs. Such verbs owe their "snappy" quality to the natural speech rhythm of the English language. In *A Dictionary of Contemporary American Usage* (1957), Bergen and Cornelia Evans say about such verbs: "They are simple and forceful and are generally preferred to their Latin equivalents. So *give up* is often preferred to *relinquish*; *give in* to *acquiesce*; *call out* to *evoke*; *take up* to *assume*; *bring in* to *introduce*."

Garner's Modern American Usage (2003) shows phrasal verbs in some typical contexts:

> ... politicians *put up with* the press, and vice versa; striking workers *hold out* for more benefits; arguing family members *work out* their problems; campers must *make do* with the supplies they have; legacies are *handed down* from one generation to the next; gardeners work to *get rid* of weeds; overworked employees, like candles left too long, *burn out*. ...

Phrasal verbs, sometimes also called *compound verbs* or *verb phrases*, have an informal feel that fits the style of humor writers and hard-boiled novelists. James M. Cain's classic novel, *The Postman Always Rings Twice*, begins this way:

> They threw me off the hay truck about noon. I had swung on the night before, down at the border, and as soon as I got up there under the canvas, I went to sleep. I needed plenty of that, ... and I was still getting it when they pulled off to one side to let the engine cool.

This simple narrative by Cain's fictional drifter and ex-con is built on a string of phrasal verbs: *threw off, swung on, got up, pulled off*. Later in the novel, there are sentences like this: "I ran back, picked her up, and slid down the ravine," where every action is described by a phrasal verb.

GETTING UP AND OTHER PHRASAL VERBS

Consider the phrasal verb *get up*, which has several meanings, including: "to rise from a sitting position"; "to rise from bed"; "to go up or ascend"; "to rouse, as one's courage"; "to prepare or arrange, as an exhibit." In a humorous essay, "Advice to Youth," written in 1882, Mark Twain built an entire paragraph on one of these meanings:

> Go to bed early, get up early—this is wise. Some authorities say get up with the sun; some others say get up with one thing, some with another. But a lark is really the best thing to get up with. It gives you a splendid reputation with everybody to know that you get up with the lark; and if you get the right kind of a lark, and work at him right, you can easily train him to get up at half past nine, every time—it is no trick at all.

As the examples show, a phrasal verb is a verb that consists of more than one word (usually a verb and an adverbial particle), such as *add up, break down, come on, dress up.* Ask any foreign student of English which is the biggest problem in learning the language, and he or she will tell you, mastery of phrasal verbs. There seems to be no logic involved in their forms and meanings, and using or understanding them can be difficult and confusing. Teachers of ESL (English as a Second Language) urge students to simply memorize the most common phrasal verbs, often providing them with lists of the verbs to be learned by heart. To create some order among the phrasal verbs, teachers often break up the list into the following four categories:

Transitive: A phrasal verb that is followed by an object, e.g., *pass up* (*an opportunity*), *try on* (*a garment*), *break into* (*a conversation*), *make up* (*a story*).

Intransitive: A phrasal verb that is not followed by an object, e.g., *blow over* (*The scandal blew over*); *show up* (*The guests finally showed up*); *die away* (*The noise died away*).

Separable: A transitive phrasal verb in which the object can come between the verb and the particle, e.g., *calm down* (*Calm down the child; Calm the child down*); *give back* (*He gave back the money; He gave the money back*).

Nonseparable: A transitive phrasal verb in which the particle can't be separated from the verb, e.g., *look after* (= "take care of"), as in *Please look after the children* (Incorrect: *Please look the children after*); *run against*, as in *She is running against the Mayor in the election* (Incorrect: *She is running the mayor against in the election*).

There is nothing in the forms of the phrasal verbs that would indicate whether they are transitive or intransitive, separable or nonseparable. Here, too, foreign students have no recourse but to memorize the use and meanings of these verbs.

This brings up the problem of meaning. Many phrasal verbs have more than one meaning (sometimes as many as five) and the meanings can be both literal and figurative. For example:

check out. (literal) *I checked out of the hotel* (= I left the hotel). (figurative) *Check out the bank before you open an account* (= investigate the bank).

come across. (literal) *I came across an old friend at the store* (= I met by chance). (figurative) *She comes across as very shy* (= She gives the impression of being very shy).

hold up. (literal) *The traffic jam held us up* (= The traffic jam delayed us). (figurative) *He was held up at gunpoint* (= He was robbed at gunpoint).

let down. (literal) *She let down the hem of the skirt* (= She lowered the hem). (figurative) *They let us down by not helping out* (= They disappointed us by not helping out).

make out. (literal) *I made out a check for $50* (= I wrote out a check for $50). (figurative) *How's he making out in business* (= How's he succeeding in business?).

put off. (literal) *We put off the wedding till May* (= We postponed the wedding). (figurative) *They were put off by his coldness* (= They were perturbed by his coldness).

Garner's Modern American Usage warns users to watch out for three pitfalls when using phrasal verbs: (1) Be sure to include the entire phrase, not just the verb. For example, use *cut down on* instead of *cut down* (expenses), *make up for* instead of *make up* (a loss); (2) Avoid a phrasal verb in which the adverbial particle is not essential but merely a useless appendage. Avoid, for example, phrases like *measure off* or *out, select out, divide up, separate off* or *out*, where the verbs *measure, select, divide, separate* will do by themselves; (3) Even though noun compounds derived from phrasal verbs are written solid or hyphenated, the corresponding verb forms should be written open, as two separate words. Thus, *breakdown* (n.) but *break down* (v.); *follow-up* (n.) but *follow up* (v.); *dropout* (n.) but *drop out* (v.).

The formation of compound nouns from phrasal verbs is well established in English, as in the following examples:

phrasal verbs	compound nouns
black out	blackout
break away	breakaway

break down	breakdown
break in	break-in
break out	breakout
break up	breakup
build up	buildup
drive in	drive-in
drive through	drive-through
fall back	fallback
get away	getaway
get together	get-together
go ahead	go-ahead
go between	go-between

Another type of formation is one in which the phrasal verb is inverted to form the compound noun, as in the following:

phrasal verbs	*compound nouns*
break out	outbreak
burst out	outburst
flow out	outflow
keep up	upkeep
lay out	outlay
put out	output

rush on	onrush
spill over	overspill
take up	uptake
throw over	overthrow

THE LOWDOWN ON DOWNPLAY

Some noun compounds formed by inversion, like *outlay* and *output*, are also used as verbs, but such uses are restricted to technical contexts, so they go mostly unnoticed. Adjective compounds formed by inversion, such as *upcoming* ("the upcoming election") and *ongoing* ("an ongoing conflict") are more conspicuous and therefore sometimes disparaged as "journalistic." A controversial case of an inverted phrasal verb is that of *downplay*. The standard verb is *play down*, but some time in the 1950s journalists began using *downplay* as a verb, as in *He tried to downplay his part in the controversy*. Despite being disparaged as "journalese" by some critics, the word has since come into general use. William Safire used it in a column in the early 1980s, but in a later column he changed his mind and explained why:

Downplay is telegraphese, like *downhold* (U.P.I. editors used to end messages to foreign correspondents with the not-so-cheery "Downhold expenses"). The word is elbowing its way into dictionaries, but the inversion of two words into a single-word substitute is offputting. *Play down* is a clear compound verb, offering a contrast to *play up*. To *play down* is to de-emphasize, minimize, and break a press agent's heart. We don't say *upplay*, why say *downplay*? Why not leave well enough alone and play down the controversy? *Downplay* is inelegant, trendy, and puts me off. I promise henceforth to play down stories (but not to hold down expenses) and never to use *downplay* again.

And, as far as we can tell, he has kept his word.

Many phrasal verbs function like idioms, i.e., like fixed phrases whose meaning differs from the individual meanings of its words. Such verbs have usually one or more figurative meanings and are used informally. The verb *get* has generated many phrases of this kind, including:

get *around* "circumvent or outwit (a rule, an order, etc.)"

get *away with* "go unpunished for (a crime, etc.)"

get *by* "manage with minimal effort"

get *down to* "attend to (business)"

get *in with* "enter into close association with"

get *off* "finish (the workday)"

get *on* "advance (in years)"

get *out of* "avoid doing (something)"

get *over* "recover from (an illness, etc.)"

get *through* "finish"

get *to* "contact"

get *up* "arise or ascend"

Compare these phrasal verbs with established idioms, such as the following:

get a kick out of "find (something) amusing"

get it "understand something," as in *I don't get it.*

get lost "go away," as in *I wish that bore would get lost.*

get nowhere "fail despite trying hard"

get on one's nerves "irritate or upset (someone)"

get real "be serious or realistic"

get there "reach one's goal"

Similar comparisons can be made with many phrasal verbs and idioms that begin with a verb, for example, *be, bring, carry, cut, do, go, have, hold, keep, make, pass, put, run, set, take.*

Native English speakers absorb such usages with their mother's milk. Foreign learners of English, however, must learn them by rote, unless they are lazy enough or patient enough to wait until they assimilate them through practice.

Dr. Timothy Leary's bizarre ideas have been long ago discredited, but there's no denying that he had a knack for expressing himself simply, in short, snappy phrases, a knack that attracted many followers in his day. Here's an excerpt from a talk he delivered impromptu at a gathering of his fans (source: *rotten.com*):

Six words: drop out, turn on, then come back and tune it in . . . and then drop out again, and turn on, and back in . . . it's all a rhythm . . . it's all a beat. You turn on, you find it inside, and then you have to come back (since you can't stay high all the time) and you have to build a better model. But don't get caught—don't get hooked—don't get attracted by the thing you're building, cause . . . you gotta drop out again. It's a cycle. Turn on, tune in, drop out. Keep it going, keep it going . . . gotta keep it flowing, keep it flowing . . .

prefixes and suffixes:

how to create a new word

in one easy step

There is no easier way to create a new word than to attach a prefix or suffix to an established and familiar word. Thousands of words have been coined in English by this one-step method. Suppose you want to coin a word that means "rip beforehand." Take the prefix *pre-*, which means "before," and attach it to the verb *rip*, and voilà! you've coined the word *prerip* (as in *Wanting to look cool, he preripped his new denims*). All right, so it's not the greatest coinage; but a coinage it is. Its chances of getting into a dictionary are practically nil, since words coined by adding prefixes or suffixes to existing words are what lexicographers call "self-explanatory," and therefore not grist for the dictionary mill.

Yet words made up by using prefixes and suffixes have the great advantage of being easily accepted as valid words. As far as we know, nobody has ever objected to words like *preadmission*, *preapprove, precool, precut, preplan, prequalify,* and hundreds like them. In 1996, Vice-President Al Gore was credited with coining the word *prebuttal* for a rebuttal to a speech issued before even the speech was given. To no one's surprise, the word resurfaced during the 2004 presidential campaign debate to describe a pre-debate rebuttal. No one has objected either to the universal displacement of the venerable term "used car" by the upstart "pre-owned car." Nor was there an outcry in the early 1970s against the bizarre coinage *prequel* for a sequel dealing with events preceding a previous work (though one solitary Canadian critic wrote that "the coining of such words should be punishable by a slow and ugly death"). Similarly, no protests have been issued against words formed ad hoc with the prefix *post-*, meaning "after," such as *postbudget, post-Freudian, postprimary, postrace, postseason,* and the like.

Compare the facility with which prefixes and suffixes slip into the language, without fuss or muss, to the protests that have met the overuse of new combining forms like *e-, i-, cyber-, techno-,* and *info-.* For instance, in their book *Wired Style* (1999), the writers Constance Hale and Jessie Scanlon lash out against the proliferation of the combining form *cyber-,* calling it "terminally overused." (See the chapter on **Combining Forms.**) Combining forms come in spates, calling attention to themselves, and irritating readers often enough to be discarded. This was the fate of the combining form *-gate,* which practically vanished once the Watergate scandals of the 1970s faded from memory. Combining forms are intrusive strangers we tolerate for a while; prefixes and suffixes are familiar figures we take for granted.

A prefix (from Latin *praefixus,* "fastened in front") is a meaningful element attached to the beginning of a word in order to form a new word. A suffix (from Latin *suffixus,* "fastened up") is such an element attached to the end of a word.

PREFIXES

Prefixes, which are far fewer in English than suffixes, are added mostly to verbs, as *un-* is added to the verb *do* to form *undo*. Other examples are *dis-* in *disrobe*, *mis-* in *mistreat*, *pre-* in *predetermine*, and *re-* in *rediscover*. The same prefixes can be used with adjectives (*uncertain*, *disorderly*, *misbegotten*, *prefabricated*, *repaid*) and nouns (*unperson*, *discomfort*, *mistrust*, *preexistence*, *remarriage*). But not all prefixes are equally productive. The prefix *a-*, meaning "not," derived from Greek, has produced only a few new words, among them *ahistorical*, *amoral*, and *apolitical*. Similarly, the prefix *ab-*, meaning "off, away from," which came into English as a component of words taken from French or Latin like *abhor* and *abjure*, has yielded less than a handful of new words, among them *aboral*, "away from the mouth," and *abnormal*, "away from the normal."

Some of the commonest of our prefixes, such as *un-*, *over-*, and *under-*, originated in Old English (before 1100). When *un-* is added to a verb, it means to do the opposite or reverse of the verb, as in *uncover*, *undress*, *unfasten*, *unfold*, *unload*, *untie*. But when it is added to an adjective or noun, it means "not," and is a synonym of another negative prefix, *in-*, which came into English from Latin. The two prefixes, *un-* and *in-*, have created considerable confusion since it is often unclear which word takes *un-* and which *in-*. As a general rule, if the adjective or noun came from Old English, the prefix is *un-*; if it came from Latin, the prefix is *in-*. Unfortunately, this rule has exceptions, found in such pairs as *unequal* and *inequality*, *undigested* and *indigestible* (both *equal* and *digest* are from Latin). The problem is compounded by the fact that a number of adjectives sometimes occur with both prefixes, and their use is often in dispute. Is it *indecipherable* or *undecipherable*? *insubstantial* or *unsubstantial*? *inelastic* or *unelastic*? *inexperi-*

enced or *unexperienced*? (The answer is: either *insubstantial* or *unsubstantial* is acceptable, but the rest take only *in-* .) If you are in doubt, your safest course is to consult a dictionary.

Another cause of confusion is that not all words prefixed by *in-* have negative meanings. For example, the word *invaluable* doesn't mean "not valuable" but rather "highly valuable; priceless" but the ambiguity in meaning often leads people to drop the prefix and use *valuable*, which of course is not the same as *invaluable*. To say that something is without value, one has to say that it is *valueless* or *worthless*, but a good synonym for *invaluable* is *priceless*. A similar situation came about, with far-reaching consequences, when the word *inflammable*, meaning "easily set on fire," was thought to be easily mistaken for its opposite, namely, "not easily set on fire." Fire departments and insurance companies, committed to safety, agreed to drop the *in-* prefix and change the word to *flammable*. The change was deplored in critical circles, where the loss of *inflammable* to *flammable* was viewed as corrupting the language. Though both words are still used, this is what *The New York Public Library Writer's Guide to Style and Usage* (1994) recommends: "Some people may . . . believe that *inflammable* means 'not flammable.' The coinage *flammable* has been used by some manufacturers as a way to show the meaning more clearly, but *flammable* is a safe choice." As for the opposite of *flammable*, a new word was coined with the indisputably negative prefix *non-*: *nonflammable*.

The negative prefix *in-* is also found in the variant forms *il-*, *im-*, and *ir-*, as in *illegitimate, impossible*, and *irrational*. The American dialectal word *irregardless*, meaning "without regard, irrespective," has been condemned by critics since the 1920s. Wilson Follett called it a barbarism, and Porter Perrin described it as "a careless duplication of meaning (negative prefix *ir-* and negative suffix *-less*); not used in reputable writing and better avoided in speech." Even though *Webster's Third* labeled the word "nonstandard," in 1961 the editors of *Life* magazine angrily denounced the inclusion in the dictionary of this "most monstrous of non-words." *Webster's Dictionary of English Usage* (1989), after showing its widespread use, especially in common speech, admits that "*irregardless* is still a long way from winning general acceptance as a standard English word. Use *regardless* instead."

Currently, the most common negative prefix is *non-*, generally considered more neutral than *un-*. Manser and McQuain, in their *Guide to Good Word Usage* (1989), give the examples *a nonprofessional golfer* and *non-Christian religions,* noting that "The prefix *un-*, attached to the same words, may have stronger negative force: an *unprofessional* or *un-Christian* act, for example, violates professional ethics or Christian principles." Since the 1960s, English has been deluged with nouns and adjectives prefixed by *non-*. The prefix is used in two senses:

1. (forming nouns and adjectives) "Not; opposite or reverse of," as in *nonblack, nonwhite, nonachiever, noncandidate, noncommitted* nations, *nondegradable* waste materials, *nonpolluting* means of transportation, *nonaddictive* drug, *noninvasive* medical procedures, *nonprint* media, *nonprofit* organization.

2. (forming only nouns) "Not real or true; sham," as in *nonbook, noncountry, nonevent, nonissue, noninformation, nonplay, non-thing.*

THE OVERUSE OF *NON-*

Criticism of the overuse of *non-* has not been wanting, especially of its frequent use to coin unnecessary antonyms, such as *nonoffensive* (for *defensive*), *nonpermanent* (for *temporary*), *nonnuclear* (for *conventional*), *nonsuccess* (for *failure*). Wilson Follett, in his *Modern American Usage* (1966), criticized

the increasing desire to classify everything into two groups like a digital computer; e.g. *fiction* and *nonfiction, alcoholic* and *nonalcoholic, age-determined unemployment* and *non-age-determined unemployment.* This tendency is to be deplored, both because of the ugly, unarticulated compounds it produces, and because the twofold division with *non-* is likely to suggest a strictness that it does not always possess.

The misuse of *non-* is perhaps most succinctly illustrated by the following exchange between Napoleon and Talleyrand, reported by Ralph Waldo Emerson:

Napoleon: What is all this about non-intervention?
Talleyrand: Sire, it means about the same as intervention.

Prefixes are either productive or unproductive. (Note: We did not say "nonproductive.") Productive prefixes are those that form new words, while unproductive ones exist only as fossils in established words. *Un-* and *non-* are productive prefixes. Other common productive prefixes are:

counter- (meaning "offsetting, opposing," and added to nouns and verbs), as in *counterattack, counterbid, counterculture, counterdemonstration*

de- (meaning "undo the action of," and added to verbs), as in *deactivate, declassify, decontaminate, de-escalate, demilitarize, demonetarize, demythify* dis- (meaning "do or be the opposite of," and added to verbs, nouns, and adjectives), as in *discredit, dishearten, disinherit; disbelief, discourtesy, disinfectant; disinterested, disorderly, dispassionate*

inter- (meaning "between, among," and added to adjectives, nouns, and verbs), as in *intercontinental, international, interpersonal; intermarriage, intersession, interstate; interact, interbreed, interweave*

mis- (meaning "wrong, wrongly," and added to verbs and nouns), as in *misaddress, misappropriate, misbehave, misguide, misjudge; misconduct, misdeed*

out- (meaning "out, away, beyond," and added to verbs, nouns, and adjectives), as in *outdo, outclimb, outgrow, outlift; outbreak, outburst, outcry, outgrowth; outbound, outgoing, outworn*

over- (meaning "over, beyond, excessive," and added to adjectives, verbs, and nouns), as in *overactive, overcautious, overdependent; overact, overburden, overcharge; overconcern, overdecoration, oversupply*

under- (meaning "under, below, beneath," and added to verbs, nouns, and adjectives), as in *undercook, underpay, underuse; undercarriage, underclass, underground; underlying, underqualified, undersea*

An example of an unproductive prefix is *ad-* (meaning "toward") and its variant forms *a-, ab-, ac-, af-, ag-, al-, an-, ap-, ar-, as-,* and *at-,* found in words taken from Latin or French, such as *adjoin, ascribe, abbreviate, accede, affix, agglutinate, allude, annul, apprehend, arrogant, assist,* and *attract.* Another unproductive prefix is *con-* (meaning "together") and its variant forms *col-, com-,* and *cor-,* found in words taken from Latin or French, such as *conceal, confess, collect, collide, compose, comprise, correct, corrode*. These prefixes are so imbedded in the words in which they came into English that they are no longer recognizable as prefixes.

SUFFIXES

Suffixes are so common in English that they are hardly noticed. Consider this opening passage from Norman Vincent Peale's best-seller, *The Power of Positive Thinking*:

> Believe in yourself! Have faith in your abilities! Without a humble but reasonable confidence in your own powers you cannot be successful or happy . . . A sense of inferiority and inadequacy interferes with the attainment of your hopes, but self-confidence leads to self-realization and successful achievement.

Without suffixes these sentences couldn't have been written, yet it takes some effort to spot them. If you try, you will find at least seven of them: *-able, -ence, -ity, -ful, -cy, -ment, -ion*. If you rewrite the last sentence to avoid suffixes: "A sense of being inferior and inadequate interferes with the achieving of your hopes, but confidence in yourself leads to realizing your potential and achieving success," you end up with a clumsily worded sentence that still includes four suffixes, *-ate, -ing* (three times), *-ence*, and *-al*.

Dictionaries rarely bother to define the words formed with suffixes, running them in instead like afterthoughts at the end of a main entry. While the word *humble*, used in Dr. Peale's exhortation, is treated royally in the dictionary, with a full complement of definitions, its derivatives, *humbleness, humbler, humblingly*, and *humbly*, are listed in the last line in secondary boldface. So if you want to know what these run-on entries mean, you have to look up the suffixes *-ness*, *-er*, *-ingly*, and *-ly* in the dictionary and attach them to the word *humble*. Luckily, most native speakers know what these simple suffixes mean, just as they are familiar with every one of the seven suffixes in Dr. Peale's pep talk. Other suffixes are less transparent.

For example, the suffix *-ee*. A surprisingly large number of words having this suffix are found regularly in print, words like *adaptee, electee, examinee, franchisee, mergee, rescuee, transportee*, but what they mean precisely is uncertain. That is because the suffix is ambiguous. Originally, *-ee* was a technical suffix in legal English, adapted from the French ending *-é*, and used along with the suffix *-or* in pairs like *appellor* and *appellee, mortgagor* and *mortgagee*, the first referring to the person who performs a particular action, the second referring to the person who is the recipient of the action. Later, *-ee* began to be used loosely in such nonce words as *educatee* (someone educated) and *releasee* (one released from jail), but also in ordinary words like *addressee* (one who is addressed), *deportee, nominee*, and *trainee*. But things got complicated when the suffix took on the meaning of one who performs a particular action (rather than being the object or recipient of the action) in such words as *absentee* (one who absents him- or herself), *escapee, retiree, returnee*, and others. This is a suffix that is not always self-explanatory.

Suffixes, like prefixes, can be productive or unproductive. The suffixes mentioned above, *-able, -al, -cy, -ence, -ful ,-ing -ion, -ity*, and *-ment* are productive, i.e., they are able to form new words. Examples of unproductive suffixes include *-or* (as in *editor, sailor, escalator*), *-ule* (as in *module, molecule, globule*), and *-ure* (as in *culture, failure, moisture*).

Suffixes often occur in associative sets, as, for example, *-ism, -ist*, and *-ize* in *terrorism, terrorist, terrorize*, or in cumulative sets, as

-ism, -ist, -istic, and -istically in *antagonism, antagonist, antagonistic, antagonistically*. Such a build-up of suffixes is called "suffix suffocation" in Jeffrey McQuain's *Power Language*.

> Wordwise, the poorest of all suffix forms is *-wise*. A charity worker says, 'We gave back volunteer-wise.' A singles group worries about the future 'relationship-wise,' while a politician tries to rebuild 'staff-wise.' Rarely does a noun benefit from this addition . . . In fact, almost any suffix helps suffocate the noun it appends; this tendency to let the ends of words grow in length draws strength away from their message.

Another problem with certain suffixes, especially the noun-forming suffixes *-cy, -ity, -ness,* and *-tion*, is their duplication of meaning. Synonymous pairs like *obduracy* and *obdurateness, aridity* and *aridness, completion* and *completeness, corruption* and *corruptness, ferocity* and *ferociousness, torridity* and *torridness* can create doubt and confusion in an inexperienced writer. "When such a pair exists," Porter Perrin suggests, "take the one that is more familiar to you or that fits best in the rhythm of the sentence."

Suffixes serve to form nouns, adjectives, adverbs, and verbs. The following is a selection of common suffixes arranged by their parts of speech:

noun suffixes

-age (added to nouns and verbs, as in *mileage, percentage; breakage, spillage*)

-an or -ian (added to place names, as in *Chilean, Moroccan; Egyptian, Iranian*)

-ance (added to verbs, as in *attendance, disturbance, performance*, and to adjectives ending in -ant, as in *elegance, relevance, vigilance*)

-ant (added to verbs, as in *assistant, attendant, consultant*)

-ation (added to verbs, as in *combination, information*)

-cy (added to adjectives ending in *-t* or *-te*, as in *accountancy, privacy*)

-dom (added to nouns and adjectives, as in *kingdom, filmdom, freedom*)

-er (added to verbs, as in *player, reader, mixer, babysitter*)

-ful (added to nouns, as in *mouthful, pocketful, tablespoonful*)

-hood (added to nouns, as in *childhood, motherhood, priesthood*)

-ian (added to nouns and adjectives, as in *comedian, historian, Freudian*)

-ing (added to verbs and nouns, as in *building, swimming, flooring*)

-ion (added to verbs, as in *collection, exhibition, protection*)

-ism (added to nouns and adjectives, as in *heroism, idealism, sexism*)

-ist (added to nouns and adjectives, as in *expressionist, novelist, humanist*)

-ity (added to adjectives, as in *originality, personality, superiority*)

-ment (added to verbs, as in *establishment, excitement, investment*)

-ness (added to adjectives, as in *clumsiness, manliness, politeness*)

-ship (added to nouns, as in *citizenship, fellowship, workman-ship*)

adjective suffixes

-able (added to verbs, as in *agreeable, imaginable, under-standable*)

-al (added to nouns, as in *experimental, musical, traditional*)

-ary (added to nouns, as in *customary, honorary, momentary*)

-ed (added to nouns, as in *bearded, bowlegged, big-headed*)

-en (added to nouns, as in *ashen, golden, leaden*)

-ful (added to nouns, as in *boastful, joyful, sinful*)

-ible (added to verbs, as in *collectible, convertible, digestible*)

-ic (added to nouns, as in *angelic, artistic, heroic*)

-ing (added to verbs, as in *compelling, entertaining, pressing*)

-ish (added to adjectives and nouns, as in *childish, fiendish; shortish, whitish*)

-y (added to nouns, as in *cloudy, greedy, earthy, jazzy*)

adverb suffixes

-ly (added to adjectives, as in *awkwardly, brightly, fluently, randomly*)

-ward (added to nouns, as in *backward, earthward, north-ward, rearward*)

-wise (added to nouns, as in *clockwise, crosswise, healthwise, salarywise*)

verb suffixes

-en (added to adjectives and nouns, as in *freshen, quicken; hearten, strengthen*)

-ize (added to nouns, as in *criticize, moralize, patronize, pasteurize*)

To sum up, prefixes and suffixes are rich sources of new words in English and in many modern languages. Without their ability to change grammatical functions and meanings, our vocabulary would be greatly diminished and devoid of variety and expressiveness. As Aldous Huxley stated (in a 1945 essay, "Words and Reality"), "Lacking a proper vocabulary, people find it hard, not only to think about the most important issues of life, but even to realize that these issues exist."

CHAPTER 32

reduplication:
flip-flopping higgledy-piggledy through the riffraff

In the chapter on **Onomatopoeia,** we touched on sound symbolism, or the indication of meaning through the sound of words. To illustrate this phenomenon, we described the initial cluster *fl-* as being associated with "quick motion" in words like *flee, flip, flit, flop, flow, flurry, flutter, fly.* A word in which the *fl-* cluster is redoubled is *flip-flop.* This word made headlines during the presidential election campaign of 2004, when the Democratic candidate was widely described by his opponents as a *flip-flopper* who *flip-flopped* on crucial political issues.

Flip-flop has been in the language for over 400 years. Starting out as a concise description of the act of flipping and flopping in the wind, as wings, flags, and shutters do, it took on several other meanings, such as a backward somersault, a backless sandal, an electronic circuit having alternative states, and, figuratively, a wavering, waffling, or indecisiveness on the part of—well, a political candidate. *Flip-flop* has sound symbolism: we can hear in the *fl-* clusters the sound of flipping in one direction and flopping in another. It is also visually suggestive, evoking the image of things that flip and flop, as a pair of sandals flip-flopping in sand on a beach. But perhaps most importantly, the word is compelling because of its emphatic doubling of the syllable *fl-*. This doubling of a syllable or word element to strengthen or emphasize meaning is called by linguists *reduplication*.

Reduplication is a productive process found in many languages, in a variety of functions. "Nothing is more natural," writes the American linguist Edward Sapir in his classic work, *Language,*

> than the prevalence of reduplication, in other words, the repetition of all or part of the radical element. The process is generally employed, with self-evident symbolism, to indicate such concepts as distribution, plurality, repetition, customary activity, increase of size, added intensity, continuance. . . . In a class by themselves are the really enormous number of words, many of them sound-imitative or contemptuous in psychological tone, that consist of duplications with either change of the vowel or change of the initial consonant—words of the type *sing-song, riff-raff, wishy-washy, harum-scarum, roly-poly.* Words of this type are all but universal.

Reduplications—or reduplicatives, as such words are often called—have been classified in various ways. Where the word or element is simply repeated, as in *bye-bye, cha-cha, goody-goody, hubba-hubba, no-no, pooh-pooh, rah-rah, so-so,* the reduplication is called a **tautonym** (from the Greek, meaning "of the same name"). This word was originally used in scientific names of animals in which the genus and species are identical, as *Anser anser* for the grey-lag goose, *Ciconia ciconia* for the white stork, and *Buteo buteo* for the common buzzard. Where the repeated word or element is modified, as in *chit-chat, dilly-dally, helter-skelter, higgledy-piggledy, hoity-toity, pitter-patter, roly-poly, shilly-shally,* the reduplication is called a **ricochet word**, a term coined by E. C. Brewer in his *Dictionary of Phrase and Fable* (1870). These two types differ from **rhyming compounds**, in which the two elements are unrelated words that rhyme, such as *bigwig, hi-fi, hotshot, humdrum, jet set, ragtag, sci-fi,* and *sky-high.*

A special kind of ricochet word is the so-called "schm-/shm- reduplication," which came into English from Yiddish (where it is used to dismiss or disparage, as in *koyfn, shmoyfn,* "to buy, not to buy, who cares?"—*koyfn,* "to buy") and entrenched itself, especially in American slang, over the last century. The prefix *schm-* or *shm-,* found in various slang words borrowed from Yiddish, such as *schlep, schlock, schmear, schmooze, schnook, schnoz,* was first used to form a reduplication in *fancy-schmancy,* which vaudeville comedians popularized in the sense of "pretentious, affected." This led to the use of *schm-/shm-* as a deprecatory prefix in many ad hoc formations, such as: (adjectives) *old-schmold, patient-schmatient;* (nouns) *love-schmove, money-schmoney, value-schmalue, revolution-schmevolution;* (verbs) *eat-schmeat, manage-schmanage, pray-schmay,* the two words often separated by a comma. True to its comic origins, these reduplicatives are often used jocularly and with a follow-up clause, as in these classic exchanges:

Woman (to Friend): I heard that Mrs. Knobl's son has an Oedipus complex.

Friend: Oedipus, schmoedipus—as long as he loves his mother.

Man (to Friend): The doctor thinks I may have cancer.

Friend: Cancer, shmancer—as long as you're healthy.

In the classifications above, the reduplicatives are grouped according to the forms they take. Another way of classifying them is according to their purpose or origin. They could be onomatopoeic, imitative of sounds, like *bow-wow, choo-choo, ding-dong, ha-ha, ho-hum, pooh-pooh, tick-tock, tsk-tsk*; or they could be words coined after such sounds, like *claptrap* ("empty action or talk," from an actor's device to get applause), *hurdy-gurdy* (a barrel organ), *hush-hush* ("secret, confidential"), *gobbledygook* ("nonsense," like the gobbling of the turkey cock), *mumbo jumbo* (probably altered from *mumble-jumble*).

Other reduplicatives are expressive, intensive, or emphatic repetitions, such as *goody-goody, no-no, pooh-pooh,* and *so-so,* but a more common type has contrastive vowels or consonants, and generally resembles rhyming compounds (except that one or both of the two parts are often meaningless), for example, *fiddle-faddle, hanky-panky, helter-skelter, hodgepodge, hoity-toity, hurly-burly, knickknack, loosey-goosey, mishmash, namby-pamby, niminy-piminy, nitty-gritty, shilly-shally,* and *tittle-tattle.*

A final group of reduplicatives are loanwords (see the chapter on **Loanwords and their Sources**), such as *beriberi* (disease of the nerves caused by a vitamin deficiency, from Sinhalese, reduplication of *beri,* "weakness"); *bric-a-brac* ("trinkets, knick-knacks," from French, a reduplication probably based on the phrase *à bric et à brac,* "any which way"); *mahimahi* (the dolphin, from Hawaiian, reduplication of old Hawaiian *mahi,* "strong"); *ylangylang* (an East Indian tree, or its oil, from Tagalog *ilang-ilang*); *couscous* (semolina dish, from Arabic *kuskus*); *lava-lava* (Polynesian garment, from Samoan *lavalava,* "clothing").

Still another way of classifying reduplicatives is according to their function or meaning. This method also suggests the development of reduplication from simple baby talk to more complex uses. It goes roughly like this:

1. **Baby talk:** This includes children's reduplications, like *bye-bye, choo-choo, doo-doo, pee-pee, wee-wee,* and words of baby-talk origin, like *baby, daddy, mama, mommy, nanny, papa, poppy.* Foreign examples: French *bébé,* Spanish *nene.*

2. **Diminutives:** Includes endearments and pet names, such as *honey-bunny, itty-bitty, itsy-bitsy, lovey-dovey,* and affectionate proper names like *Georgie-Porgie, John-John,* and *Jen-Jen.* Foreign examples: Tagalog *mahiyahiya,* "be little ashamed" (*mahiya* "ashamed"); Swahili *maji-maji,* "a little wet" (*maji,* "wet").

3. **Belittling:** Includes such forms as *claptrap, dilly-dally, fiddle-dee-dee, flimflam, hobnob, shilly-shally, wishy-washy,* and other terms denoting insignificance or contempt. Foreign examples: Dutch *mik-mak,* "worthless things"; German *Pille-palle,* "trifles"; Yiddish *gelt, schmelt,* "money-schmoney."

4. **Repetitiveness:** Includes such forms as *boogie-woogie, chitchat, pitter-patter, seesaw, walkie-talkie.* Foreign examples: Hawaiian *wiki-wiki,* "quickly" (*wiki,* "quick"); Mongolian *bayn-bayn,* "repeatedly"; Hindi *kit-kit,* "monotonous repetition"; Chinese Pidgin English *chop-chop,* "quickly" (*chop,* "quick").

5. **Discontinuity:** Includes such forms as *knickknack, hodge-podge, mishmash, pellmell,* and other terms denoting nonuniformity. Foreign examples: Japanese *tokoro-dokoro,* "scattered"; Somali *fen-fen,* "to gnaw on all sides"

(*fen*, "to gnaw at"); Chinook (Native American) *iwi iwi*, "look about carefully, examine" (*iwi*, "appear").

Grammatical uses of reduplication have been widely recorded in numerous languages, an exception being English. Examples of such uses include:

Plurals: Noun plurals are indicated by reduplicating the noun. For example: Hebrew *ish-ish*, "every man, everyone" (*ish*, "man"); Chinese *renren*, "everybody" (*ren*, "person"); Bahasa Malay *rumah-rumah*, "houses" (*rumah*, "house"); Indonesian *anak-anak*, "children" (*anak*, "child"); Ilocano (Philippines) *pingpingan*, "dishes" (*pingan*, "dish").

Verbs: Various modifications of the meaning of simple verbs are indicated by reduplication. The best-known ones are the initial reduplications in the older Indo-European languages to help form the past tense of many verbs. For example: Sanskrit *bharti*, "he bears," *bibharti*, "he bears up," *bhari-barti*, "he bears off violently"; Greek *leipo*, "I leave," *leloipa*, "I left"; Latin *cado*, "I fall," *cecidi*, "I fell."

By contrast with borrowed words, whose histories are usually transparent, most native English reduplicatives have obscure histories. For example:

chitchat "casual talk," is a reduplication of *chat*. But what is the origin of *chit*? It may be an earlier imitative word *chit*, "twitter," or an earlier *chit-chit-chat*, imitative of a squeaking sound. Most likely the words originated as a varied reduplication using the alternating vowels *i* and *a*, as in *dilly-dally*, *flimflam*, *mishmash*, *riffraff*.

dilly-dally "waste time," varied reduplication of *dally*, "act playfully."

flimflam "a deception, swindle," a varied reduplication of no known word.

mishmash "a confused mixture," apparently a varied reduplication of *mash*, "soft, pulpy mass." But compare German *Mischmasch*, with the same meaning, a reduplication of the verb *mischen*, "to mix."

riffraff "low-class people, rabble," from earlier *rif and raf*, "every bit or particle, worthless things," from Old French *rif et raf*, of uncertain origin.

shilly-shally "vacillating, wavering," varied reduplication of *shall I? shall I?*, one of the few reduplications of clearcut origin. Compare *willy-nilly*.

wishy-washy "indecisive, irresolute," varied reduplication of *washy*, "weak, thin, diluted."

fuddy-duddy "stuffy, old-fashioned person," a rhyming reduplication of no known word.

helter-skelter "in a disorderly or haphazard manner," a rhyming reduplication of no known word.

higgledy-piggledy "in disorder or confusion," a rhyming reduplication of no known word, but perhaps influenced by *pig*.

nitty-gritty "essential part, core," a rhyming reduplication of no known word.

roly-poly "short and plump," a rhyming reduplication, perhaps of *roll*.

seesaw "plank for moving up and down," varied reduplication of *saw*, "cutting tool," probably coined in imitation of the back-and-forth motion of one sawing wood.

super-duper "first-rate, topnotch," rhyming reduplication of *super*, "excellent."

teeny-weeny "very small, tiny," rhyming reduplication of *teeny.*

willy-nilly "willingly or not," rhyming reduplication of *will I, nill I* or *will he, nill he* or *will ye, nill ye.*

Reduplication was well known and much used in early Modern English. The following three examples from Shakespeare are typical:

See how yond justice rails upon yond simple thief...change places, and, handy-dandy, which is the justice, which is the thief? (*King Lear*)
(*handy-dandy*, "in quick alternation," rhyming reduplication of *handy*)

The people muddied...in their thoughts and whispers,
For good Polonius' death. And we have done him greenly
In huggermugger to inter him. (*Hamlet*)
(*huggermugger*, "in secret haste, any which way," rhyming reduplication of no known word)

First Witch: When shall we three meet again?
In thunder, lightning, or in rain?
Second witch: When the hurly-burly's done,
When the battle's lost and won. (*Macbeth*)
(*hurly-burly*, "commotion, uproar," rhyming reduplication of *hurly*, altered from *hurling*, "tumult," gerund of *hurl*)

Reduplication is a redoubling of sounds, and it is well known that the repetition of sounds is pleasurable to the ear. It is what creates rhyme in poetry. Both children and adults delight in rhymed verses such as these from Edgar Allan Poe's "Annabel Lee":

It was many and many a year ago
In a kingdom by the sea,
That a maiden there lived whom you may know
By the name of Annabel Lee;
And this maiden she lived with no other thought
Than to love and be loved by me.

(Notice the repetition in "many and many" and "to love and be loved.")

The pleasure of repetition is also illustrated by the whimsical rhymes of limericks:

A flea and a fly in a flue
Were caught, so what could they do?
Said the fly, "Let us flee."
"Let us fly," said the flea.
So they flew through a flaw in the flue.
(*Anonymous*)

retronyms:
new terms for old things

When the first automobiles made their appearance in the 1890s, they were so noisy and got stuck in the mud so often that pedestrians made it a habit to yell at the drivers "Get a horse, fellow!" Since for many centuries the only carriages were those drawn by horses, it was natural to rename the newfangled self-propelled car a "horseless carriage." A similar advance in technology caused moviegoers in the 1930s to refer to the earlier films without a soundtrack as "silent movies." Closer to our time, technological advances prompted the use of such terms as "manual typewriter" when the electronic typewriter came around, "rotary telephone" when the push-button phone became the norm, and "snail mail," "paper mail," "hard mail," and "postal mail" when electronic mail (or e-mail) practically replaced the former as the everyday form of correspondence. (Some old-timers still remember when "surface mail" was coined to contrast with the new "air mail"). All of these terms for old or outmoded things have come to be known as *retronyms.*

In *What's the Good Word?* (1982), William Safire defined *retronyms* as "nouns that have taken an adjective to stay up-to-date and to fend off newer terms." He cites as an example the word *guitar.* When *guitar* was replaced by an *electric guitar,* the old original became known by the retronym *acoustic guitar.* In his next book, *Language Maven Strikes Again* (1990), he gives as an example the noun *watch,* which originally sufficed as the word for a time-piece (derived from the idiom *to keep watch* or *vigil* and first recorded in Shakespeare's *Love's Labour's Lost*). When the word *wristwatch* appeared in the late 1800s, it became necessary to coin the retronym *pocket watch* for the earlier kind. Then, in the 1970s, when the *digital watch* (or *clock*) made its debut, a term was needed for its precursor, the old-fashioned timepiece that shows time by the position of the hands on a dial, and the retronym *analog watch* (or *clock*) was created.

Another language maven, Richard Lederer, in a January 2003 column titled "Retro-active words," writes:

> I remember being astonished when one of my students at St. Paul's School told me that he had missed my class because he has set his alarm for P.M. rather than A.M. On our old clocks, that would have been impossible, but on digital clocks it happens all the time. So what used to be just a clock (or watch) is now an analog, versus a digital, clock.

Much has been written about retronyms over the past twenty years. While the word (from *retro-,* "backward" + *-(o)nym,* "word, name") has so far eluded most standard dictionaries (though scooped in 2000 by the *American Heritage Dictionary*, 4th ed.), it has been widely discussed and variously defined by word connoisseurs like Safire, Lederer, and others. Richard Lederer's definition: "A retronym is an adjective-noun pairing generated by a change in the meaning of the noun, usually because of advances in technology. Retronyms, like retrospectives, are backward glances."

The writer Charles McGrath, in a feature article in *The New York Times* (Dec. 26, 2004), defined *retronyms* as:

> retoolings or respecifications of old words that have been made necessary by new technology, the most famous examples being 'snail mail,' 'analog watch,' and 'black-and-white TV.' With just a little stretching you could also include 'Classic Coke,' 'two-parent family' and 'free parking.'

Paul Dickson, in his book, *Words* (1982), defined a *retronym* thus:

> A noun that has been forced to take on an adjective to stay up-to-date. For instance, *real cream* and *live performance* are retronyms for cream and performance that have been brought about with the advent of nondairy creamers and prerecorded performances.

David Grambs, in *Words About Words* (1982), defined a *retronym* as:

> an adjective-noun pairing that arises because newer senses of the noun, or new products, have made its meaning less clear, requiring the somewhat redundant modifier to restore its original or earlier sense, e.g., 'hardcover book' (because of the advent of

softcover books), 'stage play' (because of the advent of the television play), 'natural turf' (after the advent of 'artificial turf').

Retronym was coined by the journalist and author Frank
Mankiewicz, who came up with the word in the 1970s while
serving as president of National Public Radio (NPR). In his
wide-ranging career, Mankiewicz had been a political adviser to
senators, a television anchorman, and a syndicated newspaper
columnist. In a March 2001 interview, he explained:

> When I came to NPR, I said I'm going to do three things. I'm
> never going to use 'impact' as a verb. I'm never going to use
> 'access' as a verb, and I'm never going to use the word
> 'telecommunications' at all. I've weakened a little on the
> telecommunications. . . . 'Retronym.' Bill Safire gives me credit
> for that regularly. It's a figure of speech, meaning a word that
> you now have to modify because of technology [or] mod-
> ernism. I heard a couple of announcers once saying that so-
> and-so would do a good job in the Super Bowl because they
> play their home games on natural turf. Natural turf? That's
> what we used to call grass. And then, within a day, somebody
> said that her son had come to a party and they had asked him
> to play. And he hadn't brought his instrument, so he borrowed
> an acoustic guitar. Which is what we used to call a guitar. So
> then I began to think about it. You know, 'real cream' and 'live
> drama' and 'print journalists.' These are retronyms.

It has become a favorite pastime of language buffs to draw
up lists of retronyms and invite volunteers to add to the lists.
The results are rather mixed, because not all so-called retronyms
pass muster. Is *classical music* really a retronym, or is it simply a
style or genre of music? Is *blue-collar worker* a retronym or does it

denote a type of worker? Is *church wedding* a retronym or merely a statement of fact? Is *natural childbirth* a retronym? Is *Old Testament?* Clearly not all adjective-noun phrases can be called retronyms. If they could, terms like *Old English, old money, old school,* and *Old World* would all have to be called retronyms.

Genuine retronyms, writes Richard Lederer, "signal that the thing double-labeled has become outmoded and obsolete, the superseded exception rather than the rule." Or, as William Safire describes them, they are "throwback compounds." Many retronyms, however, are not relics of the past but simply contrastive or distinguishing terms, as, for example, *biological parent,* coined to contrast it with *adoptive parent, birth mother,* coined to distinguish it from *adoptive mother,* and *legitimate theater,* as opposed to *movie theater.* These pairs of terms and what they denote are equally current, except that the retronym denotes the older version.

RETRONYMS AND NEONYMS

Here is a list of retronyms, alongside the new terms that propelled their coinage, which we shall call *neonyms* (from *neo-,* "new" + *-(o)nym,* "word, name"):

retronym	neonym
acoustic guitar	electric guitar
analog computer	digital computer
analog watch (or clock)	digital watch (or clock)
bar soap	liquid soap
black-and-white television	color television

cloth diapers	disposable diapers
corded drill	cordless drill
day game or day baseball	night game or night baseball
desktop computer	laptop computer
film camera	digital camera
fountain pen	ballpoint pen
hardcover book	softcover book
horse polo	water polo
human-readable	machine-readable
human translation	machine translation
impact printer	laser printer
manual transmission	automatic transmission
natural blonde	bleached blonde, peroxide blonde
natural language	artificial language, machine language
natural light	artificial light
network television	cable television
optical microscope	electron microscope
optical telescope	radio telescope
print book	e-book
print journalist/journalism	electronic journalist/journalism
propeller plane	jet plane

rotary phone	push-button phone
shell egg	dried egg, artificial egg
snow skiing/skier	water skiing/skier
stage play	TV (or radio) play
two-parent family	single-parent family
walk-in theater	drive-in theater
whole milk	skim milk

Not included in the above list are a number of retronyms that are distinguished from their corresponding neonyms by the adjectives *conventional, regular,* or *real,* such as:

conventional weapons (versus biological, chemical, or nuclear weapons)

conventional oven (versus microwave oven)

conventional photography (versus digital photography)

regular coffee (versus decaffeinated coffee or decaf)

regular gas (versus unleaded gas)

regular mail (versus e-mail, fax mail, voice mail)

real cream (versus nondairy cream)

real butter (versus a nondairy substitute)

IS THERE A NEED FOR RETRONYMS?

But is there really a need for retronyms? This question was raised in 2001 by the linguist Geoffrey Nunberg. In an article titled "Old Words, New Tricks" in the magazine *California Lawyer*, Nunberg pointed out that when a new technology renders an old one obsolete, speakers usually continue to call it by the same name they used for the old one. We still call a watch a watch, whether it's mechanical or electric, analog or digital; and we call a guitar a guitar, whether it's acoustic or electric, classical or flamenco. "We still talk about 'dialing a number,' even if it's really a matter of punching it in. And some of us still describe the large white objects in our kitchens as 'iceboxes,' even if it makes our twelve-year-old daughter look at us strangely."

True enough. Most of us would rather adapt an old word to new uses than create a new word for every innovation. Newspapers include "letters to the editor" even though the bulk of them are not letters but e-mail messages, and we're used to speaking of our video library or software library, forgetting that a short time ago the word *library* was restricted to a collection of books (from Latin *liber*, "book"). Nunberg points out that people talk loosely about "record companies" and "record labels," but that doesn't mean that the word *record* has become a generic term that encompasses CDs and audio cassettes. It just means that most people prefer to use old, everyday words rather than new, technical ones.

On the other hand, when it becomes necessary to draw a distinction between a new and an old technology, we feel compelled to expand our vocabulary. When you want to sell your old car, camera, or clock, you're forced to use a retronym to describe it: *compact car, film camera, conventional clock, standard radio.* So retronyms are useful counterpoints to loose usage.

The person who has been most responsible for the hunting, discovery, discussion, and dissemination of retronyms is the language maven William Safire. Since the 1980s he has written more columns on the subject than anyone else, including the word's coiner, Frank Mankiewicz. Safire has instituted a "Retronym Watch," in which he regularly features the most recent examples arriving on his desk. He is aided in the sport by an elite detachment of his Lexicographic Irregulars that focus on retronyms. The results of the Retronym Watch have appeared in a number of Safire's books, including *Watching My Language* (1997), *Let a Simile Be Your Umbrella* (2001), and *No Uncertain Terms* (2003).

In *Watching My Language*, Safire refers to what he calls a relative of the retronym, namely, new nouns formed from adjectives modifying old nouns. The examples he gives are *op-ed* for *op-ed page*, *zoo* for *zoological garden*, and *prefab* for *prefabricated house*. Other examples sent in by a reader are: *ad lib* (for *ad-lib remark*), *bell-bottoms* (for *bell-bottom trousers*), *bifocals* (for *bifocal lenses*), *convertible* (for *convertible-top car*), *daily* (for *daily newspaper*), *final* (for *final exam*), *glossies* (for *glossy photos*), and *oral* (for *oral exam*). We could also call them relatives of clippings like *ad, bus, cab, deli, lab, math* (see the chapter on **Clipping or Shortening**).

REVERSED RETRONYMS

By the way, there is another word-form also called a *retronym*. Puzzlers and word-game aficionados will recognize the word *retronym* as denoting a word or phrase that turns into a different word when spelled backward. For example, *desserts*, when spelled backward, becomes *stressed*; *mood*, spelled backward, becomes *doom*. This type of retronym is often called *reversal*. Trade names are sometimes formed with reversals: the name of the oral laxative *Serutan* was formed by spelling "natures" backward. Some given names and family names are retronymic: the names Nevaeh and Remle are reversals of "heaven" and Elmer, respectively. A street in Vancouver is named Adanac Street in honor of

Canada. Reversals should not be confused with anagrams, which are words or phrases formed by rearranging the letters of other words or phrases. Thus, the name *Erewhon*, coined by Samuel Butler as the name of a fictitious country in his 1872 utopian novel, *Erewhon*, though considered a reversal, is actually an anagram of the word *nowhere*.

Retronym is perhaps the most recent coinage using *-(o)nym*, a suffix meaning a name or word, and derived from Greek *ónyma*, dialectal variant of *ónoma*, "name." Most people are familiar with only a few of the fifty or more English words ending in *-(o)nym*. The words *synonym* and *antonym*, *homonym* and *heteronym*, *acronym*, *eponym*, *pseudonym*, and *toponym* are found in most standard dictionaries. But the *Oxford English Dictionary* (*OED*) and *Webster's Third New International Dictionary* (*W3*) include many more, such as *autonym* ("a book published under the author's real name"), *caconym* ("a taxonomic name that is objectionable for linguistic reasons"), *mononym* ("a term consisting of one word only"), *paronym* ("a word which is derived from another, or from the same root; a derivative or cognate word"), *protonym* ("the first person or thing of the name; that from which another is named"), *tautonym* ("repetition of the word for genus and species [as] Rattus rattus"), and *trionym* ("a name consisting of three terms; a trinomial name in botany or zoology"). The *OED* has even an entry *onym*, derived from the suffix, and defined as "a proposed term for a technical name, as of a species or other group in zoology, etc., forming part of a recognized system of nomenclature."

borrowing:

adopting words from

foreign places

INTRODUCTION

In earlier chapters, as those on **coinages, combining forms,** and **doublets,** we discussed words that came into English from foreign languages. Those words were important not just because they filled gaps in the language; they also influenced the formation of new words in English.

To take one example: the combining form *eco-*, in coinages like *ecosystem* "ecological system" and *ecosphere* "ecological sphere," would never have been created had not the American naturalist Henry David Thoreau adopted in 1858 the German word *Ökologie* (from Greek *oîkos* "house, habitation" + *-logie* "study of") to form the English word *ecology*, referring to the natural environment. Starting in the 1920s and '30s, a worldwide movement to preserve the natural environment led to the coinage of new words with the combining form *eco-*, derived from *ecology*:

ecospecies, ecotype, ecocatastrophe, ecotage "ecological sabotage," *ecoterrorism, ecotourism,* and so on. Out of one word borrowed from a foreign language came many homegrown ones.

The word *borrowing,* when used to mean a word or phrase taken by one language from another, is, of course, a metaphor. But, as the American linguist Einar Haugen (1906–94) wrote in the journal *Language* (1950):

> The metaphor implied is certainly absurd, since the borrowing takes place without the lender's consent or even awareness, and the borrower is under no obligation to repay the loan. One might as well call it stealing, were it not that the owner is deprived of nothing and feels no urge to recover his goods.

After trying out some other terms without success, Haugen gives up the effort. He writes: "The real advantage of the term 'borrowing' is the fact that it is not applied to language by laymen. It has therefore remained comparatively unambiguous . . . and no apter term has yet been invented."

German philologists of the mid-1800s introduced the borrowing metaphor with such terms as *entlehnen,* "to borrow," *Lehnwort,* "loan, loanword," *Lehnübersetzung,* "loan translation," and *Lehnbedeutung,* "semantic loan." A loanword is the same as a borrowed word, and a loan translation (also known as a calque) is a word or phrase translated from another language.

Some modern loanwords include *ballet, chic, faux pas* (from French), *delicatessen, hamburger, kindergarten* (from German), and *karaoke, sushi, tsunami* (from Japanese). Examples of loan translations include the term *loan translation* itself (from German *Lehnübersetzung*), *marriage of convenience* (from French *mariage de convenance*), and Spanish *rascacielos* (from English *skyscraper*). Semantic loans, also called *loanshifts,* are words or phrases that carry over a meaning from one language to another, as, for example, *passion*, in the sense of "suffering" (as in the *passion of Christ*), was a semantic loan from Latin *passiō*, "suffering," and *elder* (as of a church) was a loanshift from Latin *senior*, which was a loanshift from Greek *presbýteros*, which was itself a loanshift from Hebrew *zəqēnim* (literally, "old men").

Another term involved in the borrowing process is a *loanblend*, sometimes called a *hybrid*. This is a word made up of elements from two different languages, such as *automobile*, ultimately from Greek *autós*, "self," and Latin *mōbilis*, "movable, mobile," and *genocide*, a hybrid of Greek *génos*, "race, kind," and Latin *-cīdere*, "to cut, kill." (See the chapter on **Blends or Portmanteau Words**.)

Throughout its history, English has borrowed liberally from many languages. Whenever English speakers came into contact with speakers of other languages, they quickly picked up new words or phrases and made them their own. This has not been true with other language communities, such as France, which tried to restrict borrowing through its Académie française, created in 1634, or Spain, whose Real Academia was founded in 1713 on the French model. There has never been a language czar or national academy to regulate the English language, either in England or America, though sporadic attempts have been made since the 1600s to "polish and refine the English Tongue" (Daniel Defoe), "ascertaining and fixing our Language forever" (Jonathan Swift), and "promote the reformation of those translators, who for want of understanding the characteristical difference of tongues, have formed a chaotic dialect of heterogeneous phrases" (Samuel Johnson). But after ten years of research into the language in preparation for his great *Dictionary of the English Language* (1755), Johnson confessed that it was hopeless to think that his dictionary "can embalm his language, and secure it from corruption and decay."

Interestingly, modern English dictionaries have achieved much of what Samuel Johnson thought impossible. They have served to standardize the language by setting norms of spelling, pronunciation, grammar, and usage. The only area in which dictionaries play a limited role is in the creation and acquisition of new words. Every few years, dictionaries rush into print the latest "new words" that have established residence in the mother tongue, irrespective of their source. It doesn't matter whether they were coined from native stock or borrowed and adapted from other languages, if they are spoken or printed in quantifiable amounts, they become grist for the dictionary mill.

The ease with which the English language borrows and assimilates new words has been largely responsible for its astounding growth. Dictionaries reflect this growth in the number of vocabulary entries in them. Why dictionaries? Because it is impossible to pin down the exact size of the English vocabulary at any given time since it is constantly shifting through increment and attrition, and since we don't know what exactly is a "word" (are *sing, sang, sung, singing* different words or merely conjugations of the word *sing*?).

Leonard Bloomfield, in his seminal work, *Language* (1933), distinguished between two types of borrowings: *cultural* and *intimate*. "Cultural borrowing of speech-forms," he wrote, "is ordinarily mutual; it is one sided only to the extent that one nation has more to give than the other." As examples of cultural loans, he cites such words as *frankfurter* and *pretzel* from German, *sonata* and *scherzo* from Italian, and *curry* and *pundit* from Tamil and Hindi, respectively. English in turn has given to other languages such terms as *beefsteak, club, baseball,* and *golf.* On the other hand, "Intimate borrowing is one-sided: we distinguish between the upper or dominant language, spoken by the conquering or otherwise more privileged group, and the lower language, spoken by the subject people . . . In most instances of intimate contact, the lower language is indigenous and the upper language is introduced by a body of conquerors."

Since medieval times, English borrowings have been cultural, the result of increasing communication with speakers of different languages through immigration and travel. But the growth of English began with intimate borrowing, which came in two waves. The first was the Danish invasion of England in the 800s, which introduced Old Norse words into the indigenous Old English, common words like *anger, cake, egg, law, root, sky, skirt, scrape, they, them, window,* and *wing*. The second wave was the Norman Conquest of England in 1066. Before the Conquest, Old English consisted mainly of a Germanic vocabulary, with a smattering of cultural borrowings from Latin and Greek. But after 1100, the language was flooded with borrowings from Norman-French, words that touched upon every aspect of life: cooking (*boil, broil, fry*), culture (*dance, painting, sculpture*), church (*chaplain, clergy, priest*), military (*army, battle, soldier*), law (*judge, jury, verdict*), government (*country, court, state*), and thousands of other terms.

Today, over half of the English vocabulary consists of borrowings. This is partly so because it is far easier to borrow the words we need than to make them up, just as it's easier to borrow a neighbor's ladder or lawnmower than to acquire one of our own. It is also due to the openly receptive nature of the English language to the languages of our neighbors across the globe. An important effect of this receptiveness is that English has a richer vocabulary than most other languages, which is one reason why it has become a world language.

loanwords and their sources:

many tongues, many words

Not a day goes by without some English speaker picking up a foreign term and passing it on to friends or relatives. One day it's *feng shui*, the next it's *wabi-sabi*. If the term is meaningful (that is, it fills a gap in the vocabulary), it is passed around like a tasty recipe, in conversation, letters, e-mails, and instant messages, and by day's end hundreds of people have made it their own. Of course, it may just be a buzzword, a vogue word, and last not much longer than a day. But if it does endure, it becomes a genuine loanword, a foreign borrowing integrated into English.

Feng shui, "the art of creating harmonious surroundings," came into English in the 1990s from Chinese and became a major industry in interior design, complete with schools, products, and innovative ideas. The term, pronounced /fung shway/, was borrowed from a Chinese compound meaning literally "wind and water." Ten years later, *wabi-sabi*, "the art of interior design involving simple and rustic decor," made its debut. Borrowed from a Japanese compound meaning roughly "the beauty of things imperfect," it took an honored place next to *feng shui* in the bible of interior design and decoration.

These two loanwords are fairly typical of current borrowings, which come with increasing frequency from Asian and African languages. Some of the loanwords of recent years include *pashmina* (from Persian *pashm*, "wool"), a fashionable fabric made of a blend of cashmere and silk; *djembe*, "a goblet-shaped hand drum of West Africa"; *umami* (from Japanese, literally, "tasty") "a savory, meaty flavor," regarded as a fifth basic flavor (the four being salty, sweet, sour, and bitter) produced by glutamate and found in many Asian foods. In January 2005, millions of people throughout the world became instantly familiar with *tsunami*, a Japanese word meaning literally "harbor wave" and denoting a destructive tidal wave produced by an undersea earthquake. Until then *tsunami* was a relatively rare technical term, first recorded in English almost exactly a hundred years earlier, in 1904.

CULTURAL BORROWINGS

All of these are cultural borrowings, and over the centuries English has borrowed countless cultural terms from many languages. Hebrew, for example, was an early donor, influencing Old English through various Bible translations. Words and names of Hebrew origin include *amen, babel, behemoth, camel, cherub, gehenna, Goliath, hallelujah, hosanna, Jehovah, jubilee, leviathan, manna, messiah, rabbi, Sabbath, sapphire, Satan, shekel,* and *shibboleth.* Another Semitic language, Arabic, was the source of important loans from the Middle Ages on, usually through the medium of French and Latin, including *admiral, albatross, alchemy, alcohol, alcove, algebra, alkali, amber, assassin, bedouin, camphor, cotton, harem, hashish, jihad, jinn, minaret, mattress, monsoon, mosque, nadir, sheik, sultan, syrup, zenith,* and *zero.*

Persian, an Indo-European language of western Asia spoken in what is now Iran, has also contributed significant words to English. Among them are *arsenic, azure, bazaar, caravan, dervish, jackal, jasmine, khaki, kiosk, lilac, magic, mogul, musk, paradise, shawl, spinach, taffeta, talc, tulip,* and *turban.* An everyday English word, *check,* originated in Persian. The English word, first used before the 1300s as a call in chess announcing that one's move has exposed the opponent's king, came (through Old French *eschec*) from Persian *shāh,* "king," especially in the phrase *shāh mat,* "the king is stumped" (the source of English *checkmate*). The derivation of *checkmate* from Arabic *shāh māt,* "the king died," was a mistake, resulting from confusion of Persian *mat,* "astonished, stumped" with Persian *māta,* "to die." Out of the chess use of *check* came the meanings "a rebuff, repulse" and "a sudden stop." The name of the chess piece *rook* also comes from a Persian word, *rukh,* whose original meaning is uncertain.

Another Indo-European language, Hindi, an official language of India, has given English the words *bandanna, bangle, bungalow, cheetah, chintz, dungaree, guru, juggernaut, jungle, loot, mandarin, nabob, pajamas, pundit, shampoo, thug,* and *yoga.* Others came directly from the ancestral Indo-Aryan language, Sanskrit, words like *avatar, brahmin, karma, mantra, nirvana,* and *swastika.* The word *sugar* came into English (as it did in most other European languages, for example, Danish *sukker,* Dutch *suiker,* French *sucre,* German *Zucker,* Hungarian *cukor,* Polish *cukier,* Spanish *azúcar*) ultimately from Sanskrit *śárkarā,* originally meaning "grit or gravel."

The Far East has also provided English with a number of colorful words. From Chinese we got *kowtow* ("act servilely"), *pekoe* (tea), *sampan* ("boat"), *taipan* ("head of a business"), *tong* ("association"), *yen* ("craving"), foods like *chop suey, chow mein, dim sum*, plants and fruit like *ginseng, kumquat, lich, loquat*, games like *fan-tan* and *mah-jongg*, martial arts and exercises like *kung fu* and *tai chi*, and principles like *yin* and *yang*. While, contrary to legend, *ketchup* is not from Chinese (it's from Malay), the common word *tea* is. Like *sugar*, the word *tea* has cognates in many languages: French *thé*, German *Tee*, Italian *tè*, Norwegian *te*, Spanish *té*, all from dialectal Chinese (Amoy) *t'e*. The Mandarin Chinese form, *ch'a*, is represented by Greek *tsai*, Persian *chā*, Portuguese *châ*, and Russian *chaĭ*.

Japanese has given English popular foods like *soy, sushi, teriyaki, tofu*, the mildly alcoholic *sake*, martial arts like *aikido, judo, jujitsu, sumo* wrestling, the battle cry *banzai*, the suicidal *hara-kiri* and *kamikaze*, art forms like *bonsai* and *origami*, historical figures like *daimyo* (feudal lord), *samurai* (feudal warrior), *shogun* (military governor), and *mikado* (emperor), *haiku* poetry, *Zen* philosophy and its *koan* method, and the singalong *karaoke*. Other Japanese loanwords include *dojo* ("martial-arts school"), *futon* ("mattress"), *geisha* ("woman companion"), *kabuki* ("drama"), *kimono* ("robe"), *Nōh* (classic drama), *ricksha* ("vehicle"), *samisen* (musical instrument), *sayonara* ("farewell"), and *tycoon* ("business magnate"). Originally, *tycoon* (from Japanese *taikun*, "great lord") was a title given by foreigners to the shogun or military governor of Japan; the current meaning of a rich and powerful business magnate was introduced in the 1920s by *Time* magazine and is considered somewhat dated.

The languages of Africa have also made important contributions to English. The main donors have been the Bantu languages (Swahili, Sotho, Tswana, Zulu, etc.), the West African languages (Fulani, Mande, Temne, Wolof, etc.), and Afrikaans, the Dutch-based language of South Africa. From Bantu came such words as *banjo*, *bwana* ("master"), *chimpanzee*, *goober* ("peanut"), *gumbo* ("okra"), *impala* ("antelope"), *mamba* ("tree"), *marimba* (musical instrument), *tsetse* (fly), *zombie*. From West Africa came *banana*, *boogie-woogie*, *cooter* ("turtle"), *okra* (plant), *voodoo*, *yam*. *Boogie-woogie* (a style of jazz) is thought to be a reduplication of a West African word related to Mande *bugi*, "to beat drums." The word *juke* in *jukebox* was probably borrowed from a West African word akin to Wolof *dzug*, "act wicked, be disorderly." The word *jazz* is presumed to be of West African origin (compare Temne *yas*, "be extremely lively"), but the exact origin is uncertain. Afrikaans has given English such words as *aardvark*, *apartheid*, *commandeer*, *commando*, *dorp* ("village"), *kraal* ("enclosure"), *spoor*, *springbok*, *trek*, and *veld*.

Native American languages (also known as American Indian or Amerindian languages) provided English with some of its commonest loanwords, often through Spanish, Portuguese, or French: *cacao*, *cannibal*, *canoe*, *cashew*, *chipmunk*, *chocolate*, *condor*, *coyote*, *hammock*, *hickory*, *hurricane*, *igloo*, *jaguar*, *kayak*, *maize*, *moccasin*, *moose*, *muskrat*, *opossum*, *papaya*, *parka*, *pecan*, *persimmon*, *potato*, *puma*, *quinine*, *skunk*, *squash*, *tapioca*, *tepee*, *tobacco*, *toboggan*, *tomahawk*, *tomato*, *wigwam*, and *woodchuck*.

Perhaps not as exotic, but by far more important, have been the English borrowings from Latin, Greek, and French from the 1500s through the present. The influence of Latin was already thoroughly established in Old English, with some 175 loanwords before the 600s, basic words like *butere*, "butter" (Latin *būtyrum*), *cēse*, "cheese" (Latin *cāseus*), *disc*, "dish" (Latin *discus*), *pund*, "pound" (Latin *pondō*), and *strēt*, "street" (Latin *strāta*). These were popular borrowings, as distinguished from the learned or scholarly Latin borrowings in Old English between 650 and 1100, which included words like *altar*, *apostol*, "apostle" (Latin *apostolus*), *Cāsere*, "Caesar, emperor" (Latin *Caesar*), *mægester*, "master" (Latin *magister*), *messe*, "mass, eucharist" (Latin *missa*), and *temple* (Latin *templum*).

After the 1500s, the Renaissance brought into English (often via French) a great influx of learned Latin loanwords: *abdomen, anatomy, area, capsule, datum, decorum, dexterity, disc, editor, exaggerate, excavate, folio, gradation, habituate, insect, insinuate, janitor, jocular, lenient, meliorate, membrane, notorious, ossuary, parasite, physics, remunerate, sediment, torpid, transmission, ulterior, vitiate, vituperate,* and *volatile.*

Greek has also been a rich source of loanwords, though often coming into English as learned borrowings by way of Latin. Some examples of Greek loanwords are: *agnostic, arithmetic, atom, autopsy, barbarous, catalog, cataract, catastrophe, chaos, climate, comedy, drama, history, homonym, metaphor, ostracize, paradox, pathos, phenomenon, rhythm, skeleton, synagogue,* and *tragedy.*

With the Norman Conquest, French became the biggest contributor of loanwords to English as well as a conduit of innumerable Latin and Greek borrowings. Among the thousands of Norman-French and Parisian French words entering English after 1100, there were everyday terms like *change, charge, female, fruit, letter, male, mirror;* cultural terms like *art, bracelet, clarinet, diamond, fashion, fur, jewel, painting, sculpture;* cookery terms like *beef, broil, butcher, dinner, fry, pork, poultry, roast, stew, veal;* ecclesiastical terms like *chaplain, clergy, cloister, prayer, preach, priest, sacrament, saint, sermon;* judicial and legal terms like *attorney, court, crime, defendant, judge, jury, plaintiff, verdict;* governmental terms like *chancellor, country, govern, parliament, revenue, royal, state, tax;* and military terms like *army, battle, captain, defense, navy, sergeant,* and *soldier.*

From about 1700 to the present, English borrowed widely from European languages. French, the language of culture and diplomacy, continued to lead as a major source of loanwords in English, with borrowings like *apéritif, avant-garde, bidet, bourgeois, brassiere, buffet, café, camouflage, canard, chateau, croissant, cuisine, debacle, debut, debutante, dessert, etiquette, garage, gourmet,* hotel, *limousine, lingerie, pastiche, petite, pirouette, prestige, quiche, regime, risqué, salon, silhouette,* and *souvenir.* Modern French also contributed to English numerous cultural phrases, such as *faux pas,* "blunder," *haute couture,* "high fashion," *haut cuisine,* "high cuisine," *nom de guerre,* "pseudonym," *nom de plume,* "pen name," *savoir faire,* "tactfulness," *tant mieux,* "so much the better," and *tout le monde,* "everybody."

Next to French in influence was another Romance language, Italian, whose special contribution has been in music. English borrowings in this realm include *alto, aria, cadenza, contralto, crescendo, diva, falsetto, finale, forte, libretto, maestro, opera, oratorio, piano, pizzicato, prima donna, soprano, staccato, tempo, viola,* and *violin.* Italian has also given English a host of cultural terms: *arsenal, balcony, bordello, broccoli, cameo, canto, carnival, casino, confetti, dilettante, fresco, ghetto, gondola, graffiti, grotto, imbroglio, incognito, inferno, lasagna, malaria, maraschino, motto, mozzarella, paparazzo, piazza, portico, regatta, replica, stanza, stiletto, stucco, studio, torso, umbrella,* and *vermicelli.* Many Italian words were introduced into American English by immigrants of Italian origin, among them such cuisine terms as *cappuccino, espresso, fettuccine, linguini, pasta, pizza, pizzeria, ravioli, risotto, spaghetti,* and *zucchini.*

A third Romance language, Spanish, exerted its greatest influence in the Americas. Direct borrowings (with minor changes in pronunciation and none in spelling) include *adobe, armada, armadillo, bonanza, bravado, bronco, cargo, chinchilla, desperado, embargo, enchilada, guerrilla, hacienda, marijuana, matador, mesa, mosquito, negro, patio, peccadillo, pinto, poncho, pronto, pueblo, rodeo, sierra, siesta, silo, sombrero, taco, tamale, tequila, tortilla,* and *vigilante.* Loanwords adapted to English pronunciation and spelling include *alligator* (Spanish *el lagarto,* "the lizard"), *avocado* (Spanish *aguacate*), *cigar* (Spanish *cigarro*), *canyon* (Spanish *cañón*), *chili* (Spanish *chile*), *lariat* (Spanish *la reata,* "the rope"), *lasso* (Spanish *lazo*), *ranch* (Spanish *rancho*), *stampede* (Spanish *estampida*), *stevedore* (Spanish *estibador*, "loader"), *tornado* (Spanish *tronada*, "thunderstorm").

To be sure, there have been various other languages from which English borrowed at one time or another. Among the Celtic languages, Irish loanwords include *blarney, brogue, colleen, leprechaun, shamrock, shillelagh, Tory, trousers;* Scottish gave us the words *bog, clan, glen, loch, plaid, slogan;* and Welsh contributed *coracle, corgi, eisteddfod, flummery,* and perhaps *flannel.* (Welsh *bwg,* "ghost, goblin," often cited as the source of English *bug,* was most probably borrowed from Middle English *bugge.*)

In the Germanic group, English has borrowed considerably from Scandinavian, Dutch, and German.

Scandinavian: During the late Old English and Middle English period (900–1500), many basic, homespun words came into English from Old Norse (the collective name of Icelandic and Norwegian before the 1500s): *anger, cake, dirt, egg, fellow, get, happen, husband, kick, leg, rag, raise, root, skill, skin, sky, take, want, window,* and *wing.* In modern times, English has borrowed from one or another Scandinavian language the words *auk, glower, keel, muggy, rug,* and *rune.* It got from Icelandic the words *geyser* and *saga,* from Norwegian *fiord, floe, lemming, ski, slalom,* and from Swedish *nickel, ombudsman, smorgasbord,* and *tungsten.*

Dutch: The extensive commerce between the Dutch- or Flemish-speaking peoples and the English since the Middle Ages led to important English borrowings in the areas of shipping, textiles, food, and even art. Nautical and shipping terms borrowed from Dutch or Flemish include *boom, commodore, cruise, deck, dock, freight, leak, pump, scoop, scour, skipper, sloop, tackle,* and *yacht.* Textile terms include *cambric,* duck (cotton cloth), *nap* (cloth surface), *spool,* and *stripe.* English also borrowed from Dutch the word *booze* as a verb meaning "to drink heavily," along with *brandy* and *gin,* and edibles like *coleslaw, cookie, cruller, gherkin, pickle,* and *waffle.* Other common loanwords from Dutch include: *boss,* "master"; *dope,* "thick sauce" (eventually leading to "thick-headed person" and "stupefying narcotic"); *easel, etch, frolic, landscape, mart, Santa Claus, sketch, sleigh, snoop, spook, stoop,* and *uproar.*

German: A wide variety of cultural terms came into Modern English from German. Among the best-known ones are terms involving food and drink: *delicatessen, dunk, frankfurter, hamburger, kaffeeklatsch, knackwurst, lager, liverwurst, noodle, pretzel, pumpernickel, sauerkraut, schmaltz, schnapps, schnitzel,* and *zwieback.* A number of technical terms in geology have come from German: *cobalt, feldspar, gneiss, quartz,* and *zinc.* Other terms borrowed from German are the dog names *affenpinscher, dachshund, poodle,* and *schnauzer;* the musical terms *glockenspiel, leitmotif, schottische, waltz,* and *yodel;* and a handful of terms that have become fully integrated into English: *blitz, flak, hinterland, kindergarten,* and *rucksack.*

Yiddish: The mass immigration of East European Jews to Britain and America at the turn of the 20th century introduced this Germanic language to English. For a variety of reasons, Yiddish insinuated itself into the language of urban English speakers, especially in the slang register of many Americans. Well-known loanwords from Yiddish include: *bagel, chutzpah, kibitz, kosher, maven, mensch, nebbish, nosh, schlep, schlock,* and *yenta.*

In his book *The Miracle of Language* (1991), Richard Lederer attributes the unparalleled growth of English to its being "the most hospitable and democratic language that has ever existed. English has never rejected a word because of its race, creed, or national origin. Having welcomed into its vocabulary words from a multitude of other languages and dialects, ancient and modern, far and near, English is unique in the number and variety of its borrowed words." And he quotes the poet Carl Sandburg: "The English language hasn't got where it is by being pure."

CHAPTER 35

naturalization of loanwords:

how aliens become citizens

When people living in a foreign country apply for citizenship, they have to go through a process of naturalization. There are various legal requirements for naturalization such as living in the adopted country a specified number of years. Once these requirements are fulfilled, the applicants undergo a solemn ceremony in which they pledge loyalty to their new country. They then stop being aliens and become full-fledged citizens.

Foreign words are also said to undergo naturalization. After being adopted in a new country for a certain length of time, they may become naturalized. What that means is not as simple as standing up before a judge and swearing allegiance to the new country.

In fact, there are no hard-and-fast rules for a foreign word to become a naturalized citizen of another country. The naturalization of words is gradual, involving many changes and adjustments, and not always successful. Words that fail the process fail to become citizens. Countless words have met this dismal fate.

Comparing foreign words to foreign persons may sound like an absurd exaggeration, but there is considerable truth in it. Lexicographers, who agonize over new words to determine their status in the language, often can't make up their minds whether a particular word can be accorded citizenship. The authoritative *Oxford English Dictionary* (*OED*), torn by the problem, was moved in its "General Explanations" to create a new intermediate category of words called *denizens,* which it described as "fully naturalized as to use, but not as to form, inflexion, or pronunciation, as *aide-de-camp, carte-de-visite,* and *table d'hôte.*" So there you have it: Words may be aliens, denizens, or citizens, just like people.

ANGLICIZATION

The naturalization of a foreign word in English is called *anglicization.* Most people find it hard to believe that such common English words as *beef, chair, city, just, line, pay, please,* and *sure* are loanwords. But they are, being anglicized forms of Old French *boef, chaiere, citet, juste, ligne, paier, plaisir,* and *seur.* As these examples show, anglicization means making the words conform to English patterns, as of pronunciation and spelling. French loanwords like these flooded English in the Middle Ages and were quickly assimilated into the English vernacular. Later borrowings found the transition to English less of a smooth ride.

As a rule, a foreign word that fills a real need or gap in the borrowing language has an excellent chance of becoming naturalized. If it's useful, people will use it. Examples of such words are food items like *hamburger, pizza, sushi, curry, chili, mango,* and *bagel.*

But even such words undergo some degree of anglicization, whether in pronunciation, form, or meaning. Foreign proper names, especially the names of cities, are often anglicized: *Antwerp* (from *Antwerpen*), *Athens* (from *Athenae*), *Munich* (from *München*), and *Naples* (from *Napoli*).

LA RÉSISTANCE

Resistance to the adoption of new words began with the overflow of borrowings from the 1500s onward. As Robert Claiborne writes in *Our Marvelous Native Tongue* (1983), ". . . of the more than ten thousand new words brought into English during the sixteenth and seventeenth centuries, only about half are still in use." He goes on:

> Why some words survive and others, equally useful (or equally pretentious), perish is, as the philologist Albert C. Baugh reminds us, one of 'the things about language that we cannot explain.' . . . why did 'impede' survive and its opposite, 'expede,' disappear—especially since we have since had to contrive a substitute, 'expedite'? If 'disagree' and 'disabuse' are still acceptable, why not 'disaccustom'? Nobody will ever know the answer. (*Disaccustom*, by the way, has become acceptable; check your latest dictionary.)

The loanwords that survive usually undergo a certain amount of change in order to assume an English form. The most obvious change is in pronunciation. Thus, the word *marble* was borrowed from Old French *marbre*, but the difficulty of pronouncing the two consecutive *r* sounds caused the second one to be changed to an *l*. Another example is the group of words that includes *messenger, passenger,* and *scavenger,* in each of which an *n* was inserted in the original forms (*messager, passager, scavager*) before *-ger*, apparently to make pronunciation easier. Many loanwords, especially those borrowed from French and Italian, have variant pronunciations: one replicating the original and one that has been anglicized. Some examples are *bourgeois* (boor zhwah' or boor' zhwah), *crescendo* (kri shen'do or kri-sen'do), *papier-mâché* (pah pyay' mə shay' or pay'pər mə shay').

WHERE THE STRESS LIES

Another common change is in the placement of the stress on loanwords. A certain amount of wavering occurs at first between the foreign word stress and the English one. This can still be seen in the variant pronunciations of words like *ballet* (ba lay' or bal' ey), *debris* (də bree' or day' bree), *garage* (*U.S.* gə rahzh' or gə rahj' or *Brit.* gar' ij), *massage* (*U.S.* mə sahzh' or *Brit.* mas' ahzh), and *melee* (may' lay or mel' ay).

The most obvious sign that a word has been borrowed is its spelling. Non-English letters or accent marks reveal a foreign source, and incomplete anglicization is shown by variant spellings like *café* or *cafe, coupé* or *coupe, matinée* or *matinee, facade* or *façade, canyon* or *cañon, melee* or *mêlée, role* or *rôle.* In some cases, the foreign accent mark is retained to prevent mispronunciation of the word, as in *blasé* (blah zay' or blah'zay), which otherwise might be pronounced (blays); in other cases accent marks are kept to prevent confusing one word with another, as with *résumé,* which, if unaccented, could be easily confused with the verb *resume.*

Foreign plural forms are often adopted in English either unanglicized or forming variant English plurals, as in this list:

addenda, plural of addendum (there are no "addendas")

alumnae, plural of alumna (there are no "alumnas")

alumni, plural of *alumnus* (there are no "alumnuses")

analyses, plural of *analysis* (there are no "analysises")

antennas or *antennae*, variant plurals of *antenna*

appendixes or *appendices*, variant plurals of *appendix*

axes, plural of *axis* (there are no "axises")

bacilli, plural of *bacillus* (there are no "bacilluses")

beaus or *beaux*, variant plurals of *beau*

cacti or *cactuses* or *cactus*, variant plurals of *cactus*

crises, plural of *crisis* (there are no "crisises")

criteria or *criterions*, variant plurals of *criterion*

diagnoses, plural of *diagnosis* (there are no "diagnosises")

errata or *erratas*, variant plurals of *erratum*

fungi or *funguses*, variant plurals of *fungus*

hypotheses, plural of *hypothesis* (there are no "hypothesises")

larvae, plural of *larva* (there are no "larvas")

nuclei or *nucleuses*, variant plurals of *nucleus*

ova, plural of *ovum* (there are no "ovas")

radii or *radiuses*, variant plurals of *radius*

Loanwords from German belong in a special category, since German nouns are capitalized. Older borrowings from German are anglicized by dropping the initial capitals, as in *blitzkrieg, frankfurter, glockenspiel, kindergarten, kitsch,* and *sauerkraut.* But more recent loans tend to retain the capitalized form: *Anschluss, Realpoli-*

tik, Schadenfreude, Weltanschauung, Weltgeist, and *Weltschmerz.* However, the custom is to retain the German spelling without the initial capital.

Anglicization is a slow process. Though English is quick to borrow the words it needs, it is not so quick to blend them into the language. There are many reasons for this resistance. One is that foreign words are regarded as more elegant or glamorous than "plain English." The language of fashion excels in adopting foreign words and phrases, especially terms imported from France: *bijou, boutonniere, chapeau, chateleine, chemisette, faconne, marquisette, mousseline,* and *poult-de-sole.* So does the language of cooking: *à la mode, al dente, au fromage, bouquet garni, cacciatore, en brochette, flambé, parmentier,* and *vol-au-vent.* Another reason is that a loanword often has a precise meaning that cannot be rendered in an equivalent English word and so it remains uniquely foreign. *Schadenfreude,* meaning "a feeling of pleasure one gets from someone else's misfortune" (literally, "damage-joy") is such a word.

ENGLISH DENIZENS

Foreign phrases, because of their length and complexity, are especially difficult to anglicize. Here is a list of phrases that have long been "denizens" of English, some for hundreds of years, yet have remained unchanged in spelling (and to some extent in pronunciation):

AU CONTRAIRE "on the contrary"

BON APPÉTIT! "Hearty appetite!"

C'EST LA VIE! "That's life!"

ENFANT TERRIBLE "a shockingly unconventional person" (literally, "terrible child")

E PLURIBUS UNUM "out of many, one"

FOLIE DE GRANDEUR "delusion of grandeur"

HOMME DU MONDE "man of the world"

J'ACCUSE "I accuse"

LAPSUS LINGUAE "a slip of the tongue"

MIRABILE DICTU "wondrous to relate"

NIL DESPERANDUM "never to despair"

PIÈCE DE RÉSISTANCE "the chief or outstanding item"

SEMPER FIDELIS "always faithful"

TEMPUS FUGIT "time flies"

TOUT LE MONDE "the whole world"

VENI, VIDI, VICI "I came, I saw, I conquered"

VIVE LA DIFFÉRENCE! "Long live the difference!"

VOX POPULI "the voice of the people"

Strange and non-English though these phrases may sound to many English speakers, they are nevertheless established in English literary usage and can be regarded as fully naturalized in their use, though not in their spelling, pronunciation, and other aspects. In short, they are English denizens.

CHAPTER 36

the integration of foreign words and phrases:
how they find a home in English

Most of the examples in the previous chapter are recognizable borrowings, bearing the imprint of their foreign sources. Few of us would mistake them for native English words. But the fact is that English has thousands of loanwords that have become so integrated into the common vocabulary that, unless you were a language scholar, you couldn't distinguish them from what the Victorians called "Anglo-Saxon" words, that is, words traceable back to Old English. How did these loanwords manage the feat of assimilating into English without leaving behind a clue to their origins?

One way this happened was by the massive influx into Middle and Modern English of French and Latin words with similar beginnings and endings, which by reinforcing each other infiltrated the language without raising a red flag. These beginnings and endings are the prefixes and suffixes of innumerable borrowings like *abhor, abjure, abrade* (**ab-**), *adapt, adhere, adjust* (**ad-**), *baggage, carriage, damage* (**-age**), *glossary, library, military* (**-ary**), *bicycle, bifocal, bilingual* (**bi-**), *colleague, collect, collude* (**col-**), *combine, compare, commingle* (**com-**), *confer, convene, consign* (**con-**), *deface, deform, delay* (**de-**), *disagree, disband, discredit* (**dis-**), *accident, different, insistent* (**-ent**), *edible, horrible, visible* (**-ible**), *illegal, illogical, illegitimate* (**il-**), *immature, imperfect, impossible* (**im-**), *informal, injustice, insecure* (**in-**), *irrational, irregular, irrelevant* (**ir-**), *action, addition, creation* (**-ion**), and hundreds of other words beginning with *ante-, anti-, mal-, mis-, per-, pre-, pro-, re-, sub-,* and *trans-,* and ending in *-ism, -ist, -ity, -ize, -sion, -tion,* and others. (See the chapter on **Prefixes and Suffixes.**)

Word formation in English wouldn't be nearly as productive in English today without the prefixes and suffixes that came into the language through borrowing. The same can be said of combining forms like *bio-, chromo-, chrono-, eco-, mini-, photo-,* and many others. (See the chapter on **Combining Forms.**)

Another way borrowings become assimilated in English is through folk etymology (see the chapter on **Folk Etymology**). The French and Latin borrowings that saturated English with new prefixes, suffixes, and combining forms were learned borrowings, used by literate or educated people, as opposed to so-called popular borrowings, which were passed on orally by the naïve or unschooled. Often, though, learned words made their way into common talk, but in such a manner that the original word was transformed into something entirely different. Just as in the game of "telephone" a word or message whispered by the first player to the next becomes significantly altered by the time it reaches the last player, so a borrowed word uttered by one speaker can become a different word in the mouth of the fiftieth or hundredth speaker. This process is amusingly illustrated by the self-educated Mrs. Malaprop in Richard Sheridan's 1775 comedy, *The Rivals.*

Mrs. Malaprop's name was derived by Sheridan from French *mal à propos*, "inappropriate," which represents the way this character misused words, usually by substituting similar-sounding but completely inappropriate ones for them, with ridiculous results. Sheridan's audience belonged to the intelligentsia of his day, who found great hilarity in the stupid mistakes of the uneducated Mrs. Malaprop. Today her malapropisms (a word derived from her name) sound contrived, as indeed they were, but in Sheridan's time they seemed like the typical verbal blunders committed by those of the lower classes who aspired to better themselves.

Here are some examples of Mrs. Malaprop's distortions of learned Latinate words:

"He is the very pine-apple of politeness!" [pinnacle]

"Why, murder's the matter! slaughter's the matter! killing's the matter!—but he can tell you the perpendiculars." [particulars]

"Sure, if I reprehend any thing in this world it is the use of my oracular tongue, and a nice derangement of epitaphs!" [apprehend, vernacular, arrangement, epithets]

Unlike malapropisms, which result from ignorance, the verbal errors known as spoonerisms are usually temporary slips of the tongue. Spoonerisms, named after William Archibald Spooner (1844–1930), an Oxford clergyman and lecturer, are unintended transpositions of the initial sounds of words or syllables, resulting in some truly humorous phrases. It appears from anecdotal evidence that Spooner was habitually prone to commit spoonerisms. When World War I ended, he told a friend, "When the boys come back from France, we'll have the hags flung out." He meant, of course, that they'd have the flags hung out. One day he walked into the Oxford dean's office and asked the secretary, "Is the bean dizzy?" On another occasion he reprimanded a student, "You hissed my mystery lecture," and once he referred to Queen Victoria as "our queer old dean." One time he confounded an audience by remarking, "We all know what it is to have a half-warmed fish inside us." It turned out that he meant "a half-formed wish."

The vocabulary changes produced by folk etymology are not due either to errors of ignorance or of speech pathology, but result, paradoxically, from the thorough assimilation of a borrowed word. When such a word becomes established and familiar, people try to account for its origin by associating it with other familiar words. So the Algonquian word for a common North American rodent, *otchek* or *otchig*, is changed by folk etymology to *woodchuck*. Similarly, the Spanish *cucaracha* is associated with the familiar English words *cock*, "male chicken," and *roach*, "a freshwater fish," to give us *cockroach*, though this insect has little to do with either a chicken or a fish.

Still another reason for the smooth transition of loanwords into English is that most borrowings are nouns and noun phrases, which are easily integrated into English sentences. A noun like the French-origin *ricochet* can simply replace the English noun *rebound* in the sentence *The bullet's ricochet struck the wall.* The conversion of the noun to the verb *ricochet* (*The bullet ricocheted*) occurred in English (see the chapter on **Functional Shift or Conversion**). The Latin-origin noun *genuflection*, "bending on one knee in reverence or worship," is harder to replace with a synonym, but it was easily converted by back-formation to the verb *genuflect* (see the chapter on **Back-Formation**).

The preponderance of noun borrowings is not altogether remarkable, since studies have shown that nouns are more frequent in language than other parts of speech.

One of the important consequences of borrowing from foreign languages and of building new words from foreign elements is the creation of large numbers of synonyms. Peter Mark Roget (1779–1869), the author of *Roget's Thesaurus of English Words & Phrases* (1852), undertook his classic work in order to organize the vast number of English synonyms into a coherent and logical system. He writes in the book's Introduction:

> I have admitted a considerable number of words and phrases borrowed from other languages, chiefly the French and Latin, some of which may be considered as already naturalized; while others, though avowedly foreign, are frequently employed in English composition, particularly in familiar style, on account of their being peculiarly expressive, and because we have no corresponding words of equal force in our language. The rapid advances which are being made in scientific knowledge . . . create a continual demand for the formation of new terms to express new agencies, new wants, and new combinations. Such terms, from being at first merely technical, are rendered, by more general use, familiar to the multitude and . . . eventually incorporated into the language, which they contribute to enlarge and to enrich. *Neologies* of this kind are perfectly legitimate, and highly advantageous; and they necessarily introduce those gradual and progressive changes which every language is destined to undergo.

It is clear from Roget's remarks that he welcomed the many synonyms that borrowings brought into English and didn't regard them as intrusive or superfluous. Unlike Roget, his contemporary, the prolific English philologist William Barnes (1801–86), deplored what he considered the unnecessary doubling of words and advocated replacing loanwords with obsolete Old English terms or with new formations from native elements. To replace such Latin-origin words as *ancestor, caution, democracy, grammar,* and *perambulator,* Barnes coined the forms *foreelder, forewit, folkdom, speechlore,* and *pushwainling.* Roget resisted such purism (as did most English speakers) and included in his thesaurus synonymous pairs like *greatness* and *magnitude, height* and *altitude, length* and *longitude, lunatic* and *madman, make* and *manufacture, niggardly* and *insufficient,* and many other pairs of synonyms.

No two synonyms have exactly the same meaning or application. They may differ in use, one being formal and the other informal or slang (e.g., *insane* vs. *crazy* or *nuts*), or in connotation, or in idiomatic expression. The synonym studies found in college-level and unabridged dictionaries draw meaningful distinctions between such synonyms as *illegal, unlawful,* and *illicit,* or *help, aid,* and *assist,* or *necessary, requisite,* and *indispensable.* It follows that many borrowings are not merely duplicates of existing words, but supply a new dimension or nuance that is lacking in the existing words. Were it not for the novel qualities they impart to our speech and communication, it is doubtful that most borrowings would find a home in the language.

CHAPTER 37

word genealogies:

reconstructing the history of a word

All borrowed words have histories. To determine a word's history one has to trace it back to its earliest source. In a way, word history is the reverse of word formation: it moves backward rather than forward. Etymologists (students of word history) trace back and reconstruct the history of words, and their work is reflected in the etymologies of dictionaries.

One of the coolest features in dictionaries is the etymology, usually found between brackets at the beginning or end of a dictionary entry. We are all fascinated by where words come from—the origins of words such as *Halloween* or *octopus* or *democracy*. Some dictionaries try to offer an origin for every word. If they do, you will be surprised at all the abbreviations used, but again, this is something one learns to use easily with practice. Other books give word origins for fewer words but describe them in more detail. If you are reading that type of book and cannot find the origin of a particular word, there are plenty of dictionaries and other word-origins books to look in, and Internet dictionaries and search engines can also be helpful.

A dictionary etymology tells us what is known of an English word before it became the word entered in that dictionary. If the word was formed in English, the etymology shows, to whatever extent is not already obvious from the shape of the word, what materials were used to form it. If the word was borrowed into English, the etymology traces the borrowing process backward from the point at which the word entered English to the earliest records of the ancestral language. Where it is relevant, an etymology notes words from other languages that are related ("akin") to the word in the dictionary entry, but that are not in the direct line of borrowing.

A FAMILY HISTORY OF WORDS

An historical dictionary like the *Oxford English Dictionary* (*OED*) devotes itself to giving "complete" etymologies. Most unabridged and many college-level dictionaries also offer full etymologies. But the fact of the matter is that all or most modern dictionaries draw much of their historical and etymological information from the *OED*.

Etymologies are similar to genealogies, and the vocabulary of etymology is borrowed from genealogy. One speaks of languages and words as being "related," belonging to the same "family," and as being "descended." Etymology is one of the oldest and most established branches of language study. Classical Greek investigators of words looked for the *etymon* or true meaning of a word. In Spain, Isidore of Seville compiled a multivolume encyclopedia named *Books of Origins or Etymologies*. In the

18th century, Nathaniel Bailey was the first to explain the etymologies of English words in a dictionary, but lacking a complete understanding of the interrelations of languages, he made many errors. In the 1800s, Noah Webster furthered etymological work but, again, made many errors.

When the British became a large part of the affairs of India in the 1700s, they became interested in the classical language, Sanskrit. This interest led to a study of a Sanskrit grammar made about 400 B.C.E. by Panini, whose study was compared to the grammar of Greek and Latin, revealing many similarities among the languages. Eventually, it was concluded that the likenesses were not accidental and that the three languages, as well as Gothic, Celtic, and others, were descended from a common source, of which no record has survived: Indo-European. Linguists have been able to reconstruct the earlier stages of Indo-European languages and their work has influenced today's studies of etymologies. Sir William Jones (1746–94), W. W. Skeat (1835–1912), and other modern linguists transformed the study with painstaking analysis of textual evidence from many languages, converting etymology from guesswork to a scholarly branch of historical linguistics.

An etymologist must know a good deal about the history of English and also about the relationships of sound and meaning and their changes over time. Knowledge is also needed of the various processes by which words are created within Modern English. Etymologists look for the following in their quest to provide a correct etymology: an explanation of the differences in sounds between a word and its supposed source; a reasonable relationship of meaning between a word and its supposed source; and, in the case of borrowing, historical contact between the two cultures at the time the assumed borrowing occurred. Preparing etymologies requires the application of scholarship, skepticism, and common sense. Fact and hypothesis are involved in this work, as what is known of the origin and development of a word (or its elements) is a matter of chance.

When all attempts to provide a satisfactory etymology have failed, an etymologist may have to declare that a word's origin is "uncertain" or "unknown." The label "origin uncertain" or "origin unknown" in an etymology does not necessarily mean that the etymologist is unaware of various speculations about the origin of a term; rather it means that no single theory is backed by enough evidence to warrant its inclusion in a serious work of reference.

The information gathered by etymologists is given in a kind of shorthand in a dictionary's bracketed etymology. The etymology will usually specify the period or year the word first appeared in English, what it meant, how it was spelled, what other languages it appeared in, and what language it came from if it was borrowed. It is the purpose of the etymology to trace a word as far as possible in English and to trace the pre-English source as far back as possible.

ANTEDATINGS

Etymology is a painstaking discipline, described by Barbara Wallraff as "the archaeology of words." When you do see a date in a dictionary etymology, do remember that it only indicates the earliest written or printed use that the editors were able to discover. That means that the date is subject to change if and when evidence of earlier usage is found. Editors of the *OED* are constantly searching and calling for antedatings of words and phrases, and are surprisingly successful in their quest. Here is a list of some recent antedatings published in the *Oxford English Dictionary News* of June and September 2005:

PATIO (antedated to 1776 from 1800)
PASTRY-COOK (antedated to 1656 from 1712)
PASSWORD (antedated to 1799 from c. 1817)
PAWNSHOP (antedated to 1656 from 1712)
PEDICURE (antedated to 1839 from 1842)

An etymologist tracing the history of a word must review the etymologies in previous editions and those in other dictionaries. A useful piece of information that has been previously overlooked can be added or new evidence used to review the account of the word's origin. Such evidence may be unearthed by the etymologist or may be the product of published research by other scholars. In writing new etymologies, the etymologist must have knowledge of the languages from which a new term may have been created or borrowed, and must research and analyze a wide range of documented evidence and published sources in tracing a word's history. The etymologist must sift through theories and try to evaluate the evidence conservatively but fairly to arrive at the soundest possible etymology that the available information permits.

HOW TO READ ETYMOLOGICAL ABBREVIATIONS

The abbreviations in dictionary etymologies are sometimes difficult to understand, so we will try to clarify them in the following examples:

abandon, *v.* [ME *abandonen;* OFr. *abandoner* <*mettre a bandon*>, to put under (someone else's) ban, relinquish; see BAN]

This says: The verb *abandon* has been in English since the Middle English (ME) period (approx. 1125–1475), at which time the usual form was *abandonen.* It came into Middle English from Old French (OFr., approx. 800–1400) *abandoner,* a word which resulted from the shortening of the phrase *mettre a bandon,* to put under (someone else's) ban, to relinquish. For further information about *ban,* see that word in the dictionary.

Or try this one:

infantry *n.* [MF & OIt; MF *infanterie,* fr. OIt *infanteria,* fr. *infante* infant, boy, footman, foot soldier (fr. L *infant-, infans* infant) + *-eria* -ry - more at INFANT]

The noun *infantry* came into English from either the Middle French (MF, approx. 1400–1600) *infanterie* or the Old Italian (OIt) *infanteria.* The Middle French word came from the Old Italian *infanteria,* a military term derived from the word *infante,* which can mean a foot soldier in addition to the sense of an infant, boy, or footman. This Old Italian word developed from the Latin (L) root *infant-,* stem of *infans,* meaning "an infant." Finally, there is more information to be found under the entry for *infant.*

There, that was not so hard. The key to reading the etymologies in dictionaries is (1) to read the part of the Guide to the Dictionary so you can understand how etymologies are presented, and (2) practice!

In reading etymologies, you may also see that the word consists of various parts, each with its own meaning. If, for example, you look up the word *ambidextrous,* meaning "able to use both hands equally well," you will see that it came from the Latin word *ambidexter,* and that it is made up of two parts: *ambi,* which means "both," and *dexter,* which means "right hand." Such information can help you to remember the word's meaning and to learn new words. By associating this word with *ambivalent,* which means "unable to choose between two things," and *ambiguous,* which means "open to two or more meanings," you can learn three words for the price of one.

Outside of using respectable dictionaries, one can attempt to find etymological information through a search engine. By searching on + "the whole nine yards" + "origin," or + hamburger + etymology, you can read some interesting theories regarding a word's or phrase's history. Some dictionaries on the Internet could be used and relied upon for etymologies, like the *OED* or the Merriam-Webster's dictionaries or the *American Heritage Dictionary.*

Etymology is history, and history embodies the wisdom of the ages. "Words are the only things that last forever"; wrote the essayist William Hazlitt, "they are more durable than the eternal hills."

PART 7

conclusion

genetic drift:
English around the world

There's some truth in George Bernard Shaw's famous quip, "England and America are two countries separated by a common language." Well-known differences exist between the English of England and that of America in such areas as spelling (*eon/aeon, center/centre, favor/favour*), in vocabulary (*bus/coach, truck/lorry, gas/petrol*), in syntax (*to the hospital/to hospital; I don't have/I've not got*) and, of course, in pronunciation.

A good example of divided usage is the diagonal line (/) used above to show divided usage: the Merriam-Webster's dictionaries call it a "diagonal," while the Oxford University Press called it a "shilling mark" before Great Britain converted to decimal currency, but since then has opted for "oblique." Even in the United States, the Government Printing Office's Manual gives you a choice between "virgule, solidus, separatrix, shilling";

while the *New York Public Library Writer's Guide to Style and Usage* calls it a "slash," but lets us know that "The slash goes by many names: virgule, cancel, shilling, diagonal, slant bar, stroke, solidus, and separatrix." In short, I/we or he/she can opt for either/or or any/all of the above.

Since English usage is not regulated by an academy, as is French or Spanish, different varieties of speech and writing are common and acceptable in English. In this book, the word formations and patterns we have explored are in the variety of English known as Standard American English. One reason for using this variety is the fact that we, the authors, are Americans and feel more at home in American English than in any other kind of English. Another compelling reason is that at present American English is the most widely used variety of English, spoken by a population of over 295 million. By contrast, British English is spoken by 58 million people. The other major varieties, including Canadian, Australian, South African, Indian, and West Indian English, have comparably fewer speakers. And a third significant fact is that, since World War II, American English has steadily grown in prestige and influence, to the extent that it has by now become the chief contributor of new vocabulary to the English language.

DOUBLE STANDARDS

But not all Americans communicate in Standard American English, and one might reasonably ask whether the processes of word formation we've been describing apply also to other varieties of English. "Standard English" itself is not clearly defined. While the term is generally used to mean the established speech and writing of educated people, linguists have distinguished between *Formal Standard* (e.g., "I have none"; "This is she") and *In-*

formal Standard (e.g., "I don't have any"; "It's me"). Moreover, we distinguish Standard English from nonstandard English, which includes dialectal varieties, popular slang, and the jargons of many fields (business, journalism, science, etc.).

In general, the processes of word formation which we find in Standard English operate also in nonstandard English. Just because a word is considered slang, the *form* of the word need not be slang. For example, the word *gagman*, meaning "a humorist," is slang, but the *form* is a standard compound of *gag* and *man*. It may seem paradoxical, but, unless they are borrowings, most nonstandard words derive from standard ones. The approximately 1,000 slang synonyms for "drunk" (e.g., *boozed, loaded, soused, stinko*) in Lester V. Berrey and Melvin Van Den Bark's *American Thesaurus of Slang* (1947) derive from standard words and phrases. The slang and jargon of bloggers (writers of Web logs) are similarly based on the standard vocabulary, for example, *deadtree media*, "printed newspapers and magazines," *ego-googling* (or *e-googling*), "Looking up one's name in the search engine Google to check on its prominence," *to flame*, "to hotly attack or criticize (someone)," *idiotarian*, "an advocate of ideas considered idiotic."

The following are some examples of nonstandard (mainly slang) words listed under various types of formations:

Acronyms and abbreviations:
AC-DC (a bisexual)

A.K. (an old fogey, from Yiddish *alter kaker*)

M or *em* (morphine)

TABU ("typical army ball-up")

Back-formations (most commonly *back slang*, the reversal of the letters of a word):

epar (rape)

mur (rum)

reeb (beer)

yob (boy)

Blends or portmanteau words:
blaxploitation (black exploitation)

scuzzy "disgusting" (perhaps blend of *scummy* and *fuzzy*)

swingle (a swinging single)

Clippings or shortenings:
ki (kilogram of marijuana)

Hebe (Hebrew)

perv (pervert), *vert* (pervert)

tranks (tranquilizers)

Compounds:
airhead "fool, dolt"

coffin nail "a cigarette"

homeboy "close friend"

looney tunes "a lunatic"

Derivatives:
airheaded "stupid"

bitchin (or *bichin*) "excellent, great"

discombobulate "annoy"

worriment "annoyance"

Diminutives:
bitty, bitsy

eentsy-weentsy

itsy-bitsy, teeny

teeny-weeny,

yummy

Eponyms:
Doctor Hall (alcohol)

Doctor White (cocaine)

Raggedy Ann (LSD)

Robin Hood (a philanthropist)

Sam Hill (the devil)

Euphemism:
catched (pregnant)

landowner (dead person)

nut factory (insane asylum)

Folk etymology:
coconut (cocaine)

cuckoo (a cuckold)

twilight (a toilet)

Inheritance or pattern formation:
IMFU (immense military foul-up)

JANFU (joint army-navy foul-up)

SNAFU (situation normal, all fouled-up)

Loanwords:
schicker (drunkard)

schlemozzle (a brawl)

schlock (junk, narcotics)

schlub or *zhlub* (oaf, dolt)—all from Yiddish

Metaphor:
cash in one's chips (to die)

Do they grow corn in Iowa? (sure)

flog a dead horse (discuss, debate)

tough nut to crack (problem)

Neologisms:
crunk (crazy drunk)

drailing (drunk e-mailing)

e-mauling (stalking by e-mail)

mouse potato (a computer addict)

whip (a fast car)

Nonsense words:
bumfluff (nonsense)

doozandazy (gadget)

tootledum (fool)

Onomatopoeia:
barf (vomit)

keck (to cough, retch)

puke (vomit)

smooch (kiss)

Reduplication:
bibble-babble (jabber)

dumdum (stupid person)

rowdy-dowdy (noisy)

yackety-yak (jabber)

We pointed out above that marked differences exist between Standard American English and Standard British English. But these differences rarely interfere with communication, especially since, thanks to television and transatlantic travel, many equivalent words and usages have become familiar to both Britons and Americans. Even where differences exist—and there are dialectal differences within the United States (Northern, Midland, Southern, etc.) and within Great Britain (Lancashire, Midlands, Yorkshire, etc.)—the language is uniformly English, as are the ways in which words are formed.

A WORLD OF "ENGLISHES"

Contrasted with American and British English is the global network of "Englishes" that make up World English. According to the *Oxford Guide to World English* (Tom McArthur, ed., 2002), English is a significant language in 104 countries, from Anguilla to Zimbabwe, from Antigua and Barbuda to Zambia. In at least 75 of these countries, English has an official or semi-official status. There are noticeable differences in the vocabularies of many of these countries.

Canadian English is unique in showing the influence of both American and British English: American *gas, truck, wrench* (instead of British *petrol, lorry, spanner*), but British *braces, porridge, tap* (instead of American *suspenders, oatmeal, faucet*).

The vocabulary of Australian English tends to be informal, freely shortening words (*Aussie,* "Australian," *barbie,* "barbecue," *Chrissy,* "Christmas") and attaching the suffix *-o* to many words: *compo,* "workers' compensation," *derro,* "derelict," *reffo,* "refugee," *smoko,* "a work break."

African English has a varied vocabulary, including the English of West Africa (Ghana, Nigeria, Liberia, etc.), of East Africa (Kenya, Tanzania, Uganda), and of Southern Africa (Botswana, Lesotho, Republic of South Africa, Zambia, Zimbabwe, etc.). Typical formations are compounds, such as West African *chewing stick,* "wooden stick used for brushing teeth," *highlife,* "a style of jazz music and dance," and *tight friend,* "close friend"; and hybrid forms, such as East African (Swahili) *mbenzi,* "rich person," *wabenzi,* "rich people" (literally, "owner(s) of a Mercedes-*Benz*"); and Southern African *muti medicine,* (Zulu) "folk medicine," *larney party,* "ostentatious party."

Indian English has also been creative in word formation, with such English-Hindi hybrid forms as *kaccha road,* "dirt road," *policewala,* "policeman," *relgari,* "railway train," use of the suffix *-ji* as an honorific form of address (*Gandhiji, sahibji*), new compounds (*batch-mate,* "classmate," *head-bath,* "hair wash"), new verbs (*condole* "offer condolences," *prepone,* "not postpone"), and archaic or obsolescent forms like *issueless,* "childless," and *needful,* "the needy."

Then there's also *Euro-English,* the use of Americanisms and anglicisms in Continental Europe. Despite the many languages represented in the European Union, English has unofficially become the lingua franca of this organization. As a result, many English words have infiltrated most languages of Europe.

Since the 1960s, *franglais* (a blend of *français* and *anglais*) has denoted the French language "contaminated" by many anglicisms, such as *drugstore, flashback, fun, okay,* and *striptease.* In 1966, *Time* magazine described it this way: "Franglais permits a Frenchman to do *le planning et research* on *le manpowerisation* of a *complexe industrielle* before taking off for *le weekend* in *le country.*" One of the ways the French regulators of the language dealt with the influx was to Gallicize the most common anglicisms, changing words like *meeting, rocket,* and *ticket* into *métingue, roquette,* and *tiquet.*

German has been by far more open than French to borrowings from English, especially American English, either adopting the loanwords to German, as in *babysitten,* "to baby-sit," *Beiprodukt,* "by-product," *boxen,* "to box," or leaving them unchanged, as *feedback, image, rally,* and *team.* Dutch has also borrowed extensively from English, especially technical terms like *crucial, informatie,* "information," *management, research,* and loan translations like *diepvries,* "deep freeze," and *gouden handdruk,* "golden handshake."

The impact of American English on the Scandinavian languages has been extensive, including loanwords, loan translations, idioms, and semantic transfers. Examples given in the *Oxford Guide to World English* include English *strike,* rendered as *strejke* in Danish, *streike* in Norwegian, and *strejk* in Swedish; *self-service,* loan-translated in Danish and Norwegian as *selvbetjening* and in Swedish as *självbetjaning*; *communication*, found in Danish and Swedish as *kommunikation*, and *kommunikasjon* in Norwegian.

The term *Spanglish* (a blend of *Spanish* and *English*) has been used informally since the 1960s for various mixtures of Spanish and English found among Spanish-speaking peoples. The influence of English on Spanish is most prominent in loanwords, such as *bistec*, "beefsteak," *boicot*, "boycott," and *boicotear*, "to boycott," *boxeo*, "boxing," and *boxear*, "to box," *droga*, "drug," and *droguero*, "druggist," *parquear*, "to park," *pushar*, "to push," and *troca*, "truck." Many loans have not been Hispanicized, for example, *agenda*, *bus*, *cake*, *jazz*, and *jet*. Also common are loanshifts (semantic loans), in which the meanings of English words are attached to similar-sounding Spanish words, for example, *atender*, "take care," shifting in meaning to "attend (school)"; *elevador*, "a hoist," shifting in meaning to "elevator" and competing with *ascensor*.

English-influenced Italian has been called informally *itangliano* (a blend of *italiano*, "Italian," and *anglo*, "English"). Several hundred English loanwords have been recorded in Italian, most of them popularized by the media, for example, *budget*, *club*, *design*, *know-how*, *market*, *shopping*, *show*, and *style*. Italianicized forms include *bluffare*, "to bluff," *un night*, "a night club," and *uno snob*, "a snob."

Slavic languages, especially Russian and Polish, have been influenced by English chiefly in the areas of sports, food, business, and technology. The influence has been largely lexical, with loanwords like *futbol*, *khokkey* (hockey), *match*, *sprint*, *bifshtek*, *puding*, *boykot*, *miting*, *tanker*, and *kompyuter* in Russian, and *playoff*, *tennis*, *bit*, *hardware*, *interface*, and *monitor* in Polish.

It is generally recognized that at the start of the 21st-century English is well on its way to becoming an international language, at least in the sense of being the language of choice in global communication. That is probably as close as the world can get to what the creators of artificial languages like Esperanto, Interlingua, and Volapük dreamed of in the 19th and 20th centuries. And whatever its imperfections, English has the advantage of being a natural language, with millions of speakers who are able to modify, shape, embellish, and expand it at will.

CHAPTER 39

summing up:
a review of word formation

The road of word formation is a winding and often surprising one filled with byways, detours, and unexpected discoveries. In his book, *Language* (1933), the great American linguist Leonard Bloomfield called word formation "the stepchild of traditional school grammar," because of its neglect in education. Apparently the variety and seeming unpredictability of word formation stymied schoolteachers. Yet, as we have seen, a close study of word formation reveals patterns and processes that are eminently teachable and, in the end, rewarding to most pupils.

A REVIEW OF *THE LIFE OF LANGUAGE*

What follows is a recapitulation, in alphabetical order, of some of the patterns and processes of word formation we have discussed throughout the book:

Abbreviations and **acronyms** are more productive sources of new vocabulary that they might seem at first glance. A look at the daily paper will spot numerous abbreviations, such as DWI ("driving while intoxicated"), GOP ("Grand Old Party," nickname of the Republican Party), CDs (compact disks), and DVDs (digital versatile disks, formerly digital video disks). Some words formed from abbreviations are based on earlier words derived from abbreviations (e.g., *guppie* for "gay urban professional," based on *yuppie*, "young urban professional"). The abbreviation ID for *identification* is also used as a noun (*Show me your ID*) and as a verb meaning "to identify" (*The detective ID'd the suspect*). Acronyms, formed from the first letters of a series of words and pronounced as one word, include examples like *dink*, for "double income/no kids," *POTUS* for "President of the United States," and *NIMBY* for "Not In My Back Yard."

Do you consider the invented words of Dr. Seuss (*It-Kutch, Preep, Proo, Nerkle, Nerd* in "If I Ran the Zoo") to be "real words?" What about **baby talk**? These types of speech, used by children and adults, adopt simplified grammar and special vocabulary to convey information. Some of these have actually taken hold and become part of the vocabulary, like *tummy* for "stomach," *doggie* for "dog," and *choo-choo* for "train." This simplified speech is imperfect and modified by small children learning to talk; but baby talk also encompasses the consciously imperfect or altered speech used by adults in speaking to small children. This type of language is also heard when people talk to animals and (to a lesser extent) when people who are on intimate terms tease or speak playfully to each other.

A **back-formation** is a shorter word derived from a longer one by removing a part of it, such as a suffix or prefix. Thus *gloom* came from *gloomy, donate* from *donation, resurrect* from *resurrection*, and *burgle* from *burglar*. The editor of the *Oxford English Dictionary* (*OED*), Sir James Murray, coined the term **back-**

formation for words like these. Back-formations are created mainly to fill a gap in the language, as where certain nouns lack a corresponding verb (e.g., the verb *televise*, "back-formed"— itself a back-formation—from *television*, or *copy-edit*, from *copy editor*).

A **blend** is a combination of two words or word elements to make a new one. Blends are also called portmanteau words, amalgams, fusions, hybrids, or telescoped words. Such words, like *racino* (blend of *racing track* and *casino*), *netiquette* (blend of *Net*, "the Internet," and *etiquette*), *guestimate* (blend of *guess* and *estimate*), *telecast* (blend of *television* and *broadcast*), and the classic *motel* (blend of *motor* and *hotel*), develop in several ways: as unconscious or unintentional speech errors, as true coinages, in analogy with other words, and as spelling variations. Blends can occur spontaneously when two words are closely associated, as *exercise* and *bicycle* blending into *exercycle*.

Clipping or **shortening** is the creation of short variants of complex words. In some, the initial or first part of the longer word is used: *ad* from *advertisement*, *chimp* from *chimpanzee*, *deli* from *delicatessen*, *lab* from *laboratory*. In others, the beginning of the word is dropped: *burger* for *hamburger*, *phone* from *telephone*. Occasionally, only the middle part is retained to create an "elliptical word," such as *flu* from *influenza*.

A **coinage** is an invented word or phrase. Coinages such as *quark* (a subatomic particle), *waitron* (neutral word for a waiter or waitress, after *patron*), *cinemuck* (the muck found on the floor of movie theaters), *cruciverbalist* (crossword-puzzle designer), and *plerk* (blend of *play* and *work*) are created to give a name to a previously unnamed concept. The process of coinage often involves the creation of unmotivated, completely arbitrary words. Invented words like *conversate* and *dolphinarium* are also called **neologisms**.

The joining of **combining forms**, as *bio-* and *-logy* to get *biology*, is important in word formation. A combining form can join another combining form (e.g., *bio-* and *-graphy* to form *biography*) or a free word (e.g., *mini-* and *skirt* to form *miniskirt*). There are hundreds of combining forms in English and other languages and they, by definition, cannot stand alone as free words (though there are many modern exceptions, such as *auto, bio,* and *phone*). Combining forms often form scientific and technical terms.

A word made up of two or more words—*bathroom, bookworm*—is a **compound**. Compounding, or composition, is one of the most productive ways of forming words. Most English compounds are of two types, either based on native formations, like *coffeehouse, livingroom, steamboat,* or on Greek and Latin patterns, as *agriculture* and *macrobiotic*. There are families of compounds—sets of compounds based on the same word, like *cross* or *house: crossbar, crossbreed, crossover, crossroad; houseboat, housecoat, houseguest, household*. Many compounds are formed by the use of hyphens, such as *bridge-building, city-state,* and *Irish-American*. Compounding is considered one of the most important types of word formation.

Contraction is a shortening of a word or word-form, often so that it can be attached to an adjacent form or fused, with the addition of an apostrophe. Examples are *don't, they're, who's, isn't*. Traditional poetry has made use of contractions, such as *'tis* for *it is* and *'twill* for *it will*. Words like *away, aground,* and *ashore* were originally contractions of *on way, on ground,* and *on shore*. Words slurred in speech are often represented in writing as contractions, for example, *gonna* ("going to"), *wanna* ("want to"), *outasight* ("out of sight"), as do "eye dialect" words like *br'er* ("brother") and *bo'sun* ("boatswain"). Advocates of spelling reform have long tried to simplify contractions by omitting apostrophes (*dont, didnt,* etc.) but have been so far unsuccessful.

Derivation is the process of adding a prefix, suffix, or other word element to an existing word. Through derivation adjectives are created from nouns (*lovable* from *love*), nouns from verbs (*computer* from *compute*), adjectives from verbs (*conceivable* from *conceive*), nouns from nouns (*indexation* from *index*), and verbs from nouns (*containerize* from *container*).

A **diminutive** is a word denoting something small or endearing of its kind. There are many words denoting a smaller or affectionate version of an original (e.g., *auntie, sonny, starlet*). Diminutiveness is sometimes contained in etymologies and is not evident to those using the words (e.g., *catkin*, originally "little cat"). Examples of diminutives are *cigarette* from *cigar, rivulet* from *river*, and *princeling* from *prince*. Diminutives are also formed by the addition of a combining form like *mini-*.

A **doublet** is one of two or more words derived ultimately from a single source: *abbreviate/abridge, fragile/frail, guardian/warden*. The doublets may or may not show much resemblance and they also vary in closeness of meaning. A doublet can also be described as one of two words in the same language representing the same ultimate word but differentiated in form. There are also triplets, such as *royal/regal/real* and *gentile/genteel/gentle*.

An **eponym** (from Greek, "named for") is a word or phrase derived from a person's name, such as *sandwich, boycott, Melba toast,* and *peach Melba*. Often a person's name is the impetus for creating the word, for example, *leotard,* named for the aerialist Jules Léotard, who wore such a garment; or the *Heimlich maneuver* for helping a person who is choking on food, named after Henry J. Heimlich, a surgeon who devised the maneuver. The term *Webster* or *Webster's* as a synonym for "dictionary" derives from the name of Noah Webster, who published a famous American dictionary in 1828. Derivatives such as *bowdlerize,* clippings like *dunce,* and blends like *gerrymander* have come from people's names.

Many words are derived from place names, such as *champagne, sherry, calico, bikini, copper, hamburger, jeans, mayonnaise,* and *rugby.*

A **euphemism** (from Greek, "speaking good") is a mild or acceptable word or phrase used to replace a harsh or inappropriate one. Euphemisms are usually used to avoid offending the feelings or sensibilities of one's listeners (e.g., *underachiever* instead of "poor student," *flight attendant* instead of "steward(ess)," *seniors* instead of "old people," *attendance teacher* instead of "truant officer"). Derogatory names for homosexuals, including the word *homosexual* itself, have been changed to the neutral "same-sex" (*same-sex marriage*), practically replacing the earlier *gay* and *lesbian* epithets in certain contexts. Ethnic names are especially prone to change through euphemisms: *Native American* and *African-American* have largely replaced names now considered disparaging, such as, respectively, "American Indian" or "Redskin," "Negro" or "Colored" or "Black." And old ethnic slurs like *Mick, Wop, Dago, Yid,* and *Hebe* are no longer tolerated in print and only used jocularly.

Folk etymology is a term for words and phrases that have resulted from changes based on "folk" or "popular" notions. Folk etymology explains the name *sparrow-grass* for *asparagus, spitting image* for *spit and image,* and *penthouse* for Middle French *appentis.* A folk etymology arises when a word is assumed to derive from another because of some association of form or meaning, but in fact the word has a different derivation. Foreign words taken into English are especially likely to be changed through folk etymology in order to make sense of them. Some examples are: *crayfish* (from Old French *crevisse*), *mushroom* (from Old French *mouscheron*), and *woodchuck* (from Algonquian *otchek*). But native words have also been affected by folk etymology, for example, *acorn* (Old English *æcern*), *bridegroom* (Middle English *bridegome*), and *wormwood* (Old English *wermōd*).

Functional shift or **conversion** is the process by which words change parts of speech without the addition of a prefix or suffix, as in *soldier on*, the verb, being created from *soldier*, the noun. The change in part of speech can occur to a base word (*to drive* becoming *a drive*) and also to compounds (*sandpaper* becoming *to sandpaper*). The commonest shift is from noun to verb (*to access data, to contact someone, to anchor a show*). This can even happen to an auxiliary verb like *must*, which became the noun *a must*.

Generalization is a fairly slow process in which the meaning of a word or phrase is widened. Many examples of this can be found in religion, where words like *doctrine, novice, office* have come to mean more general, secular things. A word like *fantastic*, which originally meant "based on fantasy," has been generalized to mean "extremely good." Another example is *virtue*, which meant at first a desirable male attribute (derived from Latin *vir*, "man"), then was extended over time to apply to both sexes.

Inheritance is a process in which characteristics of word parts are transferred to a new whole, as the element *Mc* in *Mc-Donald's* (the fast-food company) taking on the meaning "mass-produced" or "cookie-cutter" and used to form *McNews, McJob, McMansion,* and *McWord*. The process includes many words and phrases that are formed on the model or pattern of older words or phrases, such as *animal lib, gay lib,* and *kids' lib,* inherited from *women's lib*. The inherited word part often becomes a suffix or combining form, as *-speak* (in *Newspeak* and *doublespeak*) used to form such words as *adspeak, artspeak, businessspeak, Eurospeak,* and *-net* (in *Arpanet*, for Advanced Research Project Agency network) used to form *Internet, Ethernet, Intranet,* and so on.

Loanwords and borrowings are words assimilated from one language into another, as *chic* and *restaurant*, borrowed from French. Borrowing is a process similar to adoption and it usually occurs when no term exists for a new concept, object, or state of affairs. Languages influence each other because we are keenly aware of foreign cultural, economic, political, and social developments—especially with the influence of the Internet, television, and travel. English has borrowed words from many languages, including French, German, Hebrew, Italian, Japanese, Russian, Spanish, and Yiddish. Borrowing is reciprocal. The aforementioned languages have acquired many loanwords from English.

Metaphor is the process of adding new, extended meanings to words having concrete or literal meanings. The new meanings are often called figurative or transferred. Metaphors are pervasive in English because every word or phrase with a literal meaning can be used figuratively. The transferred meaning is either added to the original meaning (e.g., a *circus* is now also "any noisy, confusing place or activity," as in *The convention was a circus*) or it displaces the old meaning partially or completely (*blank* originally meant "white," *corn* referred to grain in general). Metaphor is often seen in phrases (*Iron Curtain, on Easy Street, play second fiddle*) and in titles like *Joe Sixpack* and *Digest* in *Reader's Digest*.

Neologisms are words that are clearly new, and are so identified by speakers and writers. The term *neologism* is often used as a synonym for "new word." Neologisms tend to be disliked when they first appear and considered ungrammatical, pretentious, offensive, unnecessary, and the like. For years the neologisms *finalize* and *hopefully* were criticized and condemned by language purists. But, like hundred of others before them, these words eventually became integrated into the standard language (although from time to time someone raises an objection to using *finalize*). Dictionaries and language journals keep track of neologisms, publicizing them periodically, and a language society even runs a contest for the neologism of the year.

A **nonce word** is any word with a special meaning used for a special occasion, like *catastrophize*. Usually the word is formed for an object or situation that was previously unknown. The term *nonce word* was coined by the editors of the *Oxford English Dictionary* for words that were "apparently used only for the nonce" ("for the time being," "for one thing"). Nonce words are often designed to be economical in describing a complicated concept (*antidisestablishmentarianism*), to fill a lexical gap (*space walk*), or to describe something new (*petishism*, "love of pets").

Not to be confused with nonce words, a **nonsense word** is one that is meaningless but simply created for effect, usually humorous. Lewis Carroll and Edward Lear in Great Britain, and Dr. Seuss (Theodor Seuss Geisel) in the United States, were famous composers of nonsense verses that included many nonsense words. Examples of nonsense words are Carroll's *Jabberwock*, *Jubjub bird*, *Bandersnatch*, *vorpal*, *galumph*, *frabjous*, and *chortle* (all from the nonsense poem *Jabberwocky*), some of which have become part of the common vocabulary. Related to nonsense words are speech and writing consisting of meaningless phrases and sentences, characterized as *gobbledygook*, *bafflegab*, *gibberish*, *mumbo jumbo*, and *babble* (especially in such compounds as *psychobabble*, *technobabble*, *Eurobabble*).

Onomatopoeia is the formation of words through the imitation of sounds from nature and technology, such as *buzz*, *clunk*, *cock-a-doodle-doo*, *meow*, *murmur*, and *splash*. In these words, sound and sense echo and reinforce each other through either alliteration or assonance.

Phrasal verbs like *take up*, *guard against*, *pile on*, and *turn out* are word formations created mainly to express figurative and idiomatic meanings. However, phrasal verbs also have literal meanings and many (like *break up*, *run out*, and *tear down*) can have both literal and figurative meanings. Phrasal verbs frequently change into compound nouns: *to drop out* changes to *a dropout, to break up* changes to *a breakup*. Such changes are often accomplished through inversion: *overflow* from *flow over*, *uptake* from *take up*, *input* from *put in*. Due to the ease with which they are formed by combining common verbs (*be, do, go, keep, make, put, take, turn*) with prepositional and adverbial particles (*back, down, in, off, on, out, up*), the number of phrasal verbs have increased greatly in English since the 1800s. Today phrasal verbs are among the most productive types of word formation in the language.

Prefixes and suffixes are elements that become attached to the beginning or end of a word to produce a new word. Prefixes tend to be used with verbs and produce new verbs (e.g., the prefix *mis-* + *treat* produces the verb *mistreat*). Prefixes are also used with nouns and adjectives (the prefix *un-* + *wise* produces the adjective *unwise*). Suffixes attach themselves to nouns, verbs, and adjectives (e.g., *-er* makes nouns from verbs). This creation of new words by the adding of prefixes and suffixes is part of the processes of conversion and derivation, as well as compounding. Suffixes often occur in chains, as *-istically* in *antagonistically*, but prefixes do not and they usually occur singly (*disengage, unkind*).

Reduplication is the doubling of a sound, word element, or word, as in *goody-goody, hanky-panky, hunky-dory, mishmash*, and *walkie-talkie*. This is usually done to form a compound word or to strengthen an expression by the repetition of a sound or element. Reduplications could be imitative of sounds (like *choo-choo* or *ding-dong*), or emphatic and intensive (*no-no, so-so*), or loanwords (*beri-beri, bric-a-brac*), and are common in baby talk (*bye-bye, wee-wee*).

Retronyms are phrases created because an existing term that was once used alone needs to be distinguished from a term referring to a new development or variation, for example, *snow ski-*

ing (to contrast with *water skiing*), *acoustic guitar* (to contrast with *electric guitar*), and *conventional weapons* (to contrast with *biological, chemical, or nuclear weapons*). We use them and create them almost every day, but most people don't even know what they are and they are often not included as dictionary entries. With color television came the retronym "black-and-white TV" and with cable television we now have the retronym "network television."

Specialization is the process that narrows the meaning of a word or phrase. It is the opposite of generalization. This process may occur due to cultural or social need. Another reason is the existence of words having the same or similar meanings. When synonyms exist, speakers try to distinguish between them and, gradually, each word takes on a specific meaning. *Deer* once meant "four-legged beast" and *pigeon* was once used generally to mean "a young bird." Both words became specialized.

Why do we need all of these processes? Because we never have enough words to express ourselves differently or originally, and these processes help us create the words we need. Rudolf Flesch, the author of the controversial *Why Can't Johnny Read?* (1955), put it this way:

> A favorite proverb of the picture-and-diagram lovers is 'One picture is worth more than a thousand words.' It simply isn't so. Try to teach people with a picture and you may find that you need a thousand words to tell them exactly what to look at and why.

word death:

as with all living
things . . . an ending

In the foreword to a delightful book about obsolete words (Susan K. Sperling's *Poplollies and Bellibones*, 1977), the prolific writer of books about words and wordplay, Willard B. Espy (1910–99), writes this about words that have disappeared from the language:

> And when did the dead words die? The vital statistics on births are mostly available, give or take a hundred years. . . . As soon as a new locution emerges to cock a snook at society, *Time* or the *Reader's Digest* leaps on it with a glad cry and flings it into the central current of the language. But it is more difficult to be certain when a doddering word slips from public ken. It generally lingers in old reference works, sometimes with a note of the year it was first sighted:

Hoddyspeak, n. Simpleton, blockhead. [1505]
How much more satisfactory if the reference encompassed the word's entire lifespan!
Hoddyspeak, n. Simpleton, blockhead. [1505-1733]

Mr. Espy goes on to eulogize many of the excellent words that have met an untimely death. "Never again, alas," he laments, "will we hear a crane *crunkle*, a sheep *blore*, or a donkey *winx*. Never again will we see a *shiterow* flap along a stream, though herons may abound. Nor shall I ever, however great the provocation, dare call one of my sons-in-law an *odam*, with the accent on the last syllable."

FORGOTTEN ENGLISH

Another lover of lost words is Jeffrey Kacirk, who for a number of years has been authoring a yearly calendar called *Forgotten English*, each day of which features a word that has vanished, or is about to vanish, from English as we know it. Here are a few examples from the *Forgotten English* of 2005:

JANUARY 1. *stepmother's-breath.* "Of weather, coldness, frostiness. A cold morning is said to 'have a step-mother's breath'" (Joseph Wright's *English Dialect Dictionary*, 1896–1905).

JANUARY 8. *flesh-tailor.* "A surgeon" (Edward Lloyd's *Encyclopedic Dictionary*, 1895).

FEBRUARY 2. *burke.* "To kill, to murder, secretly and without noise, by means of strangulation. From Burke, the notorious Edinburgh murderer who . . . used to decoy people into the den he inhabited, kill them, and sell their bodies for dissection. . . . The term *burke* is now usually applied to any project that is quietly stopped or stifled—as [in] 'The question has been burked.' " (John Camden Hotten's *Slang Dictionary*, 1887).

APRIL 21. *ostentate.* "To make an ambitious display of, to show or exhibit boastingly. . . . [Hence] *ostentator,* one who makes a vain show; a boaster" (Noah Webster's *American Dictionary of the English Language*, 1828).

WHY DO WORDS DIE?

Words like *crankle* and *blore* seem quite good, worth mourning for. Why did they die? Why in general do words die? This may happen for a number of reasons. For instance, a new word may come into the language and supplant an older word. This happens often with place names: *Burma* is replaced by *Myanmar, Ceylon* by *Sri Lanka, Bombay* by *Mumbai.* Similarly, *witcraft* was replaced by *logic, inwit* by *conscience, patrocinate* by *patronize, expulse* by *expel,* and *frush* (from Latin *frustum,* "fragment") by *crush.*

Words that have become obsolete in Standard English may survive in some dialects. *Firedogs,* "andirons," known since the 1700s, is now used chiefly in the American South; *bismark,* "jelly doughnut, danish," is found mainly in some Northern dialects. Change, be it in cultural, social, or political institutions, in values, in science and technology, or in fashion, is a factor in the death or loss of words. New technology replaces old. Foreign words replace native words. Or perhaps words, like old soldiers, simply outlive their usefulness and fade away. The process of word death is usually gradual and long—taking decades or even several generations.

For example, because few men (except monks) shave their heads to create a bald patch, the word *tonsure*, which describes this, is no longer in everyday use. In medieval times, when the practice of shaving such bald patches was common, *tonsure* was a useful word.

Breeches gradually fell into disuse when fashion changed and *trousers* replaced *breeches* in the 1600s as the garment covering the legs. The word was retained in the dialects of northern England and in Scotland, though.

A similar phenomenon occurs when there are changes in social institutions. With the end of feudalism, associated words like *bondsman, serf,* and *vassal* disappeared from common use. But as long as feudalism is discussed in history classes, these words will remain in the language. They are rare words, but are neither archaic nor obsolete.

When scientific and technological concepts and objects are superseded by new ones, the terms for earlier concepts and objects go out of common use. Think of *alchemy, spinning-jenny,* and *rotary telephone.* Some words naturally fell out of use with the objects they denoted, as *gofe* ("pillory") and *chermadic* ("heavy weight used as a projectile"). But, in many cases, the exact reason for disuse is obscure. Why does *eructation*, that long synonym of *belch*, remain in use, while another synonym, *nidorosity* (from *nidorous*, "resembling the smell of burnt meat," from Latin *nidorosus*), included in Noah Webster's 1828 *American Dictionary of the English Language*, fell into total oblivion? Nobody knows.

Archaisms are words and phrases that retain an aura of the past, yet continue to be used. Some that fit this description are: *behold, damsel, ere, forsooth, hither, ne'er, sire, smite, 'twas, unto,* and *yonder.* This type of word is found in historical novels, plays, poems, and films—as well as in religious settings and documents, nursery rhymes and fairy tales, and in trade names and commercial advertising. Rural dialects also retain words that have gone out of use in the standard language, words like *burbles,* meaning "small pimples" in East Anglia, *streek,* "to stretch," in northern England, *scraffle,* "to scramble," in Scotland.

Unfortunately, we have lost many words that have no real counterparts in today's English. Do you know of a single word meaning "instinctive parental affection?" There was a word for this: *storge.* How about a word for "stamping the feet in disapproval?" That would be *supplosion.* We might sometimes lament that these words are no longer used. Finding them again allows us to understand how our ancestors lived hundreds of years ago.

Words are creatures of a sort. Words we now consider verbal "fossils" were once used in speech and writing, were alive. Some may have never taken wing but became part of our recorded language. One type of word that may die quickly is the slang or jargon used by a small group whose vocabulary is very specialized or temporal. A word of this nature may be born and die within weeks or months. After some slang terms fall out of use, they may be found buried in a few lexicons or glossaries. They are not quite extinct; they go on existing as artifacts, but are no longer alive. For example, during the Prohibition era, terms like *bathtub gin, bluenose, bootlegger, feds, hooch, moonshine, rum runner,* and *speakeasy* were everyday slang words; today they may appear only in period movies and history books.

CHECKING FOR A PULSE

Deciding that a word is "dead" or "lost," is not easy. The presumption is that no one uses it anymore. But when can we be sure that people are no longer using a word? How much time should be allowed before we can say that a word has stopped being obsolescent (in occasional use by a few) and has become obsolete (used by no one)? Lexicographers have quite a time keeping up with the expansion of language as well as the simultaneous diminution of language. Before their disappearance, words and phrases are often recorded in a variety of published writings, including dictionaries and glossaries.

It is sometimes hard to determine if a word is really obsolete, for it may linger in obscurity and then suddenly emerge. *To thieve,* found in Old English, then for long unrecorded, reappeared in the 1600s. Through their occurrence in the Bible and in Shakespeare's plays, many expressions, though disused in ordinary speech and writing, have remained in literature and can hardly be termed obsolete. The Romantic Movement of the 18th and 19th centuries restored old words to literature, some of which have returned to general use. To this class belong words like *dight,* "to adorn," nearly lost in the 1700s but revived a century later; *elfish,* "elflike," altered from *elvish; hue,* archaic about 1600, afterward reintroduced as a poetic synonym for *color;* and *to jeopard* "to risk, imperil," *murrain,* "plague, pestilence," and *soothfast,* "true, truthful," brought back by Sir Walter Scott.

Standard and college-level dictionaries—and even unabridged ones—discriminate against the retired words of English, the archaic, obsolete, and rare, because there is only so much space in a printed dictionary. The "dead" words may appear in specialized books, often compiled because of the author's fascination with such words, not really in an effort to revive them. These books are simply collections of colorful but obscure words that one could use in place of their modern counterparts. Such a book, mentioned earlier, is *Poplollies and Bellibones,* which is subtitled "A Celebration of Lost Words." (A *poplolly* is defined in the book as "A little darling [from the French *poupelet*], a female favorite, special loved one, or mistress." A *bellibone* is defined as "A lovely maiden, a pretty lass," an anglicization of French *belle et bonne,* 'fair and good.' ")

Obsolete and archaic words offer insights into the nature of our language while simultaneously illustrating older beliefs and customs. It's fun to look at odd groups of once-common adjectives, adverbs, nouns, and verbs that, while similar to modern words, look and sound strange to us today. No one these days would refer to water as "Adam's ale," and that's a pity, because it's a humorous reference to the only kind of drink Adam knew. And some of us would cheer the return of the *skimmington*, which was a form of public ridicule to punish a wife-beating husband by staging a parade in which actors impersonating the husband and wife rode through the streets in a cart beating each other with ladles and skimming spoons; in some parts of England it was the guilty party who was carried through the streets and exposed to humiliation.

Finally, it is a fact of life that words, even the most common ones, develop new meanings that push aside or replace old ones. An example of this type of semantic change is seen in the first line (and title) of a famous hymn based on Psalm 100 by the English hymnist Isaac Watts (1674–1748), "Before Jehovah's Awful Throne."

Before Jehovah's awful throne
Ye nations, bow with sacred joy;
Know that the Lord is God alone;
He can create and He destroy.

We cringe at the word *awful* in this hymn, because in modern usage it has come to mean "extremely bad, unpleasant, terrible," as in *I hated that show; it was just awful.* But in earlier times the word meant "inspiring awe, majestic." A number of other solemn, reverential words have undergone a similar weakening, including *terrible,* "causing terror," *horrible,* "causing horror," *dreadful,* "causing dread," *horrid,* "bristling with fear," and even *lousy,* "infested with lice." In all of these cases, the weakened meaning has rendered the original strong meaning obsolete.

We can rarely observe the birth of a word and never its death. Linguists often discuss the death of languages. While it is true that many languages have disappeared over the centuries and millennia, other so-called "dead languages" continue surviving in one form or another. Latin and Sanskrit are examples of such languages. The same can be said of words. Some words may indeed die, never to be heard or seen again; vogue words, slang terms, jargon, are by definition short-lived. In general, however, the words of a language never die as long as they are enshrined in the stories and poems of a people, and as long as they continue to grow, change, and be revived over time. Words are the lifeblood of a living language.

suggested reading

Adams, Valerie. *An Introduction to Modern English Word-Formation.* New York: Longman/Pearson Education, 1973.

Ayers, Donald M. *English Words from Latin and Greek Elements,* 2nd ed. Tucson: University of Arizona Press, 1986.

Bauer, Laurie. *English Word-Formation.* New York: Cambridge University Press, 1983.

Bauer, Laurie. *Introducing Linguistic Morphology.* Edinburgh: Edinburgh University Press, 1988.

Burridge, Kate. *Blooming English.* New York: Cambridge University Press, 2004.

Crystal, David. *The Cambridge Encyclopedia of Language.* New York: Cambridge University Press, 1987.

Crystal, David. *The Cambridge Encyclopedia of the English Language,* 2nd ed. New York: Cambridge University Press, 2003.

Finegan, Edward. *Attitudes Toward English Usage: The History of a War of Words.* New York/London: Teachers College Press, 1980.

Jackson, Howard. *Words and Their Meaning.* New York: Longman/Pearson, 1988.

Lieber, Rochelle. *Deconstructing Morphology: Word Formation in Syntactic Theory.* Chicago: University of Chicago Press, 1992.

Lodwig, Richard R., and Eugene F. Barrett. *Words, Words, Words: Vocabularies and Dictionaries,* 2nd ed. Rochelle Park, NJ: Hayden, 1973.

Matthews, P. H. *Morphology,* 2nd ed. New York: Cambridge University Press, 1991.

McArthur, Tom. *The Oxford Companion to the English Language.* New York: Oxford University Press, 1992.

McArthur, Tom. *The Oxford Guide to World English.* New York: Oxford University Press, 2002.

McQuain, Jeffrey. *Never Enough Words.* New York: Random House, 1999.

Metcalf, Allan. *Predicting New Words: The Secrets of Their Success.* New York: Houghton Mifflin, 2002.

Plag, Ingo. *Word-Formation in English.* New York: Cambridge University Press, 2003.

Seyles, Dorothy U., and Carol J. Boltz. *Language Power,* 2nd Ed. New York: Random House, 1982.

Stockwell, Robert, and Donka Minkova. *English Words: History and Structure.* New York: Cambridge University Press, 2001.

Zuckerman, Marvin S. *Words Words Words,* 2nd ed. Encino, CA: Glencoe, 1980.

DICTIONARIES, USAGE BOOKS, AND TEXTBOOKS CONSULTED

Barnhart, Clarence L., Sol Steinmetz, and Robert K. Barnhart. *The Barnhart Dictionary of New English since 1963.* New York: Barnhart/Harper & Row, 1973.

Barnhart, Clarence L., Sol Steinmetz, and Robert K. Barnhart. *The Second Barnhart Dictionary of New English.* New York: Barnhart/Harper & Row, 1980.

Barnhart, Robert K., Sol Steinmetz, and Clarence L. Barnhart. *The Third Barnhart Dictionary of New English.* New York: H. W. Wilson, 1990.

Barnhart, Robert K. *The Barnhart Dictionary of Etymology.* New York: H. W. Wilson, 1988.

Bloomfield, Leonard. *Language.* New York: Henry Holt, 1933.

Bussman, Hadumod, Gregory P. Trauth, and Kerstin Kazzazi. *Routledge Dictionary of Language and Linguistics.* New York: Routledge, 1996.

Collins COBUILD English Guides 2: Word Formation. London: HarperCollins, 1991.

Crystal, David. *A Dictionary of Linguistics & Phonetics,* 5th ed. New York: Blackwell, 2003.

Crystal, David. *An Encyclopedic Dictionary of Language and Languages.* New York: Penguin, 1992.

Dickson, Paul. *Words.* New York: Delacorte, 1982.

Evans, Bergen, and Cordelia Evans. *A Dictionary of Contemporary American Usage.* New York: Random House, 1957.

Follett, Wilson. *Modern American Usage.* New York: Hill and Wang, 1966.

Fowler, H. W., and E. G. Fowler. *The King's English,* 3rd ed. Oxford: Oxford University Press, 1931.

Garner, Bryan. *Garner's Modern American Usage.* Oxford/New York: Oxford University Press, 2003.

Grambs, David. *Words About Words.* New York: McGraw-Hill, 1984.

Hartmann, R. R. K., and F. C. Stork. *Dictionary of Language and Linguistics.* New York: Wiley, 1972.

Hartmann, R. R. K., and Gregory James. *Dictionary of Lexicography.* New York: Routledge, 1998.

Manser, Martin H., with Jeffrey McQuain. *Guide to Good Word Usage.* New York: World Almanac, 1989.

McQuain, Jeffrey. *Power Language.* Boston/New York: Houghton Mifflin. 1996.

The New York Public Library Writer's Guide to Style and Usage. New York: HarperCollins, 1994.

Pei, Mario, and Frank Gaynor. *Dictionary of Linguistics.* New York: Philosophical Library, 1954.

Perrin, Porter G. *Writer's Guide and Index to English.* Chicago: Scott, Foresman, 1959.

Pyles, Thomas, and John Algeo. *The Origins and Development of the English Language,* 3rd ed. New York: Harcourt Brace Jovanovich, 1982.

Random House Webster's College Dictionary. New York: Random House, 1997.

Robertson, Stuart, and Frederic G. Cassidy. *The Development of Modern English.* Englewood Cliffs, NJ: Prentice-Hall, 1957.

Safire, William. *On Language.* New York: Times Books, 1980.

Sapir, Edward. *Language.* New York: Harcourt, Brace, 1921.

Webster's Dictionary of English Usage. Springfield, MA: Merriam-Webster, 1989.

Index

af-, 275
affixes, 33–34
African languages, 17
  African English, 344
  loanwords, 308,
    310–11
ag-, 275
-age, 278, 324
agri- or agro-, 186
-aholic, 185
ain't, 71–72
-al, 199, 276, 277, 280
al-, 275
Algeo, John, 89, 148
Alice's Adventures in
  Wonderland
  (Carroll), 242
alphabetisms, 42
amalgams, 160, 350
amelioration, word, 104
American Dialect
  Society, 218,
    219–23
American Dictionary of the
  English Language,
    154, 362
American English,
    337–38
American Heritage
  Dictionary, 10, 22,
    293, 335
American Heritage
  Dictionary of Indo-
  European Roots, The
  (Watkins), 84
American Heritage
  Dictionary of the
  English Language, The,
    84
American Language, The
  (Mencken), 60,
    162
American Speech, 39, 159
American Thesaurus of Slang
  (Berrey and Van
  Den Bark), 339

-an, 278
an-, 275
anagrams, 12, 237,
    300
analogical forms, 29
analogy, generalization
  by, 130–33
-ance, 278
anglicization, of foreign
  words, 317–18,
    321
Anglo-saxon times, 153
"Anglo-Saxon" words,
    323
animal sounds, 254–55,
    256
"Annabel Lee" (Poe),
    290
-ant, 279
ante-, 324
anti-, 199, 324
antonyms, 180
ap-, 275
apostrophes, 7, 66–67
ar-, 275
Arabic, loanwords,
    308–9
-arch, 23
archaisms, 362–63
-arian, 199
Aristotle, 4, 11, 139
Arrival and Departure
  (Koestler), 137
Art of Composition, The
  (Twain), 6
Arte of English Poesie, The
  (Puttenham), 166
artificial languages, 347
-ary, 280, 324
as-, 275
Asian languages
  loanwords, 303,
    307–8, 309–10
  neologisms, 216
association, accidental,
    109

associative sets, suffixes
  in, 277
-aster-, 20, 76
astro-, 180
astron-, 23
at-, 275
"at" symbol @, 173
-ate, 276
-athon, 184–85
-ation, 122, 200, 279
atlas/Atlas, 127, 208
augmentatives, 75, 79
Australian English, 344
  diminutives, 74, 77
Autobiographical Study, An
  (Freud), 137
autonyms, 300
Ayesha (Morier), 246

B
Babbitt, George F., 208
Babbitt (Lewis), 208
babble, 157–58,
    245–46
baby talk, 79, 118,
    155–57, 158, 349
  common words in,
    157–58
  reduplications, 286
back-clippings, 63–64
back-derivations, 49
back-formations,
    48–56, 58,
    349–50
  derivatives, 199
  neologisms, 224–25
  nonstandard English,
    339–40
  noun borrowings
    and, 327
Bacon, Sir Francis, 237
Bailey, Nathaniel, 331
Barber, Benjamin, 31
Barnes, William, 328
Barnhart Dictionary of
  Etymology, 84

company names
  abbreviations and
    acronyms, 42
  new root formation
    and creation of,
    13
complex words, 13
compounds, 188–89,
  351
  compound nouns,
    122, 123,
    263–65
  compound verbs, 55,
    260
  compound words,
    13, 20
  eponyms, 204
  how to make a
    compound word,
    193–95
  neologisms, 226
  Newspeak, 189–90
  nonstandard English,
    340
  power of, 190–93
computers
  coining of "Google,"
    166–67, 175
  cyberspeak, 183–84
  derivatives, 202–3
  Internet coinages,
    172–74
  neologisms, 216
  spam, 25
  specialized meanings
    of technical terms,
    103, 105, 144–46
con-, 275, 324
conjunctions, 125
connotative
  diminutives, 75
context, word usage in,
  103–4, 106–7
contractions, 66–68,
  351
  ain't, 71–72
  common, 68–71

conversion
  functional shift and,
    101, 121–24, 354
  total and partial
    conversions,
    124–25
Copy Editor, 218–19
cor-, 275
-cosm, 19
counter-, 274
Coupland, Douglas, 30
Coverdale, Miles, 36–37
cryptographers, 236
-cule, 76
cultural borrowings,
  305, 308–15, 326
-culus, 76
cumulative sets, suffixes
  in, 277–78
-cur-, 20
-cy, 276, 278, 279
cyber-, 88, 270
cyberspeak, 183–84

D
Danish, loanwords, 309
de-, 274, 324
dead languages, 366
dead metaphors,
  108–9, 138–39
death
  euphemisms for,
    114, 117
  word death, 359–66
Decline of the West
  (Spengler), 136
Defoe, Daniel, 304
degradation, 149–50
  See also derogatory
    words
denizens, 317, 321–22
denotative diminutives,
  75
Derby, earl of, 210, 244
derivation, 196, 352
  addictive derivatives,
    197–99

compounds, 193
examples of
  derivatives, 13
formation of
  complex words
  via, 13
functional shift, 124
how to make
  derivatives,
  199–203
metaphorical
  meanings of
  derivatives, 141
neologisms and
  derivatives, 226
nonstandard English
  derivatives,
  340–41
derogatory words
  derogatory meanings,
    106, 107–8
  derogatory slang, 77
  dysphemisms, 111,
    112–13
deterioration, word,
  104
Devious Derivations
  (Rawson), 95–96
diagonal line (/), usage
  of, 337–38
dial-a- forms, 34
Dickson, Paul, 30, 153,
  240, 293
dictionaries
  blends, origins of,
    162
  borrowings in,
    304–5
  clipped words in, 61
  combining form
    invention, 178–80
  compounds in, 195
  definitions for
    "word," 7, 9–10
  diminutives in,
    73–74, 75–76
  doublets in, 84